£6.50

D1179288

LONELY HILLS &
WILDERNESS TRAILS

LONELY HILLS & WILDERNESS TRAILS

RICHARD GILBERT

David & Charles

*For ten days we roamed throughout this rugged, beautiful and
fascinating area; climbing the mountains, crossing the Drangajokull and
exploring the valleys, corries and lakes. No matter that some expeditions spun
out to twenty hours for, being only thirty miles south of the Artic Circle,
darkness never fell. . .*

*

*As we gazed in wonderment round every point of the compass, Foinaven,
Ben More Assynt, the Beinn Dearg hills, the flat table top of Wyvis,
the Fannichs, Cairngorms, Mullach Coire Mhic Fhearchair,
the Affric peaks, Beinn a'Chlaidheimh, Torridon, the Cuillin and Flowerdale
hills all hove into view. It was like the joy of meeting long lost friends. . .*

A DAVID & CHARLES BOOK

First published in the UK in 2000

A catalogue record for this book is available from the British Library.

ISBN 0 7153 0922 6

Printed in Singapore by Sino Publishing Ltd
for David & Charles
Brunel House   Newton Abbot   Devon

Contents

Contents

The Hebrides

Wild Camping in Britain

Mountains and Memories

Contents

Stories and Legends

Introduction

My passion for mountains began at an early age when my parents moved out of London to Borth-y-Gest in North Wales at the start of the war. Family expeditions to the hills were part of life, and even when we moved back to the Home Counties in 1945, my father would carefully save up his petrol coupons to take us to the Lake District and Scotland for mountain holidays.

Every school holiday, winter and summer, during my last three years at school I would hitch-hike to Ben Nevis, the Lake District or Snowdonia and climb mountains with a group of friends that we called the 'pioneers'. We taught ourselves; guidebooks were sparse and equipment was ex-WD army surplus and tended to be heavy and badly designed.

It was a good apprenticeship, for it taught us to fend for ourselves in the mountains and to make important judgments and decisions; but above all, it was high adventure and our fitness and stamina got us out of all sorts of scrapes. I remember descending the Crib Goch knife-edge from the summit of Snowdon in full winter conditions one January day, without ice-axes and not knowing if there was in fact a feasible way off Crib Goch itself. When, in darkness, we arrived back down at Pen-y-Gwryd, some real climbers told us that we should have used ropes, ice-axes and crampons. On another occasion we descended in thick mist from Scafell Pike into Upper Eskdale, rather than Borrowdale, but later walked back by moonlight from Wasdale to Borrowdale via Sty Head Tarn, arriving at camp at 1am.

At the age of eighteen I joined the army for two years' National Service, and I soon saved up enough money from my pay of 28s a week to buy a BSA Bantam 125cc motor bike, on which I could get to North Wales on weekends. My two elder brothers, Oliver and Christopher, were now at university and starting to rock climb and they would take me climbing in the Lake District and Skye. One of our favourite cliffs was Crag Lough on Hadrian's Wall in Northumberland – by then the family had moved to Corbridge-on-Tyne.

Going up to Oxford University in 1958 I immediately joined the OUMC and found a club full of enthusiastic climbers. We met for lunch, tea and supper to talk climbing, we spent the afternoons practising on the old railway bridges at Horspath, and we went to North Wales, to Derbyshire gritstone or to the limestone of the Avon Gorge every weekend. Scooters, motor bikes and ramshackle old cars were pressed into duty, and the pubs of Worcestershire and Shropshire became regular haunts on the long drive to Wales. The summer vacations were spent in the Alps, and the Easter vacations winter climbing on the north face of Ben Nevis or Lochnagar.

After a few years I became more reflective and began to lose interest in hard, technical climbing: several of my friends had been killed, and I had had a number of narrow escapes myself. I was beginning to derive most satisfaction from multi-day expeditions exploring the remote corners of the Scottish Highlands. Several such expeditions in March and April with my friend Alan Wedgwood involved traverses of Munros (separate mountains in Scotland over 3,000ft). We would camp high up, perhaps beside a stream or a frozen lochan, and enjoy the sunset over the Hebrides, the herds of deer, mountain hares, ptarmigan and golden eagles. I devoured every book on Scotland that I could lay my hands on, and I was particularly influenced by the writings of W.H. Murray in his two classic books *Mountaineering in Scotland* and *Undiscovered Scotland*. Murray thrilled to the beauty of the Highland scene and delighted in the adventure and physical challenge that was offered by the mountains. In accordance with the pre-war Murray era we would wear tweed jackets, smoke pipes and never travel without a flask of whisky.

Even when I left university I would head for the Highlands at every opportunity, and the 277 Munros provided a cast-iron framework with which to work and an important motivator for getting me out of the tent and on to the mountains in all seasons, however bad the weather. On 21 June 1971, with a large party of friends, I climbed Bidean nam Bian in Glen Coe, my final Munro. I look back on the years which I spent climbing the Munros as the most exciting and rewarding of my mountaineering life, which left me with countless happy memories and a detailed knowledge of the Scottish hills. Although this was the end of an era, it marked the beginning of a life-long love affair with the Highlands which has sustained me and enriched my life.

Soon after I finished the Munros my wife, Trisha, and I bought a cottage on a hillside overlooking Ullapool in Ross-shire. From a balcony on the south side of the house you could look across Loch Broom to An Teallach, east to the Fannichs and the Beinn Dearg Forest, and west to the Summer Islands and the Outer Hebrides. The cottage made a base for countless wonderful holidays with our family of four children, and we never tired of exploring and climbing the exceptional hills of Wester Ross and Sutherland. We visited every bay and inlet of the indented coast and camped on lonely strands, in remote glens and in high corries.

Fraser Darling's inspirational books, *The Highlands and Islands*, *Island Years*, *Island Farm* and *Naturalist on Rona* sparked off a deep love of the Hebrides. When our children were still very young we hitched a lift in an Ullapool prawner to the uninhabited Priest Island, in the mouth of Loch Broom, and camped for several nights, eventually being taken off in a Force 8 gale. This was so successful that we repeated the exercise a few years later on Tanera Beag, another of the Summer Islands. The sound of the wheeling, screaming sea birds and the smell of thrift and sun-warmed bog myrtle, while we fished for mackerel off the rocks, will always rekindle memories of those island camps.

The hills of the North-West proved an ideal training ground for the children, who later accompanied us on many family holidays in the Alps. The fact that both Trisha and I were teachers and had long holidays which we could share with the children, was a great bonus.

In addition to mountain holidays with my own children, and when they left home, to more ambitious expeditions with Trisha, I ran the mountaineering and expeditions club at Ampleforth College. My policy was to introduce the boys to remote, unfashionable mountain country; thus we visited many wild corners of the world including Iceland, the Lyngen Peninsula of Arctic Norway, the Himalaya and the High Atlas Mountains of Morocco, as well as fitting in numerous shorter meets in the Highlands. Regular exertion in the hills, when I could fill my lungs with sharp, pure air, became an essential part of my life and a necessary safety valve from the frustrations of being a chemistry teacher in a stuffy, fume-filled laboratory.

Introduction

Throughout the 1980s, in my spare time, I worked with Ken Wilson on three large-format, heavily illustrated books, *The Big Walks*, *Classic Walks* and *Wild Walks*. This task took me all over Britain to seek out remote and rugged country, and many were the days when I would leave home at 4am, drive to Scotland or South Wales, complete a challenging walk, and return home the same evening. When *High* magazine started publication in 1983 the editor, Geoff Birtles, asked me to write a monthly column: 'Richard Gilbert's Walking World'. I have written this column ever since, and it has, like the Munros, acted as a stimulus to get me out into the hills in order to have something worthwhile to write about.

A large part of this book of essays is based on articles that I wrote for *High* magazine over the last sixteen years. I have attempted to include a selection that has world-wide appeal, such as the Rockies, Alaska, the Alps, the Caucasus, the Himalayas and Iceland; but inevitably, the North-West Highlands of Scotland and the Hebrides are heavily represented. When I look back to fifty years of activity in the mountains it is those sparkling spring days in the Western Highlands, with snow on the tops, the burns brimming with meltwater and the birch and alder coming into leaf, that come foremost to mind.

The thirty-nine articles published here show the immense diversity of experience that is available to anyone who is reasonably competent in the hills. You will not find here any 'life and death' epics on the highest mountains in the world. My experiences are those that are regularly enjoyed by the thousands of average, but enthusiastic, hill walkers and mountaineers who seek out wild places.

In spite of gloomy talk about the commercialisation and despoliation of wild country there are plenty of places off the beaten track where solitude can be assured. I often think back to our descent from the Mestia Pass into the beautiful lost world of Svanetia, and to the morning when we crested a ridge on the Hornstrandir Peninsula of North-West Iceland to see the sun glinting on the polar ice-sheet. Such memories, and many others, sustain one through life.

I am not ashamed to admit that I have been much happier and more at peace with myself when waking up in a small tent in an upland valley in the Cheviots to the sound of curlews, or on a grassy alp in Austria to the music of cowbells, than on the Hispar La in the Karakoram to the menacing rumble of avalanches.

Thankfully we are free to find our own level and to do just what we want in the hills. The extreme rock climber, the fell runner, the Skye ridge record holder and the Lake District rambler all derive enormous personal satisfaction from their activities – and long may it remain so.

DISTANT HORIZONS

*'Avalanches broke away from the impossibly steep snow
faces above the pass with a crump and a roar.'*

Svanetia: The Legendary Kingdom of the Caucasus

In the late 1980s, partly as a result of the development of glasnost but more importantly from a need to obtain hard currency, certain Soviet mountaineering clubs advertised climbing and trekking holidays in various ranges of their vast country. Thus in 1989, Trisha and I applied for an international climbing camp in the Altai range of Siberia – but having received a letter of acceptance, we fell foul of Soviet bureaucracy. Letters, faxes, telexes and phone calls met a brick wall and our visa applications landed on stony ground. However, in 1990, Karakoram Experience managed to overcome the red tape and obtain permission for a party of eleven to spend two weeks trekking and climbing in the Caucasus. Although a handful of foreigners had managed to climb in the Caucasus over the previous few years, this was the first formal group from Britain since John Hunt's expedition in 1958, described in his book *The Red Snows*.

The Caucasus range is the natural boundary between Russia in the north and Georgia in the south and, spanning 500 miles between the Black Sea and the Caspian Sea, can be said to divide Europe from Asia. Apart from the massive cone of Elbruz, a volcano extinct for two million years and rising to 18,510ft on the north side, the peaks of the Caucasus are dramatic in form, their rock spires rising steeply from deep wooded valleys. The permanent snow level is at a height of between 8,200ft and 9,800ft; thus most mountains are festooned with hanging glaciers and glistening ice-fields, while vast boulder-strewn glaciers fill the upper basins. In scale the Caucasus could be placed between the Alps and the Himalaya.

One of the principal joys for us was the wild and unspoilt nature of the range. There is a minimum of development in the valleys, only the most rudimentary paths, no tree-felling and virtually no system of mountain huts or refuges apart from the monstrous Priut hut on Elbruz. The grassy alps are seamed by bubbling streams and are ablaze with flowers. We picked wild raspberries and redcurrants, and saw ibex, known locally as *tur*, on the moraines. Wild boar and bears are said to live in the forests.

KE had agreed a programme of trekking and climbing with officials in Moscow. We were to be based at Baksan Camp, but the implementation of the plans in the mountains was another matter. Vitali Medvedev, our guide, interpreter and mentor, managed to secure the help of the leader of Baksan's mountain rescue squad, a huge bull of a man whom we christened Kojak because he had not a single hair on his head. Kojak was immensely kind and co-operative and, believing us to be incompetent, assigned several of his best henchmen to us for the duration of our stay. Our two leaders from KE, Glenn Rowley and Terry Ralphes, were hardened Himalayan and Alpine climbers and the entire party were fit and committed, but I suspect that Kojak was mindful of the horrific avalanche on Peak Lenin in the Pamirs a week or two earlier which had swept forty-two climbers, many of them foreign visitors, to their deaths.

Baksan Mountaineering Camp is a cross between a 1950s Outward Bound school and a Butlin's holiday camp. The peace and tranquillity of the pinewoods is broken at 7am by the loudspeakers announcing reveille. Soon afterwards long streams of extremely fit young men and women can be seen queuing up at the cold water taps to complete their ablutions before setting out on a run through the trees. At 8am they are summoned to muster parade where they line up in rows for the day's briefing.

As privileged guests we were excused such rigours, and at 9am, having rubbed the sleep from our eyes, we reluctantly joined the scrum for breakfast in the canteen. The food was quite awful, but with strenuous days ahead we had to eat what we could of the lukewarm congealed semolina, bread, sweet black tea, prune juice and a watery yoghurt called *kefir* . On special occasions we were offered meatballs of fat and gristle, unripe apples and slices of water melon. Our kind Russian hosts were apologetic and embarrassed: very little food was coming into the valley, they explained, and with corruption rife, any palatable items disappeared well before they arrived at Baksan.

Emerging, blinking, into the sunshine we were assailed by the most excruciating caterwauling, which went under the name of Soviet pop music, blaring across the campus. This, more than anything, made us impatient to leave for the mountains.

Climbing in the USSR is highly organised. If you are lucky enough to secure a place on one of their climbing courses in the Caucasus you must prove your competence by working progressively through the grades from I to VI. There is no easy way forwards, and no place for young tearaways to short-circuit the system and make straight for a grade VI north face. As a result the top Soviet climbers, having served a long apprenticeship, are extremely sound practitioners with a wealth of experience and hard routes behind them.

Trekking seemed to be unknown in Russia, and certainly our hosts had no notion of what was involved. However, after a day of negotiation, we left Baksan with two cooks, a guide, an interpreter and four stalwart porters for a six-day trek to cross the 12,011ft Mestia Pass over the spine of the Caucasus into Georgia, and to return over the Betsho Pass. With the complete absence of convenience foods the porters were lugging sacks of fruit and vegetables, including water melons, over snow bridges, crevasses, glaciers and moraines for up to thirteen hours a day. The whole exercise was ludicrous, and the state of a sack of ripe pears after being manhandled for two days is best left to the imagination. Vegetable soup and bortsch without any seasoning was our staple diet and this was cooked on petrol stoves, the fuel for which was bartered for Western goods and then syphoned from vehicles. However, it is not my intention to carp: far from it; the trek was one of the highlights of our lives. The mountains were truly magnificent, the surrounding valleys scarcely touched by man, the weather impeccable and the Russians highly entertaining, intelligent, generous and anxious to do all that was humanly possible to make the expedition a success.

There was Igor, agile and strong as an ox, with biceps and thighs like tree trunks, who could have arm-wrestled Geoff Capes into submission or taken his place in a troupe of Cossack dancers. Igor was always first into camp, lighting the stoves and putting on the tea. He would only wear his prized plastic boots on the steepest of snow-slopes, otherwise he padded along in old baseball boots.

Sergei was tall and handsome with dark, shoulder-length hair; he always seemed to have two or more girls hanging round his neck! When he wasn't climbing, Sergei was earning good money in Kiev, either as a professional photographer or by cleaning the windows of multi-storey office blocks by abseil.

We hardly noticed Smargiel for the first few days because he covered both his massive load and his head with an unfolded tent to keep off the sun. He was a student at Pyatigorsk who was working during the summer months at Baksan, and he spoke reasonable English. We shall never forget arriving at a high col, collapsing exhausted on the ground, and marvelling at Smargiel who dropped his pack and hurtled back down the screes like a mountain goat, to relieve the last member of the party of his rucksack. Steve, too, may remember dressing a deep and festering blister on his foot caused by his latest, expensive, multi-coloured Gore-tex boots while Smargiel, smiling broadly, lined his own tatty, split, holed but eminently comfortable boots with a thick layer of *Pravda*.

It was surprising that no one from the large Baksan Mountaineering Camp had ever crossed the Mestia Pass into Georgia, but enquiries by Kojak produced Nikolai, from Ulu Tau Mountain Camp in the neighbouring Adyr Su valley to act as our guide. Nikolai was wiry and fit, a very accomplished mountaineer who happily shouldered a mammoth pack to help with the portering. He reckoned that we were the first Europeans to cross the Mestia Pass since the end of the war. Our descent from the pass would take us into an unknown region of Georgia called Svanetia, an ancient and romantic kingdom completely surrounded by mountains which, until a road was built in 1932, was inaccessible for nine months of the year. This mountain enclave has, for hundreds of years, offered a refuge from warring nations. Svanetia was said to be so isolated as to be little affected by the revolution, and our Russian companions were thrilled to have the opportunity of visiting it.

The approach to the Mestia Pass lay along a high hidden valley, the Adyr Su, which had been closed at its mouth by a landslide. The ingenious Russians had built a 200ft high ramp at about 45°, up which ran a platform on wheels which could take a vehicle. A winding engine could therefore lift a jeep to the rough road which ran up the Adyr Su for eight miles to the Ulu Tau Mountain Camp.

We ambled along the exquisite valley enjoying the carpet of flowers, a myriad coloured butterflies and tiny, furry, stoat-like creatures called *Laska* scurrying amongst the rocks. A milky glacier torrent roared beside us, the sun shone, fleecy clouds drifted by, we caught glimpses of rock and ice spires towering into a blue sky, the aroma of pine needles filled the air, and we passed Russians with baskets collecting mush-rooms, raspberries and wild strawberries. On a platform of boulders in a side valley a rusty 88mm gun, with a long and menacing barrel, pointed skywards, a relic of the German occupation of the Russian Caucasus in 1942.

After a night at the climbing camp we zigzagged up inter-minable moraines, crossed a glacier tongue and camped on the summit of a rock island. Our tents were poised high above an extensive glacier system at the centre of a huge amphitheatre of stupendous peaks with horrifyingly steep north faces: notably Adyr Su Baschi and Ulu Tau, first climbed from the south by Tom Longstaff and L.W. Rolleston in 1903. In the early evening the valleys filled with mist which rolled around the peaks and we sat, hypnotised, drinking our hot fruit juice, as the sun set diffusing the snow-fields with a ruddy glow.

At 5.30am the 45° snow ramp was firm and we cram-ponned up with ease, spurning Sergei's rope handrail which he had tied off to a titanium ice-screw. These ice-screws are tough and light, and are the only items of Soviet gear that are prized in the West and can be exchanged for fleece jackets and

Gore-tex anoraks. The titanium metal is filtched from factories making fighter planes and recast into pitons in hidden sheds and workshops.

Weaving around the crevasses of the upper névé we gained the Mestia Pass after two hours and sheltered from the icy wind in a snow scoop. Away to the north-west rose the twin-topped peak of Elbruz, bathed in sunshine, far above the sea of cloud. But our eyes were drawn down to the south, towards Svanetia. The Leksyr glacier, the second largest in the Caucasus, spread out its tentacles below us and then, in a series of icefalls, ran away south-eastwards for many miles until it turned south and spent itself above the woods and pastures of Svanetia.

One of the great frustrations of trekking in Russia is the almost complete lack of any sort of map. Sergei had a small-scale map showing the principal passes across the Caucasus, but only the largest mountains were named and we could only identify the most characteristic peaks such as Elbruz, Shkhelda and graceful Ushba, one of the most beautiful mountains in the world, which points its twin horns to the heavens like a crescent moon. It was a strange experience for us to have to relinquish our independence and rely entirely on our guide, Nikolai, for without him we would never have worked out which way to go.

The Leksyr glacier was overlooked by relentlessly steep mountains with loose rocky sides which posed a threat of stonefall, so we sped over the ice and across scoured rocks and moraines, and skirted the icefalls; it took several hours to reach the wide, grey river of ice. Here we could relax and enjoy the scenery: waterfalls cascading over rocky lips from hanging glaciers, and a skyline of black teeth and sheer precipices of yellowish rock towering literally thousands of feet above us.

As the valley narrowed, a deep layer of dusty boulders covered the ice, and then we were forced down to the side of the glacier river. Here a chaos of razor-sharp boulders, possibly released from above by a recent earthquake, had to be negotiated by a tortuous route before we could reach the scrub vegetation. Crashing through the undergrowth we ploughed down, at one point crossing a subsidiary torrent by a tree trunk. At 7pm, with green pastures just below, we camped for the night beside the river. In spite of our fatigue we were overjoyed by our first taste of Svanetia; the journey had been through the most wonderfully untamed country we had ever experienced.

Nikolai's son was up at first light picking wild raspberries from the hillside for our breakfast. It was bliss to be sitting in the warm sunshine, feasting on the fresh fruit, with a leisurely exploration of the village of Mestia to look forward to.

Svanetia was distinctly different from Russia. Terraced fields were being scythed and the hay stooked, most houses had potato patches and orchards heavy with fruit, cattle were grazing the steep pastures, and hairy pigs roamed at will through the streets and wasteground, rooting at whatever took their fancy. It was refreshing to see some self-sufficiency, for Svanetia did not appear to be suffering from the dead hand of the collective farm's system. Many houses in the village of Mestia were extremely old with stone watch-towers, three or four storeys high, built (at one end) for defensive purposes. In Mestia we could buy sweet Georgian wine and apricot brandy, and help ourselves to carbonated mineral water from springs in the ground. We visited the tiny museum at the birthplace of Mikhail Khergiani, the USSR's most famous climber, and saw the frayed rope which caused his death in 1967. The display of his equipment reminded me very much of my own, still being used in 1990!

It is interesting to recount some of the adventures of Douglas Freshfield who visited Svanetia in 1868. In that year Freshfield, with three companions, Tucker, Moore and the guide Devouassoud, made a bold exploratory expedition to the Caucasus. At that time the range was unknown to European geographers: its peaks were all unclimbed, and many were unmapped and unmeasured. Having successfully climbed Kasbek, the second highest peak in the Caucasus, Freshfield's party headed west to Elbruz, a difficult and dangerous journey of 120 miles which took nearly a month. Their route led through Svanetia, described as a large basin forty miles long and fifteen wide surrounded by glacier-crowned ridges. The terrain guarding Svanetia was appalling, described by Freshfield as dense, uninhabited forest with shoulder-height vegetation, with only bear tracks to help them through the tangled wilderness of swamps, thickets and torrents. He was not impressed by the people of Svanetia, either, describing them as little short of bandits. When threatened by a ruffian he took stern action: 'The application of a revolver barrel to his face made him retire hastily.'

Their path from Svanetia, leading to a 10,800ft pass over to the Baksan valley and Elbruz, again impressed Freshfield: 'It winds under woods of birch, ash, oak and fir, through thickets of rhododendron and azalea; where, at every break in the forest, the eye catches glimpses, on one side of the green meadows and white towered villages of the Mushalaliz valley; on the other the deep wooded ravine of the Ingur, and the snowy heads of the Leila group... A climb up the hillside above reveals the double-peaked Ushba, which I can describe only by likening it to several Matterhorns, piled on the top of one another.'

The magnificent weather held for our two-day return journey to Baksan over the 10,990ft Betsho Pass. It was a long pull up through dark forests, upland pastures, moraines and glaciers, but it was technically easy; a plaque on the summit commemorates the crossing of 230 Russians in 1942, fleeing from the German advance up the Baksan valley. On the first night we were able to buy a pail of fresh milk from an old crone tending a herd of cows; on the second day Igor and Smargiel dashed on ahead to prepare tea and potato scones beside a stream running through flower-covered moraines − it had been eight hours since breakfast and we were famished.

Since Elbruz so completely dominates the Caucasus for sheer size and height, it irritates and motivates and makes a necessary target for the climber. It is not a difficult climb, but since few of its would-be assailants are adequately acclimatised, it takes an exiguous effort; in addition the weather is often bad, and the exposed slopes are raked by freezing winds. Sadly Elbruz regularly exacts a heavy toll; for instance in May 1990, twenty climbers died of exposure when a sudden and prolonged storm hit the mountain.

A series of two cable cars and a chairlift deposits sightseers on a bleak and soggy snowfield at a height of 12,470ft. Of course there is no shelter, let alone a warm chalet dispensing coffee and Gluhwein − yet such a building would have an unrivalled panoramic view of the Caucasus range. Maybe when the free market economy extends south to the Caucasus, matters will change. Just 1,300ft higher up, perched on a rock band, sits the outrageous Priut hut. This extraordinary incongruity is a three-storey sausage built of concrete in 1939 and covered with a skin of aluminium sheeting. It can sleep a hundred people in four-bedded rooms; it is carpeted throughout, but is freezing cold, and you are only allowed to cook in the basement. A trickle of meltwater down the rocks appears when the sun gets up in summer, otherwise you must melt snow. Toilets are primitive in the extreme. Nevertheless, in Russia you are thankful for small mercies, and we were surprised and delighted at the relative comforts that the Priut offered.

Freshfield's party, on the first ascent of Elbruz in 1868, had to make do with a camp at 11,900ft. They left for the climb at 2.10am; it was bitterly cold as they tramped across the glacier to reach the snow-cone above. Then Freshfield suddenly fell from sight into a crevasse, and '... Considerable hauling was necessary before I could get out'. At 16,000ft they seriously considered turning back, since the cold seemed to be threatening their morale and was presenting a strong possibility of frost-bitten fingers. However, when two of the porters, in their big sheepskins, indicated that they were willing to carry on, Freshfield said, 'If a porter will go on, I will go with him.' 'If one goes, all go,' said Moore, and that settled the matter.

From the top Freshfield recounts, 'We saw the mountains of the Turkish frontier between Batonur and Achaltzik, I believe the Black Sea and the great peaks between us and Kazbek, which looked magnificent. The Pennines from Mont Blanc are nothing compared to the east chain seen from Elbruz. The Caucasian groups are finer, and the peaks sharper. We were on the top from 10.40 till about 11.00; before leaving we built a stone man on the first peak which appeared a trifle the highest.'

One of the more unusual ascents of Elbruz took place in 1942. The German army, their lines of supply seriously stretched, were striving to cross the Caucasus to win control of the oil wells to the south. Alpinists from the first and fourth Mountain Division, led by Captain Groth, obtained permission to attempt Elbruz. The Red Army were holding the Priut hut, but the garrison of eleven men soon surrendered and the German troops took over. After three days of acclimatisation the assault party set out for the summit at 3am on 21 August. The weather was poor, a gale was howling over the icy flank of the ridge, it was bitingly cold and the men's eyes were caked in snow. Visibility was down to thirty feet. But by 11am the climbers had reached the summit, and rammed the shaft of the Reich war flag into the snow. Later, the world was told that the swastika was flying from the highest peak in the Caucasus.

Thankfully our experience on Elbruz was much pleasanter than that of the Germans nearly fifty years ago. It was a bright and starry night when we left the Priut hut at 3am, cramponing up the frozen snow. A nagging wind was scouring the open slopes, and I was glad of two pairs of Dachstein mitts with overgloves, two balaclavas and three pairs of trousers. Many of our party were on Diamox to help their acclimatisation and were forging ahead, but I dropped into a slow and steady rhythm enjoying my own thoughts and the pool of light from my headtorch. Passing through Pastukov's rocks at 15,750ft I recoiled at the stink of sulphurous fumes emerging from vents in the earth's crust – but at 6am the sun burst over the horizon and lit up every peak for a hundred miles.

Again it was Ushba which drew my eyes – its sublime shape and air of arrogance will be forever imprinted on my mind. Now that I could look down on it from above I felt a degree of triumph, and this helped me progress along the endless and exhausting upward traverse of the eastern peak of

Elbruz. At 9am I collapsed on the snow saddle between the east and west peaks, and contemplated the final 800ft cone. My companions were ahead and out of sight, my water bottle clinked with lumps of ice, and my teeth could make little impression on my rock-hard Mars Bar.

At this moment, to my utmost surprise, Sergei appeared from nowhere, and with an irresistible smile, clapped me on the back saying, 'We go now to the top; it is not far.' With confidence boosted and energy dredged up from the reserves, we made good speed up the final slopes of mixed snow, ice and rocks, and soon Sergei was proudly unfurling the Ukranian flag on the arctic summit plateau. To the north, brown hills gave way to distant and arid plains, while to the south, high mountains rose above mist-filled valleys and rolled on to blue horizons. Behind Ushba and Shkhelda we could make out another range of snowy mountains: the range enclosing the legendary region of Svanetia which it had been our privilege to visit, and which had provided the highlight of this unforgettable expedition.

From Baltistan to Hunza
Across the Karakoram

In the colourful brochure the trek looked irresistible: a three-week expedition into the heart of the Karakoram to visit the legendary Snow Lake, to climb the Hispar La and to traverse the entire length of the Biafo and Hispar glaciers linking the stark, almost desert country of Baltistan with the lush green valleys and orchards of Hunza. In other words, a complete crossing of the Central Karakoram.

This could be the experience of a lifetime, our swan song, a last major effort before we relaxed into graceful retirement, we mused. The 17,000ft pass should pose no real problem of altitude; this had never seriously affected us in the Alps or on the memorable Caucasus expedition when we crossed the Mestia Pass into Svanetia and later ascended Elbruz. The accompanying gorgeous photograph of a full moon rising over The Ogre, as seen across the Snow Lake, clinched it. We would go.

It wasn't until the deposits had been paid that a few clouds appeared on the horizon. The map showing our route was of an awfully small scale, and the detailed itinerary contained worrying descriptions of the trek: challenging, sustained, remote and difficult country, the largest continuous glacial system outside of the polar ice-caps, crevasses, tricky moraines, cliffs and river crossings. Nevertheless, some weeks later, complete with visas and sundry jabs, we left a sunny Manchester Airport for Pakistan.

Research into the literature showed us the fascination which the early travellers had for the Snow Lake area. Sir Martin Conway, in 1892, was the first Western explorer to climb the Hispar glacier and look down to the vast plateau, which he called Snow Lake, and he estimated its size as 300 square miles. 'Before us lay a basin or lake of snow. From the midst rose a series of mountain islands, white like the snow that buried their bases, and there were endless bays and straits as of white water nestling amongst them.'

Seven years later Hunter and Fanny Workman ascended the Hispar Pass from the Biafo glacier and confirmed Conway's Snow Lake without having time to explore it. This privilege fell to that most intrepid of explorers, Bill Tilman, who, with Eric Shipton, undertook a major traverse of the Central Karakoram in 1937. Eric Shipton's book *Blank On The Map* gives a stirring account of the 1937 expedition to the Biafo–Snow Lake–Hispar La region.

I have always found Tilman's and Shipton's books to be enthralling, but you need to be sitting in front of a roaring log fire with a full stomach before reading of their privations and spine-chilling adventures. Tilman, in particular, has the reputation of being the uncompromisingly hard man but he did have weaknesses: acclimatisation did not come easily to him and he recounts going down for a week with sickness and fever just two days out of Askole on his Karakoram expedition. I thought ruefully of Tilman when I was ill at Askole but, unlike him, I had a tight schedule and a plane to catch and could not take even one day's rest.

It was at Snow Lake that Tilman described the Yeti footprints which later sparked off a lively correspondence in *The Times*: 'We saw in the snow the tracks of an Abominable Snowman. They were eight inches in diameter, eighteen inches apart, almost circular, without sign of toe or heel. They were three or four days old, so melting must have altered the outline. The beast or bird was heavy, the tracks being nearly a foot deep. We followed them for a mile, when they disappeared on some rocks. The tracks came from a glacier pool where the animal had evidently drunk, and the next day we picked up the same spoor on the north side of Snow Lake. The Sherpas judged them to belong to the smaller type of Snowman, or Yeti as they call them.'

The PIA jumbo jet landed in Islamabad in a downpour. The roads were flooded, the atmosphere was thick and stifling, and the sickly smell of drains, unwashed bodies and curry brought back instant memories of my visit to Indian Kashmir nearly twenty years before. Our trek leader, Pete Royall, was gloomy about the prospects for a flight to Skardu. Because of the weather all flights had been cancelled for several days, and there was a backlog of passengers on the reserve list. The alternative was a non-stop, thirty-hour bus drive, first along the Karakoram Highway to Gilgit, and then along an even rougher and more tortuous road to Skardu.

Thus it was that our party of ten trekkers, plus Pete and Shukar (our sirdar) left the Shalimar Hotel by hired bus at 6am the next morning. We were a mixed bunch: two tough American women who had climbed just about every peak in the Rockies, Trisha and myself, and a group of six fit and determined young mountaineers and backpackers comprising a veterinary surgeon, an archaeologist, a business consultant, a journalist, a teacher and a martial arts instructor.

With prayer flags fluttering from the nearside wing mirror we thundered out of Rawalpindi scattering old men, children, hens and goats from the village streets. In torrential rain, with the windscreen wiper twisted round the side of the glass and inoperative, the driver peered ahead to locate the next sharp corner or blind summit, at which point, with horn blaring, he would overtake several more of the convoy of brightly painted lorries which were grinding their way northwards.

Miraculously we avoided death, although a stray dog was not so lucky as, with an agonised howl, it disappeared under the wheels. The driver kept awake by chewing tobacco, clearing his throat with a disgusting hawking noise and spitting out of the open window. I was sitting just behind him on the front seat as the gobs flew by inches from my face, but as I spent much of the journey clutching a polythene sick bag, it was the least of my worries.

As we entered the mountains it became clear that the bad weather was exceptional. Huge boiling rivers, brown with glacier flour and sediment, roared down the ravines, while the tributaries crossing the road were becoming a problem to ford. At one point a Suzuki van had been washed into a pile of boulders and was half submerged, blocking the road entirely; it was summarily winched out by a powerful truck and dumped beside the road with one wheel torn off and left in the river bed. In places fallen rocks, mud and slurry blocked half the road and we crept by with the nearside wheels merely inches from the crumbly edge of the precipice; the faces of the passengers on that side of the bus turned from green to white.

Inevitably, four hours out of Islamabad, we screeched to a halt behind a seemingly endless queue of stationary vehicles. In heavy, persistent rain we walked on to inspect the damage, and discovered that for several hundred metres the road had disappeared, having been completely washed away. In its place was a shifting bank of scree and mud, with boulders bouncing down from impossible heights into the gorge below; it was not a place to linger. With some skill the driver turned the bus around in the width of the road and we began our journey back towards Islamabad, stopping briefly for a cup of sweet tea, dahl and chapatis at a fly-ridden roadside café with an open, stinking drain running down the side of the street.

After two nights at an hotel, one hour south of the landslide, where we shared the bathroom with frogs and were terrified by cockchaffers the size of saucers, we heard that the road had been bulldozed clear. We also heard that two hundred people had been drowned in the floods, and a bus had been swept into a gorge. At the hotel we slept the night on charpoys in tents, protected from bandits by an armed guard. It was somewhat unnerving to wake in the middle of the night to the sound of gunfire, while later the wailing of the muezzin, calling the devout to prayer, echoed around the valleys.

Eventually, four days after leaving Islamabad, we arrived at the splendid K2 hotel in Skardu. It had stopped raining, patches of blue sky appeared, and we were much cheered by meeting a jubilant Alan Hinkes hot foot from climbing K2. The bad weather had arrived soon after his descent and he had walked for seven days from Base Camp through snow and rain.

The jeep road beyond Skardu had been cut in a dozen places, and it took another two frustrating days of dusty walking in broiling sun and intermittent jeep rides through the Braldu Gorge before we reached Askole. The gorge was hot and arid and, new to the Karakoram, we found the scale of the landscape intimidating. Lizards basked in the sun and scrubby sage brush grew amongst the rocks, reminding us of the Wind River range in Wyoming. Scree slopes ran up dizzily to jagged ridges many thousands of feet above the gorge, down which thundered a mighty glacier river grey with sediment. Rockfalls were commonplace and on several sections of the path it was advisable to hurry along, keeping an eye out and an ear cocked for signs of danger. As the storm clouds rolled back and the sky cleared, hanging glaciers could be seen on the higher peaks of about 18,000ft. Askole, a primitive village of mud and stone houses built into the hillside was thronged with children and goats. Skilfully constructed irrigation channels provided a few terraced fields of barley and maize.

We were now at the start of the trek proper, many days behind schedule and with most of the party ill and living on Imodium and Dioralite sachets. Pete held a council of war. He reckoned that if the recent snow had melted from the lower glaciers, and if we did several double days to make up for the time lost, we could still complete the planned trek, but there would be absolutely no leeway and acclimatisation could be a problem. With nervous smiles we swallowed our first dose of Diamox tablets and agreed to go for it.

Two hours beyond Askole the valley divides: straight on lies lies the Baltoro glacier leading to Masherbrum, K2 and Concordia, while the icefall from the Biafo glacier descends from the left (north) side. Our route lay up the moraines beside the Biafo glacier, sometimes along the ablation valleys between the ice and the steep mountainside or, on special days, along smooth and undulating ice in the middle of the glacier. We became used to double days with a 4am reveille to claw back lost time. The days would start with the smiling face of the cook, Abdullah, outside our tent: 'Morning, chai, sugar?' About two hours later the porters would have been organised by Shukar, our sirdar, and we would be off.

The terrain was undoubtedly the worst that any of us

had ever experienced. The trouble with the Karakoram is that everything is unstable and you are constantly aware of the imperceptibly slow but inexorable grinding together of continents. Whereas in Britain – say, on the Glyders or Scafell Pike – the scree- and boulder-fields will have settled and bedded down over a period of 10,000 years since the last ice age, in the Karakoram the boulders are constantly on the move. It is impossible to trust a particular boulder not to shift or roll over when you tread on it, and after two weeks of such ground we all suffered cuts and bruises. Waves of ice with blocks and flakes the size of houses are often covered with stones or gravel and you must stumble and weave your way through, nicking steps in the bare ice when necessary. Even on the exposed ice a tortuous way must be threaded through the crevasses, or narrow gaps found to be jumped across, while sizeable streams of meltwater coursing down runnels in the ice can pose further problems. It is easy to lose contact with porters and other trekkers, particularly if you are at the rear of the party, and a three-mile wide glacier like the Biafo can be a lonely and frightening place. This happened to our two American colleagues one evening when they became detached from the rest of the party. Finally they were found in a distressed condition by some porters after a three-hour sweep search.

After two exhausting nine-hour days we arrived at the idyllic oasis of Baintha, a patch of green grass in an ablation valley with a clear, sparkling stream flowing through it. Baintha provided an excuse for a much needed rest and acclimatisation day, for we were now at a height of 14,500ft. Energetic members of the party climbed a hill behind the camp and were rewarded by the sight of a herd of ibex and spectacular views of the Latok peaks. I remained in camp, and while washing my socks in the stream the water ran red: the cooks had just slaughtered the two goats that had accompanied us from Askole, and delicious fried liver, followed by wild rhubarb crumble, was on the menu for lunch.

Just beyond Baintha a large side glacier joins the Biafo glacier; it runs up towards the huge and complex peak of Baintha Brakk, or The Ogre (23,900ft), first climbed by Chris Bonington and Doug Scott in 1977. It was down this glacier that Scott crawled for three miles with two broken legs before meeting a rescue party of porters from Askole. The Biafo glacier narrows beyond Baintha, and being enclosed by vast walls of rock on either side, we felt particularly puny. In spite of another arduous double day we were all enthralled by the ferocious mountain scenery which was awe-inspiring and humbling. Dozens of rock and ice spires between 20,000 and 23,000ft high thrust towards the sky, and none more impressive than the twin-pronged Sosbun Brakk, or Conway's Ogre, on the west side of the glacier.

Camp that night was in an elevated position on chaotic moraines looking back down the Biafo glacier. Ahead, within striking distance, lay the Snow Lake and the Hispar La: just one more day to the point of no return and the start of our long descent to Hunza. In the early hours the snow was crisp and firm, and it was a joy to walk across the western edge of the Snow Lake. I could not keep my mind off the early explorers who had first visited this extraordinary plateau in the heart of the Karakoram: Martin Conway, the Workmans, Shipton and Tilman. An almost level snowfield, the Sim Gang glacier, runs east for many miles, while the main Snow Lake forms the upper basin of the Biafo glacier; on this occasion it gleamed and sparkled in the intense rays of the sun. Each branch of the 'lake' was ringed by fabulous peaks which have hardly ever been explored, let alone named. Shipton's 'blank on the map' is an apt description.

Our pace slowed to a crawl as the snow became a pudding and steepened below the crest of the Hispar La at 17,000ft; yet in spite of the blistering sun and our rasping breath, we could marvel at one of the wildest and remotest mountain sanctuaries in the world. But the weather was changing rapidly. Black clouds rolling up the Hispar glacier, with flickers of lightning, soon gave way to swirling snow which obliterated the view and began to build up on the tents. It was eerie to sit huddled in the mess tent with the porters' prayers to Allah rising and falling from their bivouac-cum-snowholes, while avalanches broke away from the impossibly steep snow faces above the pass with a crump and a roar. Although we were out of range of the avalanches we felt exposed and vulnerable.

Pete, the trek leader, announced that our schedule was now so tight that whatever the conditions we would have to strike camp and begin the descent of the Hispar glacier the next morning. Although the storm was brief, the weather remained unsettled for our six-day descent of the Hispar glacier to Hunza. Conditions underfoot were, if anything, more severe than the ascent of the Biafo glacier. Firm snow soon gave way to soft snow, crevasses and, finally, deep wet slush before we regained the hard ice. The middle of the glacier was too chaotic to be feasible, and so our route kept to ablation valleys, moraines and the steep sides of the mountains themselves. On the far (south) side of the Hispar glacier a long line of towering snow peaks formed an unbroken wall, and during the first two days of our descent from the Hispar La avalanches of new snow poured down from these heights almost continuously.

Our route along the north side was interrupted by huge feeder glaciers which filled the side valleys, cutting deeply into the hillsides, before merging with the Hispar glacier: the Khani Basa, Yutmaru, Pumari Chisch and Kunyang glaciers. We were thrilled to peer up these side glaciers to glimpse some of the gigantic peaks of the Karakoram: Kanjul Sar (24,411ft), Pumari Chisch (24,580ft), Kunyang Chisch (25,761ft) and Trivor (25,354ft). However, reascending from the side glaciers to the pencil-thin traverse paths that clung to the hillsides beyond, caused much heart fluttering, even amongst the porters. Horrendously steep faces up to 500ft high, of unstable conglomerate and mud with crudely shaped steps hacked out for your boots, gave more than a touch of exposure: the result of a single slip would have been disastrous.

I had suffered from the altitude on the Hispar La and found it hard to recover on the descent of the glacier. Swollen hands and ankles, a painful chest, hacking cough and persistent nose bleed on top of eight or nine hour days left me as exhausted as I have ever been, and it was with huge relief that we finally reached yak pastures and climbed above the glacier snout to the green fields of Hispar village. But again, the jeep track linking Hispar to Nagar had been destroyed by floods, and it was another long and dusty day's walk to reach the tiny, picturesque summer settlement of Huru. Here a weeping willow overhung a pond of ice-cold water, an old man was churning butter in a hollowed-out log, children were picking apricots, and a lammergier circled effortlessly overhead – and even more importantly, three jeeps were waiting to transport us to Karimabad and the Karakoram Highway.

We had successfully traversed the Hispar La, but with no time and little energy to spare. A bus took us through the exquisitely beautiful Hunza valley with its orchards, vines and terraced fields overlooked by the sensational peak of Rakaposhi. At Gilgit we transferred to a mini-bus for a shattering non-stop drive of sixteen hours to Rawalpindi, with most of us too tired to eat more dahl at flyblown and extremely dubious roadhouses. A fitter, wiser and slimmer party (I lost one-and-a-half stones in weight) caught the plane back home from Islamabad the next morning.

The Wind River Mountains
of Wyoming

There comes a time in life when your children leave home and you and your spouse can once again plan climbing holidays entirely to your own liking – provided, of course, that your brood has not irrevocably damaged your health and you have kept arthritis at bay. Thus it was that Trisha and I joined a team of old friends – their average age well in excess of fifty – on a three-week expedition to Wyoming. At Gatwick Airport we glanced shiftily at each other. Three were walking with ski sticks for support, in addition we had a pulled hamstring, a rebuilt shoulder, a case of hypertension, and confessions of obesity. Later, camp breakfasts resembled pill dispensaries.

The Wind River Range of Wyoming: the name was emotive and enticing enough, but when two of the team, Mike and Sally Westmacott, who had extensive climbing experience in remote ranges throughout the world, rated it top of their list for sheer scenic beauty, we knew we were in for something special. In addition, Alan and Janet Wedgwood – who had borne the brunt of the organisation of this holiday – had visited the southern Wind Rivers five years before with their children, and spoke glowingly of a cirque of stupendous granite towers deep in an area of remote wilderness, rising into the heavens above an emerald lake.

The Wind Rivers are predominantly granite mountains which extend for 120 miles, their crest making up the

Continental Divide: the western streams drain into the Green River–Colorado River system, finally emerging into the Gulf of California, while those to the east flow to the Mississippi. Glaciation and erosion have scoured out classic U-shaped valleys with high, boulder-strewn corries, extensive granite slabs and myriad lakes containing succulent rainbow trout.

The vast Bridger Wilderness encompasses the western side of the Wind Rivers, and we found that the 'wilderness' designation was highly effective at preserving the integrity of the ecosystem. Bulldozed tracks and motor vehicles are completely banned, although pack animals can be taken along some of the principal trails to assist with the stocking of camps if a permit has been obtained. Regulations such as no camping within a quarter of a mile of certain (popular) lakes, or within 200ft of trails and streams, and no lighting of fires or shortcutting of trails and switchbacks, are backed up by Draconian penalties of a $500 fine or six months' imprisonment, or both.

A seventeen-mile backpack in hot and sultry weather established us beside a shallow lake at a height of 10,500ft. A trickle of ponies, llamas and trekkers with dogs fitted with panniers accompanied us as far as Island Lake where they dispersed, each party disappearing into the wilds. From the nearest car park at Elkhart Park we had padded through forests on a bed of pine needles, descended to green valleys with tumbling streams, climbed to stony cols giving enticing views of the north Wind Rivers, and wound our way around tranquil lakes of clear water ringed by water lilies, where fish rose constantly, sending ripples to the shore. The contrast to our dusty drive north from Utah's Salt Lake City through a semi-desert of dried-up water courses, sage brush and sandstone outcrops could not have been more dramatic. In a few miles we had moved from the typical country of the 'Westerns' to a make-believe land more akin to that of the Austrian Tyrol.

As we gained height the trees thinned and the clearings were bright with flowers: Indian paintbrush, mountain aster and daisy, elephant's head, bog asphodel, grass of Parnassus and yellow mountain saxifrage. Little furry animals scurried about everywhere to such an extent that they rarely warranted comment: squirrels, chipmunks, stoats and pikas carrying flowers in their mouths because they were already – in mid-August – lining their burrows prior to winter hibernation. Other sightings worthy of note were a pine marten and a beaver dam (but no beaver). As in the Alps, marmots kept sentry duty, shrieking out warnings from exposed lookout points.

At our bare high camps it was difficult protecting food from the attentions of inquisitive small animals, and we became adept at separating mouse droppings from muesli at breakfast time. But at least the Wind Rivers are free of grizzlies, although black bears are occasional visitors to camps. A lone American backpacker told us about the menace of marmots: 'I once met a marmot that was so intelligent that he untied the drawstring of my rucksack, unzipped the food bag, selected a tin of peanuts and bit round the edge to get at the contents!' 'Really,' grunted Terry, 'and I suppose he left you a thank-you note after his meal.'

Little furry mammals may be picturesque, but they have spread an intestinal parasitic disease called *giardia* to surface water in the Wind Rivers. We were strongly advised to boil all water for five minutes, or to use a close-mesh filter. However, to save time and fuel, Alan had bought an efficient Swiss-made filter pump which, although requiring energetic hand-pumping, served us well and kept us entirely free of *giardia*.

In the north Wind Rivers the sun beat down day after

day, at times driving us into the lake, but by mid-afternoon clouds tended to gather quickly over the mountains to give short but dramatic thunderstorms. Evenings were unforgettable, with a whisper of wind keeping off the mosquitoes, and the low sun highlighting every rib and buttress of the great wall of the Wind River mountains rising behind the tents: Jackson Peak, Fremont, Sacagawea and Mounts Helen and Woodrow Wilson, all over 13,500ft high. On most nights our fishermen – Alan's twenty-one-year-old son, Tom, and Sally – produced trout as an extra course to supplement our favourite dishes of bacon and hash browns followed by pancakes, and we washed this down with either Scotch, port or Cointreau. If we'd learnt something in our dotage, it was how to eat well.

But problems soon emerged, for a combination of malfunctioning Primuses and a miscalculation on meths for the Trangia stoves meant that we desperately needed more fuel. So while the rest of the party climbed Jackson Peak via its broad south-east ridge, Trisha and I dashed down to Elkhart Park, drove to Pinedale, and returned to camp in the late evening with rucksacks of fuel. At midday in Pinedale we requested a motel room for half-an-hour; in all innocence this was to have a shower, but we were met with surly and suspicious looks of disbelief – until we told the receptionist that we'd just walked in seventeen miles from the mountains, and it was clear that we weren't up to any other activity. Back in camp Alan, one of the toughest and most Tilman-like of expedition leaders, actually brought cups of tea to our tent the next morning in recognition of our efforts!

The huge and rather intimidating South Face of Fremont dominated our immediate area and made an obvious objective. A wide rocky rib split the face into two relentlessly steep walls, and from Jackson Peak, Alan had noticed a single scrambly way to the base of the rib. Firstly, therefore, we moved a high camp into the barren wilderness of the Indian Basin, directly under Fremont, whence the rock rib proved relatively sound and easy-angled, giving a straightforward, if exposed scramble directly to the summit ridge. We lunched off Trail Mix and chocolate sitting on a narrow ledge while swinging our legs over a 300ft drop to the Fremont Glacier on the north side. But it was the snow-covered Gannett Peak, the highest in Wyoming at 13,804ft, that captured our attention, rising several miles away to the north beyond Dinwoody Pass. Access to Gannett would be via the Titcomb Basin, Dinwoody Pass and the Dinwoody and Gooseneck glaciers. Gannett looked a long day, and we began to understand why climbers we had met on the trail had taken between twelve and sixteen hours to climb it.

Again we would need a higher camp, and thus we moved to the north end of the Titcomb Basin. This stupendous amphitheatre holds several beautiful lakes, while rock peaks tower up on all sides. We likened it to a giant-sized Coruisk basin. We were fortunate to find a magnificent campsite on the last level area of grass before moraines and boulder-fields took over, and by the rays of the setting sun, were able to identify the ribbon of snow that led to the Dinwoody Pass, rising from beds of Parry's primulae which were attracting blue, yellow and brown butterflies and fritillaries.

In the event Gannett Peak took us thirteen strenuous hours, largely because the numerous changes of terrain — from rock ridges to snow gullies to glaciers — necessitated the constant taking off and putting on of crampons. The 1,500ft of reascent from Dinwoody Glacier to the top of the pass at the end of the day was particularly trying in the boiling sun and soft snow. Yet Gannett's summit ridge was exposed and narrow, with steep convex snow slopes giving way to sheer walls on the east side, and an even longer and more precipitous face on the west. We were lucky that in 1992 Gannett's bergschrunds and crevasses were obvious and safely bridged in several places.

Without being too technical, Gannett gave us a long day's mountaineering on a truly Alpine scale, and we returned to camp tired but tremendously happy

The Cirque of the Towers

Our next move was to the southern Wind Rivers, which are not glaciated but are noted for their steep granite walls up which run several bold and classic rock climbs. Then a two-day trek over the Lester Pass and via Pole Creek, with an exquisite overnight camp beside Wall Lake, took us back to Elkhart Park by a different route.

Leaving early, before the sun rose, we marched through meadows white with hoar frost, watching a pair of hunting eagles and marvelling at the reflection of the peaks in the still lakes. After restocking in Pinedale we shouldered mammoth packs at Big Sandy Opening and staggered eleven miles over Jackass Pass, to camp near Lonesome Lake under the legendary Cirque of the Towers. It took some time to come to terms with our new surroundings, bending our necks to gaze in wonder at the fantastic rock architecture, dominated by the prow of Pingora whose sheer rock walls sweep 1,750ft down to Lonesome Lake. Appropriate names have been given to the principal peaks of the Cirque, enhancing their aura of impregnability: Warbonnet, Warrior, Pylon, Shark's Nose, Overhanging Tower, Wolf's Head, Pingora (the Shoshone Indian name for 'high, rocky and inaccessible'), Camel's Hump and Lizard Head.

The climbers warmed up by 'bouldering' on Skunk Knob which rose close behind Lonesome Lake, a cliff of smooth granite which could have accommodated all of the Llanberis Three Cliffs combined. Yet Kelsey's guidebook dismisses Skunk with disdain, not considering it worthwhile to include any route descriptions or grades. Declining to attack the rock I explored the Cirque and its hidden lakes, enjoying the profusion of flowers and watching a humming bird collecting nectar.

Mike and Sally had climbed in the Cirque on a number of occasions in the 1970s and they recommended several routes. Thus by common consent, the first major objective was to be Pingora. When Frank Bonney, one of the early climbers to visit the area in 1940, first saw Pingora he declared it unclimbable – only to make the initial ascent twenty-four hours later. His route, the South-East, is still the easiest way up the peak and is now graded 5.4; Jane, John and I settled for this one, while Terry, Alan and Tom decided on South Buttress at grade 5.6.

Access to the east face of Pingora is via a ramp on the south side, which leads to a shoulder about two-thirds of the way up the mountain. A narrow ledge is the start for both climbs, and while the others changed into PAs or close-fitting sticky shoes and adjusted and arranged their racks of gear, I tightened the laces of my big boots and tried to adopt an air of confidence. At heart I was extremely apprehensive, for I hadn't climbed anything harder than the Skye Ridge for over ten years. Nevertheless I took comfort from Alan who was suffering from a swollen and festering big toe; he was sitting further along the ledge arranging a PA on one foot and a training shoe on the other.

I need not have worried, for Jane took charge of our rope and led every pitch with aplomb, claiming not to hear my bleats of protest and my half-hearted suggestion that we retreat when confronted by a particularly vicious-looking crack — this when we were perched on a ledge above a terrifyingly awesome drop and my head was spinning with vertigo. Remembering that Alan had led his fourteen-year-old daughter Ruth up this climb a few years ago I was able to pull myself together and continue. Near the top of Pingora, we met the other rope who were able to give us encouragement on the last few pitches. Pingora had been the summit of my ambition, and I felt deliriously happy sitting on the apex of this great peak, surrounded by more bare rock than I had ever seen before. The six of us then tied on to two 50m ropes and, safeguarding each other, climbed down the way we had ascended; strangely the route seemed easier in reverse. Terry, on top form, climbed down last, removing the running belays.

Terry and Tom were now fired up, and the following day, while the rest of us climbed Mitchell Peak discovering white trumpet gentians, spring gentians and delicate blooms of aquilegia, they set out for the North-East Face of Warbonnet, graded 5.7. Perhaps, above all other peaks, Warbonnet influenced the mood of our camp. It was always the last to lose the sun's rays in the evening when it appeared in startling relief, its concave face rising above a massive detached pinnacle called the Plume, to end in vertical exit chimneys. But when the afternoon's thunderclouds gathered, Warbonnet's powerful image, as it lowered over the tents, sent a grim shudder through us all. Terry and Tom were away for nearly twelve hours, returning scarred but triumphant just before dark; it was Tom's first-ever major climb, and Terry's first for over ten years.

Sally's next recommendation was Wolf's Head via the razor-sharp East Ridge which rose like a knife blade from the col under Pingora. However, after two weeks of brilliant weather, the pattern was changing, with clouds blowing in from the west bringing rain. Reluctantly, therefore, we struck camp and moved back over Jackass Pass to Big Sandy Lake for fresh trout. For the first time we noticed a chill in the air, and the leaves on the grass were yellowing with the coming of autumn.

Acres of rock remain to be climbed in the Wind Rivers, but the rate of exploration is slow. The mountains are too far from the roadhead to attract many of the top Yosemite climbers, although the guidebook records past visits by Royal Robbins and Yvon Chouinard. The summer season in the Wind Rivers is short but sweet, yet the mountains can provide some of the most delightful climbing and trail walking to be found anywhere.

Dawn Raid on the Grossvenediger

Frustration is sitting in the smoke-darkened Gastube in the Defregger Haus, at 9,721ft one of the highest huts in the eastern Tyrol, while snow falls steadily from a leaden sky. I push aside the pile of grubby old copies of *Deutscher Alpenverein* and *Der Bergsteiger*, reach for our polythene bag of Tetley tea bags and ask for another litre of *teewasser* (boiling water), cut a few more slices from the salami sausage and peer outside. The summit of the Grossvenediger, Austria's third highest mountain, is only three hours away, but bad weather has dogged us now for four days.

Boredom is relieved by the noisy entry of six jovial Swiss climbers aged about sixty, and in a considerable lather from their five-hour slog from Hinterbichl in the valley far below. They hang their wet clothes on racks around the stove and order many litres of beer and *Schiwasser* to swill down with their supper, toasting the hut, the mountains and other climbers with gusto. But suddenly one of the party, queing at the hatch for another round of drinks, collapses unconscious on the floor. Pandemonium ensues, and there is talk of helicopters being summoned, but the patient is carried to an adjacent room and laid out on a bench where he opens his eyes. He has suffered a temporary blackout and the immediate crisis is over.

Back in the Gastube the remaining five Swiss order more beer, produce a guitar and a piano accordian, and start yodelling and singing folksongs. This is not the usual semi-drunken singing that occurs regularly in Alpine huts, but a wholly musical and moving recital by professionals.

At 5am the next morning it had stopped snowing, but there was complete and thick cloud cover. Indecision reigned in the hut, with nobody wanting to make the first move, but eventually Trisha and I decided to set out. On the lower glacier it was just possible to make out the line of old tracks weaving round a few crevasses, in spite of the fresh snow. Higher up, in thick white mist, this was not possible, and we proceeded on a compass bearing with visibility at times down to one or two metres. Under these conditions one has to tentatively prod the snow at every step in case of crevasses or cornices, and progress becomes exceedingly slow. Any changes in the surface or texture of the snow enables some perspective to be seen, which is a great boost to morale.

We knew we should be heading up towards the summit ridge, but we had strayed onto a steep face. Luckily the fresh powder snow had blown off, leaving snow/ice which was excellent for cramponing. Suddenly our probing ice-axes penetrated a bank of powder snow, plumed to a razor's edge, and met air. This was indeed the narrow summit ridge and we traversed northwards, glad that the lack of visibility eliminated the obvious exposure.

At last the huge summit cross loomed up out of the mist, but it was not the occasion to linger, so we turned round gingerly, balancing on the knife edge, like crossing a river on a tree trunk, and descended quickly, following our crampon indentations down the snow. To have been the first party up this popular peak on such an unprepossessing day gave us a feeling of satisfaction, particularly as on our descent we passed other parties coming up from the Defregger Haus in our footsteps, and a large rope of Austrian soldiers zigzagging up the snow from the Neue Prager Hutte on the east side. This feeling made up slightly for the disappointing weather, for the name Grossvenediger is said to arise from the fact that Venice can be seen from its summit on a clear day.

Back at the hut the clouds were lower than ever and rain was falling. It was time to cut our losses, descend the zigzags to the Johannishutte, and continue on down to the overwhelmingly beautiful Virgental valley. At the quiet picture-postcard village of Pragraten we found a comfortable room in an old chalet attached to a farm. A profusion of colourful flowers grew in window-boxes and hanging baskets. We sank into soft beds with deep duvets, and with the prospect of delicious home-made bread, butter and jam for breakfast, it was like going back to the Alpine way of life as described so often by writers such as Frank Smythe, Janet Adam Smith and Dorothy Pilley in the 1930s.

Bad weather was the bugbear of the eastern Alps that year; indeed, we had moved over to the Venedigergruppe in the High Tauern because of storms in the Dachstein just south of the Salzkammergut. But this was not before we had enjoyed several days of hot sunshine in this dramatic region of giant limestone peaks which rise above green and flower-bedecked pastures to a height of 9,840ft. The main peaks of the Dachstein are strung out along a fifteen-mile-long ridge running roughly east—west, with two smallish glaciers on the north side, and although the area is noted for its long and sustained rock climbs, it also provides very exciting walking.

We traversed under the vast south face of the range between Ramsau and the Hofpurgl Hutte, staying an intermediate night at the Dachsteinsudwander Hutte. Many subsidiary ridges and spurs had to be surmounted and many miles of limestone screes traversed, but it was fine, high-level walking with expansive views south to the Grossglockner, and the alkaline soil encouraging a rich flora. The heat reflected off the limestone, and every day our water bottles were soon empty; maddeningly, streams gurgled through caves and passages deep beneath the rocks and only rarely appeared on the surface. However, on one scorchingly hot but memorable day the sound of cow bells led us to a spring of ice-cold water bubbling up from under a wide fan of scree.

From the Hofpurgl Hutte, set beneath the twin fangs of the Bischofsmutze, a steep scramble over the main spine of the Dachstein leads to the modernised Adamekhutte under the Hoher Dachstein. Seemingly vertical cliff faces are surmounted by hidden ramps and ingenious tortuous routes, together with the liberal use of fixed cables and iron stanchions.

The Adamekhutte is a showpiece for Austria, with heating and power provided by a complicated interlinked system of solar and hydro power together with a diesel generator. We stood on the terrace after supper tracing the easy route for the next morning up the glacier to the rocky summit ridge of the Hohe Dachstein. But an hour later the sky darkened, black clouds boiled over the Gosau lake in the valley, and hail began to hiss down. Soon the terrace was deep in hailstones, and the mountains coated white. This storm was the precursor of a spell of atrocious weather which lasted nearly a week, and next morning we walked disconsolately down through the rain to Gosau.

Zillertal Traverse by Wanderweg 502

You must hand it to the Germans, they never do anything by halves. When, in the 1880s, the Berlin section of the Deutscher Alpenverein decided to build a hut over 6,500ft up in the Zemmgrund Valley of the Zillertal, they constructed a truly massive edifice of huge blocks of stone that will surely last for ever. The Berliner Hut stands four stories high, and has never conceded a tremor, even to the severest winter storm. In the same way that the Franz-Senn Hut is the focal point of the Stubai Alps, the Berliner commands attention and respect from every visitor to the Zillertal. From its imposing position on the moraines high above the glacier river it looks across at the great peaks of the Berliner Spitze, Hornspitze, Turnerkamp and Grosser Moseler.

Unfortunately the roadhead at Breitlahner is not too far away, and hordes of *Alpenwanderer*, wearing green felt hats and lederhose and carrying walking sticks plastered with metal badges, besiege the Berliner. They arrive for lunch, quaff copious quantities of lager on the balcony in the sunshine, dine generously and monopolise the beds and *Matratzenlager* accommodation at night-time. Accommodation is allocated on a first come, first served basis; so it was that when we arrived at 5pm, limp and sore from the Greizer Hut via the Morchenscharte, we were offered only *Notlager* (mattresses in the passageway). For once our Austrian Alpine Club membership cards did not act as talismen.

However, the sheer style and tradition of the Berliner make up for any discomfort. You push open the heavy front door and enter a spacious hall which is beautifully panelled and carved. Oil paintings of past presidents of the DAV hang on the walls, and a broad staircase leads up to the first floor. There is none of the usual clutter of boots, rucksacks, ice-axes and ropes; there are special rooms for these accoutrements. The dining room is of ballroom proportions; it is lit by chandeliers of crystal glass hanging from the high ceiling, while young waitresses bearing *wienerschnitzel*, *Tiroler grostl*, *apfelstrudel* and *kaiserschmarren*, dart between the tables. But although the Berliner Hut is the showpiece of the Zillertal, it is by no means the prettiest or the best situated, and it has none of the friendliness or intimacy of the Kasseler, the Greizer or the Olperer where the Wirtin greets you with a beaming smile, shows you over her spotless domain and then sits you down with a litre of *teewasser*.

The peaks and summit ridges of the Zillertal range make up the border between Austria and Italy. For this reason traversing the mountains on the Austrian side is hard work; subsidiary ridges and spurs descend from the frontier ridge like the teeth of a comb and you are for ever climbing up and down, up and down. However, a network of huts have been built at, or just above, glacier level and the head of the valleys, and you rarely need to descend to the pastures. Footpath number 502 will take you across the main Zillertal range from near Mayrhofen in the east to the Brenner Pass. The Austrians are efficient and skilled in their path construction and waymarking; the thin line, wending its way across the snow fields, up the ridges and over the cols, is not an obtrusive feature, but a means of enjoying high mountain country in comparative safety and without route-finding problems.

It was mid-August when Trisha, my two younger children, Lucy (fifteen) and William (thirteen), and I completed the traverse in ten days, staying in eight different huts *en route*. We met surprisingly few walkers on Wanderweg 502, although the huts in the central Zillertal were crowded. The great attraction about an Alpine walking holiday is that, barring exceptionally severe weather, every day brings a change of scene, a new hut and a satisfying advance in progress. Frustrating days of hut, bivouac or tent festering are unknown. Noise, fumes and the banter in the bars, cafés and campsites are left behind. All right, there is not the unique, adrenalin-pumping action of a major climb, but neither is there the despair as precious time passes, the rock faces remain out of condition and ambitious plans fall into ruins.

Mayrhofen is the perfect Alpine resort. You alight from the toy train, which runs up the valley from Jenbach on a narrow-gauge track, and find a bustling little town where everyone wears climbing boots and breeches and carries a rucksack. The streets are lined with bakers' shops, delicatessens, restaurants and *pensions* with baskets of flowers hanging from the balconies.

We swallowed our pride and took the Ahorn cable car to Hahnpfalz, only one-and-a-half hour's walk from the Edel Hut. But fresh snow by night and damp swirling mist by day taxed the beginning of our Zillertal traverse, and the next day the conditions were sufficiently bad for us to take the valley route to the Kasseler Hut – but from there onwards the sun shone, the snowline receded and we became acclimatised. Descending from the Lapen Scharte to the Greizer Hut on a perfect summer's afternoon all the old magic was there: marmots shrieking warnings from the mouths of their burrows, chamois bounding down the screes, Alpine choughs

gliding on the updraughts, snow gentians, primulas, saxifrages, harebells and Christmas roses opening up their petals
to the sun, while the gleaming icefields of the Grosser
Loffler and the Schwarzenstein drew our gaze upwards. Our
joy was only slightly tempered by a clear view of the path for
the morrow: a 1,000ft descent to the glacier torrent, followed by an unrelenting climb of 3,500ft up scree and snow
to the Morchensharte.

I am often asked about the severity of the snowfields and
the rock scrambling, and the experience necessary to attempt
an Alpine traverse. While little or no rock climbing is
involved, the paths are often narrow and steep, and some
scrambling may be necessary to surmount rock ribs and short
buttresses. Exposure can be considerable, and there are many
places where a slip or a stumble could have serious or fatal
consequences. But this is true of many of our great mountain
traverses: An Teallach, Liathach, the Cuillin, Crib Goch and
Sharp Edge. For this reason we never took our children when
they were below the age of eleven: children like to run ahead,
they underestimate danger and they can easily trip. Also, to
reach some of the high huts, at about 9,850ft, it is necessary
to cross glaciers, and here ropes, prusiks and harnesses must
be used. But most snowfields that need to be crossed on the
major hut-to-hut paths are obvious and easy. It is vital, of
course, to use ice-axes, but crampons are rarely necessary
except early in the morning on snow glazed by frost.

The recommended guidebook times for hut-to-hut traverses always make fascinating reading: like rock-climbing
grades, everyone has an outspoken opinion on their validity.
At the start of the holiday the times are desperately difficult
to achieve; by its end they are almost insulting to one's fitness.
Of course, the times refer to perfect conditions, and under

snow when the rocks are slippery, they are wildly inaccurate. Thus a fit party we met, who set out on the Edel-to-Kasseler leg after a night of snow, took a full twelve hours and finished, exhausted, by torchlight – yet the guidebook time is eight hours.

The highest point on the Wanderweg 502 is reached east of the Berliner Hut at the Schonbichler Scharte (10,108ft), and another peak with a delightful-sounding name, the Schonbichler Horn, lies a short distance above the col. But on our visit black clouds had been building up all morning, and as we scrambled to the summit cross of the Schonbichler Horn with frozen fingers, a strong wind blew hail and sleet across the ridge. Sadly there was no view. Hastening down to the Furtschagl Haus we arrived just as the clouds were rolling away, thunder was rumbling in the valley and a rainbow hung over the Grosser Moseler.

On the west side of the Zillertal several alternative mountain traverses can be taken. From the large dammed lake, the Schlegeispeicher, you can proceed via the Olperer Hut and the Geraer Hut to St Jodok in the Brenner Pass; or you can cross to the Friesenberg Haus and take the Berliner Hohenwag back to Mayrhofen; or thirdly, you can fight your way through the ski lifts to the Spannagel Haus and continue north to the Tuxer Alps. We chose the first alternative and meandered up through the azaleas to the Olperer Hut. This is a small and extremely well run hut in a wonderful position. It looks straight up the Schlegeisgrund valley, over the lake to the hanging glaciers on the Hochfernerspitze and the Hochfeiler, at 11,482ft the highest of the Zillertal peaks. We were a day ahead of schedule and, sitting in the Gastube watching the sun setting behind the Hochfeiler and enjoying our *goulaschsuppe*, we decided to spend an extra night at the hut and attempt the Olperer (11,404ft) by the east-south-east ridge (the Schneegupfgrat).

The most frequented route on the mountain is the north ridge, but this is liberally festooned with cables and iron spikes. On the other hand, the Schneegupfgrat is superb: the approach is up a steep snowfield and a band of loose rock, but then you reach a sharp snow arête leading to the rocks of the final ridge. The rock was sound, the ridge narrow and the position airy, but the standard was only PD, and in the hot sun, it was bliss. Together with a few other climbers we felt smug moving freely along the arête, whereas across on the north ridge climbers were motionless, strung out like beads on a necklace, waiting their turn for the next pitch.

The penultimate day of our Zillertal traverse took us from the Olperer Hut, over the Riepengrat and the Alpeiner Scharte, to the Geraer Hut. The Alps were shimmering under a clear blue sky, intensely cold at first in the shadow of the Fuss-stein and the Schrammacher, and then scorchingly hot for the steep ascent to the Alpeiner Scharte (9,708ft). At the top of the pass we drank deeply from our water bottles and chatted to an old Austrian couple on their way to the Pfitscherjochhaus. I remarked that this hut was just over the border in Italy, at which they stiffened and choked: 'Not Italy, never say Italy, the Pfitscherjochhaus is in the South Tyrol.' I apologised at once for my *faux pas*. The South Tyrol was promised to Italy in the secret Treaty of London in 1915, and the Treaty of Versailles honoured that promise. But the Austrians have never become reconciled to this arrangement, and considerable animosity against the Italians of the South Tyrol remains.

The Geraer Hut is overshadowed by a semi-circle of great rock faces falling from the Fuss-stein, the Schrammacher and the Sagwand Spitze. Several times in the night we were disturbed by the roar of rock avalanches sweeping down the cliffs. When the sun rose above the rock walls we ambled reluctantly down through the bilberry bushes, past soulful cows grazing the high pastures, and finally through sweet-smelling pinewoods where large black ants scurried across the path. Hay was being scythed from even the steepest alp and hung on frames to dry, before being stored in creaking wooden chalets. Not a breeze-block or a sheet of corrugated iron to be seen. Then the lane turned a corner and the peaks of the Zillertal disappeared for another year; but soon the spire of the church at St Jodok announced the Brenner Pass, the railway station and our return to the real world.

The Worst Trail
This Side of Hell

In the year 1896 a roving Indian prospector called Skookum Jim was eking out a precarious living amongst the creeks of the Klondike river, a major tributary of the Yukon river in North-West Canada at a latitude of 64°N. While casually surveying Rabbit Creek with George Carmack he bent down and picked up a nugget of gold. This was the strike of a lifetime, because in the gravel bed of the ancient stream the gold lay thick, in quantities that were beyond the dreams of avarice. Carmack renamed the creek Bonanza Creek, and within two weeks it was staked in its entirety by the lucky four who happened to be in the Klondike area at that time. Neighbouring Eldorado Creek also yielded vast quantities of gold, confirming the Klondike strike to be the richest ever made.

With no telegraph, and the Yukon river frozen, the miners worked throughout the winter amassing fortunes in gold while the rest of the world lived in ignorance. Not until May 1897 did the thaw arrive and allow the prospectors to raft down to the sea and embark for the southern ports. Yet so huge were the distances, and so primitive the transport, that it was not until July that two rusty freighters from St Michael in Alaska, the *Portland* and the *Excelsior*, docked in Seattle and off-loaded three tons of gold. America at that time was in deep depression, but immediately it was gripped by gold fever and 100,000 people, who had nothing to lose, sold everything and stampeded north. Very few ships were available which could make the long and difficult journey north to the mouth of the Yukon and then upriver to Dawson City, adjacent to the Klondike, a tiny settlement which grew during the following six months to a town of over 40,000. Boat tickets to Dawson were changing hands at exorbitant prices and were beyond the reach of many stampeders. This, coupled with the fact that the icy grip of winter was fast approaching, meant that tens of thousands set out for the long overland route via the Chilkoot Pass.

Skagway, a small Pacific port in south Alaska, lies under a range of formidable mountains, the southern tail of the great St Elias mountains. To gain the hinterland the Indians had long used the Chilkoot Pass which runs north for forty miles from Dyea through Pacific rainforests, then climbs to 3,700ft through snow, glacier tongues and barren boulder fields, to Lake Bennett. This lake is the souce of the mighty Yukon river whence, for 570 miles, it twists and turns and foams down rapids to reach Dawson City and the Klondike. This was the route taken in the winter and spring of 1898 by over 30,000 stampeders.

The difficulties of the trail cannot be exaggerated: deep snow, ice, temperatures of -40°, blizzards and treacherous ground led to many accidents. The final 1,000ft to the summit of the pass lies at an angle of 40°, and stampeders climbed steps chopped in the ice. An avalanche killed sixty-three people in April 1898.

The Alaska–Canada boundary at the summit of the Chilkoot Pass was manned by the North-West Mounted Police, who for safety's sake would not allow anyone into Canada who was not carrying a year's supply of food and equipment, a load which exceeded one ton in weight. Supplies were weighed below the pass at a camp called The Scales. Goods were relayed in stages using caches, and this meant that stampeders had to make up to thirty ascents of the pass, staggering upwards with crippling loads. A continuous stream of backpackers moved snail-like up the icy staircase, and if one stepped aside to rest it might have been hours before he could get back into the line. Martha Black from Chicago crossed the Chilkoot Pass in the summer of 1898, wearing a long skirt, and described it as 'the worst trail this side of hell'. Martha gave birth to a son in Dawson City and later became a Canadian MP.

On the north side of the Pass a succession of small lakes lead down to Lakes Lindeman and Bennett. Huge canvas cities sprang up beside the lakes with populations of 10,000 or more. Trees were felled and the trunks whipsawed to make planks for boats and rafts. The ice finally moved away on 29 May 1898, and one of the weirdest flotillas ever launched set off down the Yukon river for Dawson City. The Mounted Police counted 7,124 boats.

Yet all was not plain sailing. Rapids between Lakes Lindeman and Bennett — at Whitehorse, Mile Canyon and again at Five Fingers — along with countless submerged rocks, reefs and sandbars, claimed many more lives and tons of supplies. Most of those that made it to Dawson met mud, high prices and disappointment, for few struck riches after the 1896 flush of successes. Dreams faded as the stampeders wore themselves out panning frozen muck from the creeks, and they were only too ready to respond, in the autumn of 1898, to rumours of a new strike at Nome in Alaska, on the edge of the Baring Sea. Moreover the enormous numbers of stampeders who tackled the Chilkoot Trail fell prey to ruthless entrepreneurs in Skagway, Dyea, Dawson and the extensive camps of Canyon City, Sheep Camp, Lindeman and Bennett. Hotels, bars, casinos, brothels and dance halls abounded.

It was not long before go-ahead companies erected overhead wires to carry goods up to the Pass summit, but it was the coming of the railway that finally finished the Chilkoot as a viable route into the Yukon. In May 1898 the White Pass and Yukon Railway Company began constructing the line from Skagway to Whitehorse. Broke and disillusioned stampeders provided a source of cheap labour, and in spite of exceptionally difficult terrain, the Skagway-to-Bennett section of the line opened in July 1899, and the extension to Whitehorse a year later. Immediately the Chilkoot Pass was deserted; it had had just two years of frantic use, and its canvas and timber settlements became ghost towns. Since 1899 the ramshackle cabins have decayed and the discarded artefacts rusted, scars have healed and the forests have regenerated. The Klondikers might never have lived or struggled through the mountains. But in 1976 the Chilkoot Pass was declared a National Historical Park and administered jointly by the United States and the Canadian Parks Services.

Today the Chilkoot is one of the great classic historical trails of the world. It provides a backpacking challenge of several days through diverse, grand, wild and exquisitely beautiful countryside, with the added fascination of literally thousands of relics bearing testament to the greatest gold rush the world has ever seen.

It was mid-August when Trisha and I left Skagway for the Chilkoot Trail, carrying a lightweight tent and food for four days. Two cruise liners were anchored in the bay and the cafés and bars were thronged with tourists; a far cry from the days when Soapy Smith and his gang ruled the town, robbing and terrifying the visitors. Escaping from commercialism with relief we entered the Pacific rainforest at Dyea and walked along the narrow path under a green canopy. Alaskan summers are desperately short, and already some of the willow leaves had turned a vivid yellow. At once our worst fears were allayed: the trail was not crowded. Perhaps another ten people left Dyea for Lake Bennett the same day that we did, but strung along a thirteen-mile leg to Sheep Camp, they were not intrusive.

It was damp, hot and humid as we pushed through ferns and hemlock, stepped over boreal toads and fungus growths, and brushed away mosquitoes beside the foaming river Taiya. At times shafts of sunlight penetrated the trees, and we had occasional glimpses of high, glaciated mountains. The park authorities have placed wooden bridges across the tributary streams, and at Canyon City, now just a few tumbledown stone walls in a forest glade, a cabin has been built so that, in the event of inclement weather, you can eat your lunch in comfort. Maps are issued free at Skagway, and rangers patrol the trail every few days so you get the feeling of being cossetted; but after two weeks fending for ourselves in the vast wilderness of the Yukon and North-West Territories, Trisha and I were not wholly averse to this.

Sheep Camp has sites for about twenty tents amongst the tree roots, and a short distance away a high steel bar with ropes has been erected so you can hoist your food out of reach of grizzly bears. At its peak Sheep Camp housed 8,000 residents with fourteen restaurants, two dance halls and a hospital. By now we were used to the tins, rusty stoves, water cans and old boots which were liberally strewn in the undergrowth, and these relics became even more prolific the next day at the site of the notorious Scales Camp.

By late summer the final slope, nicknamed the 'Golden Stairs', the ascent of which had broken so many spirits and backs, was merely a steep ramp of scree and loose boulders with patches of wet snow. In place of the Mounted Police Post was a new wooden cabin containing several Thermos flasks of hot lemonade, and a friendly note from Christine, the Canadian Park Warden, welcoming us to Canada and inviting us to a drink. The clouds were down, it was raining, our packs were leaden and we accepted the offer with gratitude.

The change from rainforest to Alpine tundra is abrupt. Once on the north side of the pass the terrain is open and rocky, with a bright flora, reminiscent of the Cairngorm plateau. The sun now appeared, turning Crater Lake to sapphire and the shallow streams to quicksilver. Lake followed lake as we made our way north, deviating from the path in places to examine ancient carts, piles of bones, rusty horseshoes and leather bridles, remarkably preserved by the cold, dry climate for nearly one hundred years. As we lost more height, juniper, azaleas, low pine and scrub birch appeared, the scenery becoming more Alpine-meadowish than Alaskan. It was no wonder that the stampeders called the next camp Happy Camp.

A Rufus humming bird flashed around our tent the next morning, and in hot sunshine we ambled down to Lake Lindeman. The smell of herbs and warm leaves pervaded the air, and white bell heather and at least five or six varieties of berry grew profusely on either side of the path. Squirrels, gophers and chipmunks scampered amongst the rocks, but however much we peered amongst the undergrowth we never saw any porcupines, even though they had stripped the bark of many pine trees. As the sun set the air became clear and sharp, and an evening spent exploring the historic sites and relics of Lindeman City was followed at midnight by our first-ever display of the aurora borealis, the flickering coloured lights moving across the northern sky.

Between Lakes Lindeman and Bennett the trail runs through pine-clad hills dotted with delightful lakes and overgrown with succulent blueberries. At Bare Loon Lake granite slabs ran into deep, clear waters, while startlingly blue dragonflies hovered over waving reed beds. But biting black flies and mosquitoes became a real nuisance, and down at Lake Bennett they were intolerable. We dared not leave the tent without applying a liberal squirt of 'Off' both to skin and clothes, for the long probosces of British Columbian mozzies have no difficulty in penetrating cotton shirts and lightweight jerseys. For the Chilkoot Trail it is essential to have a tent with a closely zipped gauze entrance to provide an insect-free zone in which to cook and sleep.

One estimate puts the population of Bennett in the spring of 1898 at 20,000; boatyards, hotels and workshops abounded, and every tree within a radius of five miles was felled. Now, piles of rusty tins, bottles, tools, ironmongery and cooking pots are everywhere to be seen, and the stilts of ancient slipways are still there, running into the lake. Historians are just beginning to identify and tag the important sites. Although a road linking Skagway to the Arctic Highway opened in 1979, the narrow-gauge railway from Skagway to Fraser still operates. Tiny railcars, carrying twelve people, run twice a day along the line to Bennett and provide a lifeline for Chilkoot Trail walkers returning to civilisation.

When you visit Alaska, the Yukon or the North-West Territories, you realise the absurdly recent history of the area. Only 150 years ago the first prospectors from the Hudson Bay Company explored the rivers, while the Indian culture was almost Stone Age. Overnight the Klondike Gold Rush changed all that, and it is understandable that the authorities take great pride in preserving what, to some people, is a mere rubbish-strewn trail, thirty years more recent than the Settle-to-Carlisle railway.

The trail is a tough challenge and it passes through wonderfully changing scenery, while the background literature and the extensive array of artefacts bring home at every step the human story of hopes, fears and suffering during that terrible winter of 1897–8.

A Circuit of
the Otztal Alps

We lounged on the balcony of the Ramelhaus in the scorching sun, nursing litre tankards of ice-cold German lager and watching the slow crocodile of climbers winding up the endless succession of zigzags to the hut. From our eagle's eyrie, 9,850ft up in the Otztal Alps, we could clearly see the church steeple and chalets of the village of Obergurgl down the valley, while beyond rose the glistening white peaks of the Stubai Alps. When the sun disappeared behind the Schalfkogel the temperature would plummet and it would be time to retreat to the wood-panelled Gastube, with its throbbing tiled stove, for goulash soup and *apfelstrudel*. But for the present we were content to breathe the mountain air and enjoy this most relaxing of surroundings, far away from traffic, telephones and the demands of modern living. The Tyrol is a tonic, where your blood pressure falls and the cares of the world slip from your shoulders.

This was our third day of a ten-day circuit of the Otztal Alps from Obergurgl to Vent. The Austrian Alps can be divided into several distinct groups such as the Stubai, Venediger, Zillertal, Otztal, Silvretta and Dachstein, all of which provide magnificent mountain walking. The Otztal is probably the largest area with the most extensive glacier systems and many of the highest peaks, and so it poses more of a challenge than its lowlier neighbours. You cannot get away without the use of a rope, crampons and ice-axe, and a knowledge of crevasse rescue is imperative. Nevertheless, a comprehensive network of paths and huts means that a hut-to-hut traverse can be enjoyed by any walker with Scottish winter experience.

Since the Otztal Circuit was to take us to well over 10,000ft it was necessary to acclimatise slowly, and the wide valley containing the Gurgler glacier, which runs south to the Italian border, was ideal for this purpose, with two intermediate level huts, the Langtalereck and the Hochwildehaus. The path up the valley from Obergurgl wound gradually up through meadows of flowers with bubbling streams, cow bells, sheep bells, shrieking marmots, chirping choughs, sparkling glaciers and hot sun. Men in Tyrolean hats were scything grass from even the steepest meadow and hanging it on stakes to dry in the sun, and the whole scene reflected the romantic image portrayed by Julie Andrews in *The Sound of Music*.

But on the third day it was necessary to cross the glacier and climb the steep zigzag path to the Ramelhaus. A further ascent involved some rock scrambling, though it was made easier by an aluminium ladder, and this led us to the top of the ridge at 10,453ft, giving fantastic views east to the Stubai and west to the Wildspitze, the highest peak in the Otztal and the second highest in Austria. After a loose descent of mica-schist screes we reached a green alp with a profusion of flowers, then the path contoured above the Niedertal valley to the Martin-Bush hut. At 8,205ft the Martin-Bush is well placed for a number of the Otztal's principal peaks, and we chose to tackle the shapely Similaun (11,830ft) via the rock ridge known as the Marzellkamm, which runs up to the summit snowfield.

By 8am the sun was blazing over the surrounding peaks

and the flowers were opening. On the lower section of the Marzellkamm, before the ridge became narrow and rocky, we walked over carpets of snow gentians, moss campion, starry saxifrage, Alpine harebells and marigolds. The summit of Similaun was at the end of a curved, knife-edged ridge of snow. A few wreaths of mist still lay in the valleys, but the mountains thrust up into an azure sky. Prominent to the north was the Wildspitze, while a 360° panorama of peaks, stretching to distant horizons, took our breath away: the Bernina Alps in Switzerland, the saw-toothed silhouette of the Dolomites, the Stubai, Silvretta and Arlbery. It took a major effort to turn for the valley, but the snow was crumbling in the sun and the snow bridges over the crevasses were becoming vulnerable.

A slushy descent of the West Ridge took us to the Similaun hut, astride the Austrian-Italian border. It was a ramshackle building, an old army post, but we enjoyed a warm welcome and a mug of hot chocolate. Just up the snow slope, behind the hut, the now famous Ice Man emerged recently from the glacier after an unusual snowmelt following a long, hot summer. This fascinating discovery pushed back the known Bronze Age by nearly 1,000 years, and the Ice Man himself is reckoned to be over 5,000 years old. A good path led us back to the Martin-Bush hut where we celebrated our climb with *wienerschnitzel* and *kaiserschmarren* (a delicious sweet pancake).

The next leg of our Otztal circuit took us over a high ridge, just below the Seikogel, before descending steeply to the Hochspitz hut in the Rofental valley. Since the path passed so close to the summit of the Seikogel, at 10,846ft, we found it worth spending a few extra minutes in scrambling to the top of this fine peak. Unfortunately the weather was changing, and the following day we left for the Brandenburger hut with clouds massing on the horizon. The path traversed high above the impressive icefall of the Kesselwanderferner, and it was little more than a scratch mark scored across rather muddy and exceptionally steep and exposed slopes. With the sky darkening we forged on with all possible speed to the hut which, at 10,735ft, is one of the highest in the Tyrol.

The Brandenburger is built on a rock island in the middle of the Weisskamm, a vast area of glaciers and snowfields, and the scene was dramatic with the sky turning a vivid purple, the light fading rapidly, a strong cold wind scouring the glacier and thunder rumbling. Half an hour from the Brandenburger, and still in the middle of the glacier, the storm broke and we were lashed by sleet and hail, lightning flashed around and thunder crashed. We felt horribly vulnerable, with the possibility of our ice-axes acting as lightning conductors. Seldom had we been so glad to reach the shelter of a hut, and soon we were steaming in front of the stove and sipping hot soup.

The storm lasted for thirty-six hours, with constant lightning and thunder and the air heavy and charged with static – even the window frames were buzzing, and at times hailstones the size of marbles drove against the windows like machine-gun bullets. But eventually the storm passed over, and the morning of the third day dawned calm. By 6am the peaks were bathed in sunshine: we were first away from the austere Brandenburger, and hastened on to the Vernacht hut via the Fluchtkogel (11,483ft).

Descending from the rock island on which the hut was perched required the greatest care, for every exposed rock and boulder was coated in verglas. However, the glacier snow was frozen hard and virgin white, and we crossed to the

Fluchtkogel in dazzling sunshine, with every ice crystal a flawless diamond reflecting the light in a kaleidoscope of colours. The air was as sharp as a needle and a real tonic, and for once there was no track or footsteps to follow in the snow which added to the exhilaration. It was a perfect mountain day.

Once we had negotiated the *bergschrund* the Fluchtkogel proved an easy conquest as our crampons bit firmly into the frozen snow. By mid-morning the sun had real strength and we were in shirtsleeves applying sun-block cream. A long and gradual descent along a path balanced on top of a lateral moraine, which effectively divided the glacier from the ablation valley, led us to the large Vernacht hut set in pastoral surroundings at 9,075ft.

The most popular mountain in the Otztal is the Wildespitze, an elegant peak with twin summits rising above narrow ridges. It is conspicuous from many of the cols and lesser mountains of the Otztal — and perhaps one should leave it at that, because our personal experience of the Wildespitze was not very rewarding. The normal jumping-off point for the Wildespitze is the Breslauer hut, which is an easy day's walk from the Vernacht hut. We were advised that the Breslauer gets very crowded, so we made an early start from the Vernacht, hastened along the path and booked into the hut by mid-morning. Streams of walkers were coming up from the valley and we soon got quite tired of the 'Gruss Gott' welcomes. By evening the hut was bursting, latecomers were being offered mattresses in the corridors and the kitchen was doing a roaring trade, while spontaneous folk singing, accompanied by an accordion, broke out in the Gastube and continued until the early hours.

The next morning dawned fine and frosty and the hut soon disgorged its occupants onto the lower slopes of the

Wildespitze. Guided parties tripped over their ropes as they pushed and shoved their way up the snow ramp to gain the Mitterkar Joch, hell bent on the summit and seemingly immune to any aesthetic pleasure. Incompetence was rife, with clients being pulled and pushed up the icy summit rocks by the guides to reach the massive iron cross. Shouts and cries rent the air, and we stayed only long enough to have our rope trampled on before making our way down. Indeed, whilst enjoying a late lunch on a large rock below the snow ramp we watched in horror as two parties, taking no heed of the rotten, sugary snow, fell 200ft to the bottom in a maelstrom of whirling limbs, axes, ropes and rucksacks. Mercifully no one was seriously hurt.

Back at the hut by early afternoon and with the day's exertions behind us, we could enjoy the hot sun and panoramic views from the terrace. We drank litres of the cheap, fruit-flavoured drink called *Schiwasser* which is sold in great quantities to replace the body fluids.

An easy descent to the village of Vent on the last day was all that remained of our hugely enjoyable Otztal circuit. After ten days in the mountains we were fit, brown, a bit leaner and felt thoroughly restored. The weather held for the 3,280ft descent through flowery meadows and sweet-smelling shrubs to the bustling village of Vent. There was just time for a bottle of wine and a pizza at the Hotel Tyrol before the afternoon bus left for Obergurgl.

Haute Provence:
The Verdon Gorge

In the late afternoon we came down from the Suech plateau in the parched limestone mountains of Haute Provence to the tiny village of Rougon. We refilled our water bottles from the fountain in the square and sat in the shade of a walnut tree, wondering how such a beautiful old village with narrow streets and ancient houses, roofed with faded red tiles and hung with creepers and vines, came to be built on such a steep hillside. Rougon is at a height of 3,000ft, and we could look down to the sinuous valley of the Verdon river to the famous gorge. Steeply wooded slopes gave way to sheer cliffs of yellowy limestone which extend on each side of the river for an astonishing seven miles. The average height of the cliffs is 1,150ft, and the whole area is a rock climber's paradise with an international reputation.

The GR4 ultra-long distance trail, which actually runs right across Southern France from Grasse to Royan on the Atlantic coast, passes through the Verdon Gorges, and Trisha and I spent a few days walking this section in mid-September when the main holiday season was over. The sun was still hot, although not oppressively so, and the evenings were deliciously cool. We needed jeans and fleece jackets to combat the early morning nip, but soon reverted to shorts and T-shirts when the sun rose. Accommodation was no problem in cheap hotels in the villages, and we could buy bread, cheese and tomatoes every day for lunch. This meant that our rucksacks could be kept to the minimum weight, although we could not afford to stint on water, taking at least two litres each for a seven-hour day.

The mountains were a revelation and a delight. From Castellane the GR4 wound its way through cool oak woodlands before emerging onto the open hillside which was covered in wild lavender, thyme and other herbs. A profusion of flowers were still in bloom, including carpets of gentians and fields of autumn crocuses, although the leaves on the birch and chestnut trees were already changing their hue. Other walkers, except in the Verdon Gorge itself, were few and far between, and the atmosphere had a touch of melancholy, like a seaside resort shutting up for the winter. Yet on our first day we were able to shelter during a brief thunderstorm at a remote pottery, high in the hills at Chasteuil, and here could still buy mouth-watering crêpes straight out of the pan.

The walk through the Verdon Gorge, between Point Sublime and La Maline, must be one of the most exciting and dramatic day's excursions in Europe. Although the distance is only seven miles, the path is a giant and tortuous switchback and does great credit to the French speleologist Edouard Martel who, at the beginning of the century, performed the seemingly impossible task of pioneering a through-route. In France the canyon is known as the 'Sentier Martel'.

From Point Sublime at the northern edge of the gorge the GR4 winds steeply down the hillside, passing under vast overhanging walls of limestone, to the water's edge. In spite of the dry weather the Verdon river was rushing along merrily because the flow is regulated by a dam and artificial lake upstream. This maintains a reasonable volume of water throughout the summer for rafting and canoeing. Only in the deep pools was the water still and green, and here fishermen were casting their flies. Cliffs soar almost straight up from the water's edge, and a series of tunnels provides the only means of progression. The longest is 2,198ft, and since there is no artificial lighting, torches must be carried. At intervals peep-holes in the tunnel walls allow views down to the river below.

Having emerged from the tunnels the path runs through damp woods, which grow thickly on the gentler lower slopes of the gorge, but before long you are climbing up steeply to circumnavigate rock bluffs and pillars – and this is the story of the day: at times you descend to river level, only to dou-ble back in giant zigzags to traverse under overhanging cliffs. In one place a series of iron ladders several hundred feet high are necessary to overcome an obstacle, and in another place fixed cables help you to traverse a loose and heavily eroded scree slope. At intervals rock platforms, like eagles' eyries, offer a clear view over the trees down to the river, giving an effective sense of scale. The main impression is one of acres of vertical rock towering up in all directions; rock faces where Malham Cove and Gordale Scar would disappear into insignificance.

Half-way along the gorge a tributary river, the Artuby, meets the Verdon river. We lunched on flat rocks just above the confluence at a place called Mescia, which was a furnace with the sun reflecting off the white limestone in all direc-tions. Indeed, at the end of the day I found the climb up to the Chalet La Maline, a good 1,200ft of ascent, to be exhausting. But it was marvellous to be sitting on the terrace of the Chalet with a cool beer, looking down on the snaking river far below. The seven-mile stretch of gorge had taken us seven hours.

We had not seen any climbers on the cliffs, but there were plenty enjoying the sunshine and wine outside the cafés of La

Palud as we walked through this little town the next morning. Perhaps they were seeking a little Dutch courage before commencing their climb, or were just having a day off relaxing in the warm sunshine. The GR4 took us way up into the hills, traversing high above the river and crossing two cols, until we could look down over broken cliffs and pinnacles to the vast, turquoise-coloured Lac de Sainte-Croix. As the path wound through thick undergrowth and scrub, we noticed many disturbed areas where the turf had been scraped off by wild boar rooting for food.

After another long and hot descent beside a crumbling precipice we walked into the incredibly beautiful old pottery town of Moustiers. The town sprawls up a deep gorge containing a cool and splashing stream. High above the narrow streets and lovely Romanesque church hangs a glittering star which is suspended on chains from the cliffs on either side.

Beyond Moustiers, the character of the landscape changes from wooded gorges and limestone cliffs to rolling hills. The GR4 led us through woods to a high plateau covered with lavender fields and orchards. Although the lavender had been harvested for the season, the hot sun released a sweet aroma from the rows of closely cropped bushes. Lavender honey was on sale at several of the farm houses. That night, sadly our last in Provence, was spent in the magnificent Roman and mediaeval town of Riez with its Corinthian columns, ramparts, squares and fountains. As we left Riez on the morning bus back to Castellane, the whole town was chock-a-block with bustling stalls and traders who had come in from far and wide for the Saturday market.

The Lyngen Peninsula
Arctic Norway

Years ago, while browsing in a secondhand bookshop, I bought a copy of *Camps and Climbs in Arctic Norway*, written in the 1950s by Tom Weir. This book had a chapter on the legendary Lyngen range, and the descriptions and photographs fascinated and thrilled me. Time and again in winter, when sitting in an armchair by the fire, I would dream about the huge Jaegevarre mountain, the rock spires of the Jaegervastind, the midnight sun and the lonely Kjosenfjord. Another inspirational book about Lyngen, also written in the 1950s, was *Mountains of the Midnight Sun* by Showell Styles, which again I devoured with relish. Styles and his friends enjoyed a truly pioneering and exciting expedition, run on a shoestring, for at that time Lyngen still contained some virgin peaks.

Lyngen peninsula is a narrow headland jutting out into the Arctic Ocean fully 250 miles north of the Arctic Circle and on a similar latitude as the north of Alaska and Murmansk. Its range of volcanic mountains rises straight out of the sea, with only short valleys running up into the interior. The mountains carry permanent glaciers which descend right down to sea level in several places but, apart from the Jaegevarre, the summits are sharp spires of rough gabbro rock with narrow ridges. There is the additional attraction of the midnight sun, twenty-four hours of daylight, and the fact that the further north you go in Norway, the better the weather.

The first ascents of Lyngen's highest peaks were achieved

at the end of the nineteenth century by Slingsby, Collie and Hastings, and even though the information that I could gather was only scant, my enthusiasm grew, for it was clear that the mountain scenery of Lyngen had few rivals in Europe. I was particularly attracted to North Lyngen where the peaks were slightly more modest, rising to about 5,000ft and resembling a larger, glaciated Cuillin of Skye. It was going to be expensive to get there: flights to Tromso were out of the question, which left the Newcastle-to-Oslo ferry, followed by a drive north of 1,200 miles. Since there are no roads up the east coast of North Lyngen it would mean chartering a fishing boat from the tiny port of Lyngseidet. Four day's travelling: would it all be worth it?

I need not have worried, because Lyngen lived up to my highest expectations. As our fishing boat made its way up Lyngen Fjord, I sat back against a pile of rucksacks and surveyed the scene. After a grey day, shafts of evening sunlight were penetrating the clouds and lighting up the snowfields and glaciers on the islands of Arnoy and Uloya to the north. The air was sharp and crystal clear, and apart from our bright anoraks, the landscape was entirely in black and white, a phenomenon I associate with northern latitudes.

We chugged our way to the inlet of Ytre Gamvik, passing under the immense rock cliffs of the North Lyngen Range which, in places, fall over 2,000ft straight into the sea. Puffins, guillemots and cormorants sat in serried ranks on tiny ledges and terns skimmed the black water. The air was chill and we were grateful for the invitation of Olaf, our kindly skipper: 'You come down here, I have something to warm you.' We descended a ladder into the wood-panelled snug where we were met by a blast of hot air. A pan of coffee was simmering on the stove and steaming mugs were thrust into our hands.

'Before coffee we drink a toast to your trip,' bellowed Olaf, reaching into a cupboard for a bottle and glasses. Paul tossed off his glass, and immediately his eyes bulged and he coughed and spluttered, gasping for air to cool his burning throat. Olaf roared with laughter. 'You like my home brew? It is 170 per cent proof!' He poured some of the pale amber liquor over the back of his hand, struck a match and lit it. Blue flames licked up towards the ceiling. Still not satisfied, Olaf poured a small measure into my coffee, struck another match, and even at this dilution, it burned.

We anchored in the bay and took off the stores by dinghy. As the last load was swung into the boat, Olaf handed down a sack of freshly caught cod. 'In case you get hungry tonight,' he said. He steamed away north to the mouth of the fjord, and we manhandled the equipment and food from the seaweed-covered rocks to a flat, raised beach of springy heather about 100ft above the shore.

After our late and substantial cod supper we slept soundly, and the sun was well up in the sky when we emerged from our tents the next morning and flexed our muscles. We were camped in an amphitheatre of rocky mountains streaked with snow. Scrub birch and willow clung to the lower slopes, and two big glacier streams coursed down from the cliffs in a welter of foam.

Our first objective had to be the conical peak of Kalddalstind, which presented a sheer face to Ytre Gamvik. An exciting scramble up the loose north-east ridge gave us our summit and, facing the keen wind, we drank in the view. Below to the south lay the Gamvik glacier ringed by toothed rock peaks, the queen of them all being the fantastic rock spire of Peppartind. Behind to the west rose Stor Galten, a huge wedge of rock rising above the snowfields and frozen lakes and topping us by 800ft. Gripping as the mountain views were, our eyes were drawn to the north, beyond the peaks of Daltind, Russelvfjellet and Lyngstuva, to the extreme tip of the Lyngen peninsula, seven miles away as the white-tailed eagle flies. Far out into the Arctic Ocean floated the mysterious island of Fugloya (Bird Island) which carries its own mountain rising to 2,500ft above the waves, and today wearing a wreath of cloud.

Another steep scramble down the appallingly loose east ridge brought us to the snout of the Gamvik glacier, and we crossed the ice and descended the lower slopes of Trommafjellet towards camp. But we were now on the wrong side of the river, and a nightmare crossing ensued; even with two climbing ropes as safeguards, several of the party were swept off their feet by the raging torrent, and speech was impossible against the roar of the water.

The inlet of Ytre Gamvik made the ideal base-camp site. Regular supplies of cod and pollack were caught off shore, we successfully climbed Stor Galten and Little Peppartind, many reindeer antlers were found, and on occasions we glimpsed small herds of these creatures. On one day we traversed the razor-sharp ridge of Russelvfjellet and continued walking across the stony wastes of gabbro to the very northern tip of the Lyngen peninsula. Then two days were written off by a ferocious storm which sprang from the north-west and continued unabated for forty-eight hours. Lyngen weather certainly went from one extreme to another – from shirtsleeves and swimming, to temperatures that nudged freezing point, rain which overnight filled the weather station gauge to overflowing, a wind of force 10.5 and fresh snow on the mountains.

One day to go, and Peppartind was still not climbed. Desperate, we took a tiny patch of blue sky as an omen, waded the lesser of the two rivers and sweated up to the Gamvik glacier. We trudged through mushy ice on the lower reaches of the glacier and then deep soft snow further up, making for Storurtind, two miles away to the west. The glacier snows rose up the walls of the cirque like a bowl of cream, filling it completely in places and rising almost to the summit of several peaks. Half-way up the glacier the clouds parted momentarily and I could see Peppartind towering into the sky: it was now or never, and we turned aside, cramponning up towards the col at the base of the south ridge. Above the snow we scrambled over steep, loose rocks to gain the col from whence we could look down sheer cliffs to another glacier set between black rock peaks in as bleak, desolate and forbidding a setting as I have ever seen. This (un-named) glacier drains into Lyngen Fjord at Indre Gamvik, four miles south of our base camp.

The south ridge of Peppartind reared above, and we roped up and set to work. The loose, wet rock needed great care, but technically the climb was straightforward, one pitch of about Very Difficult providing the crux. The considerable exposure kept the adrenalin flowing, and at 6pm we reached the pointed summit in drizzle, mist and gusting wind. At only 4,000ft, Peppartind had provided a day of almost Alpine proportions, and a worthy climax to the expedition.

Needless to say, during our two-week stay in the spectacular mountains of North Lyngen we had met not another soul. This true wilderness experience was so uplifting and therapeutic that it was not long before I returned, although this time my aim was to explore the somewhat higher mountains half-way up the Lyngen peninsula, despite the fact that they are more accessible.

The road to Lyngen stops at Koppangen, a charming little fishing hamlet consisting of a dozen whitewashed cottages, a landing stage and a few boats bobbing at their moorings. Above Koppangen rises a gorge filled with grey ice, the lower tongue of the Koppangen glacier which reaches almost to sea level. South of the Koppangen glacier, and running up to a loose and rocky mountain called Goalbarri, is the Fastdalen valley which made a convenient site for base camp.

It was rough country. The sides of the valley were either marshy or scree-covered, and when walking beside the river you had to fight your way through scrub or else scramble over huge, moss-covered boulders. The river was fast-flowing and deep, and for the duration of the expedition we fixed up a safety handrail to facilitate the crossing. Nevertheless it was a breathtaking spot, for all around were mountains, snowfields, glaciers and scree, and the rays of the sun lingered throughout the night on the upper glacier of Istind, a 5,000ft mountain to the south.

On that first evening the wind dropped at 9pm and mosquitoes appeared in swarms, whereupon there was a rush for the canisters of 'Off' – but with a superior smile, I produced my secret weapon: a Mosiquit. This was an expensive electronic insect repeller which emitted a very high frequency signal, said to discourage mosquitoes instantly. But after a few minutes, and scores of bites, I realised that the device was useless and that mosquitoes were crawling all over it. I slunk into my tent, zipped up the entrance, and scratched my bites in fury. I began to think that for the next few weeks life might be dominated by the insects. However, this first evening was the worst, for thereafter an evening breeze kept them down to no more than a mild irritant.

Chris and Robin had brought along a pneumatic igloo-shaped tent with inflatable tubes, but it became a disaster. While digging a drainage ditch round the outside, Chris spiked a vital tube with his ice-axe; the tent collapsed on Robin who was inside lighting the primus, and several holes were burnt in the tent wall.

Goalbarri provided us with a stiff and varied climb up splintered rock and firm snowfields, and we were captivated by the unfolding panorama; while 2,000ft below, down the sheer south face, the collection of tents lent a splash of colour to the scene. A magnificently sharp ridge continued towards Tafeltind, giving an exhilarating climb. The rock was tough gabbro, as in the Cuillin, and the position was airy with slopes falling away to the huge Strupbreen and Koppangstreen glaciers on the north side. All round were wonderful ridges and rock pinnacles culminating in the principal summits of Store Lenangstind and the Jaegervasstind. Northwards my eyes were drawn across the blue waters of Lyngen Fjord to the glistening white ice-caps of the Oksfjordjokelen and the Seilandsjokelen just south of North Cape and the Barents Sea. The combination of black rock peaks above white snowfields set against an azure sky cannot be beaten.

Back at base camp, as the sun dipped, we were surprised to find that the glacier torrent contained small trout. We lit fires of dead scrub willow and bilberry, and grilled the fish on hot flat stones arranged over the flames. That night we were visited by a lemming, a brown, blunt-nosed rodent with almost no tail which was tame enough to eat scraps outside the tents. Later, two foxes trotted through camp on their way up the valley.

Over the next week we climbed Rundfjellet, immediately behind base camp, and this was linked to the 4,300ft Fastdalstind by a rocky ridge. On one occasion a dot in the sky grew larger, and then to our delight it swooped low over the summit, revealing itself to be a white-tailed eagle, the first rare bird we had seen in Norway. Another expedition took us to the spectacular rock peak of Skaidivarri whose south side contained, 1,000ft above the valley floor, a hanging amphitheatre with rock walls enclosing a turquoise lake. The rock wall behind the lake had collapsed at one point into a scree slope, and this provided the key to the summit ridge and thence to the sharply pointed summit itself.

North of Koppangen the mountains fall sheer into Lyngen Fjord and effectively bar progress up the coast. However, by traversing the mountains themselves, we discovered a broad shelf which led us north for several miles – until suddenly the ground fell away and we could look down into a fantastic circle of cliffs overlooking the inlet of Strupen. A big glacier river thundered down fissures in the rocks and then hurtled into the sea, and the effect of the white, sediment-laden water could be seen far out into the fjord. A treacherous descent of loose rock and scree took us down to sea level. By this time the thought of the long, long return route was preying on everyone's mind – when to our astonishment a small fishing boat hove into view, and to our utmost delight the kind fisherman put his dingy ashore and offered us a lift back to Koppangen.

One major task remained: an ascent of Istind, the principal summit of the area. Luckily the anti-cyclone which had remained stationary over Arctic Norway for the duration of our stay continued to provide hot, sunny weather. The route to gain the north ridge of Istind lay up the Fastdalen valley: unfortunately it proved to be constructed of poor rock and was extremely exposed, and as we gained height it steepened and narrowed to a knife edge. However, although the position was dramatic, it was not much more than a scramble, and at 4.30pm we cut steps up the summit snow-cap and Istind was ours. All around us rose the peaks of our beloved Lyngen, surely one of the world's most attractive ranges of mountains.

Journey to Paradise:
The Hornstrandir Peninsula

'Can this really be Iceland, or am I dreaming?' I asked myself as I opened the flap of the tent and the sunshine flooded in. A pair of Harlequin ducks were peacefully swimming with their brood in the bay of the fjord; further out from the shore two whooper swans were distainfully preening their feathers, unperturbed by the squawking arctic terns which were dive-bombing into the water for fish and then skilfully avoiding the attentions of arctic skuas trying to harass them into dropping their catch.

The mirror-calm water reflected the blue sky and the snow-capped peaks which ringed the fjord and threw down rough screes of coarse lava to the water's edge. Beside our tent ran a swift stream, and somewhere in the tangle of scrub and boulders on the opposite bank, a golden plover was piping. On our side of the stream the boulders stopped short of the fjord's edge, leaving a fertile strip dotted with a myriad colourful flowers: butterwort, starry saxifrage, bugle, orchid, sea pink, buttercup, dwarf cornel, alpine speedwell, mountain aven and cranesbill.

The name 'Iceland' does not help that country's popular image: those endless deserts of grey lava, huge rolling glaciers, unbridged rivers laden with silt, depressing days of cloud and freezing rain, and the dust which penetrates every stitch of your clothing and jams your camera. For many years Iceland has been used to train astronauts, for the conditions are said to resemble those on the moon. It has also been the venue for world chess championships and for summit meetings between East and West. The suicide rate is the highest in Europe, there are no pubs or bars, and the price of a bottle of Scotch, if you can find one, is monstrous.

The rock is shattered, loose and crumbly and is eroding at an alarming rate; it is therefore terrible for climbing. Iceland lies on the Atlantic Ridge, the line of weakness in the earth's crust causing volcanic activity, which runs from Jan Meyen Island in the north, through the centre of Iceland, to the Azores, Ascension Island and Tristan da Cuna.

But this is the bleak picture painted by those who do not know the country. Over the years I have fallen under its spell: the primeval terrain stirs my soul, the predominantly black and white landscape is restful and makes me appreciate the splash of colour of a lichen-encrusted rock, a patch of bright moss or a community of tiny flowers. I respond to the clear, sharp air, the mighty rivers, the jagged ridges, boiling mud and plumes of steam. Oh yes, this is harsh Norse-God country where you need your wits to survive.

For the first two days at base camp Iceland had lived up to its reputation, a nagging wind from the west bringing low cloud and persistent, freezing rain – a reputation justly earned by my previous visits to Iceland, the first to the Myrdals Jokull ice-cap in the south, and the second to the Trollaskagi mountains on the peninsula north of Akureyri. But the scene which unfolded on that unforgettable July morning was like a window into paradise. That perfect morning marked the start of five idyllic days of sunshine and blue skies, with the air as clear and sharp as diamonds. We breakfasted outside in shorts, while Mike watched the bird-life on the fjord through his binoculars: great northern divers, grey phalaropes, black guillemots, glaucous gulls, ringed plovers and shags.

We were camping by a remote fjord in the Hornstrandir region of Iceland, the lobster-claw peninsula in the far north-west which carries Iceland's most northerly ice-cap, the Drangajokull. The Hornstrandir gets its name from the Horn, a great fang-shaped promontory which falls sheer for 1,700ft straight into the ocean. Vagn Hrolffson and his sturdy fishing boat *Hawkur* had ferried us to the head of Hrafnsfjordur, and we had pitched our tents on a springy bed of crowberry beside the turbulent river Skorara.

This is an area of fjords, precipitous mountains rising to nearly 3,000ft, lakes, waterfalls and rushing rivers. An occasional isolated farmstead nestles under a lee slope on the larger fjords, but in general, when you have crossed the Isafjordardjup Fjord north of the town of Isafjordur, you must fend entirely for yourself. Isafjordur, a town with a population of 3,500, is the centre for communications, its lifeline being a tiny airstrip with daily flights by Fokker Friendship to Reykyavik, while most fish landings take place twelve miles along the coast at Bolungarvik. A young fisherman, Reimar, who was only seventeen and had just left school, told us proudly in good English that wages were high: in a few months with the Bolungarvik fishing fleet he had earned enough to fly to Reykyavik and buy a brand-new Mazda car, paying the whole amount in cash.

The Hornstrandir is an Icelandic National Nature Reserve: there are no roads, and no developments are permitted. The only other walkers we met were an Austrian couple who had been dropped by fishing boat at Hornvik Bay and were backpacking to Nordurfjordur, the nearest settlement and roadhead on the south-east side of the Hornstrandir. As the crow flies the distance is only fifty miles, but they were allowing ten days for the journey because the severe nature of the terrain makes walking a daunting task.

For ten days we roamed throughout this rugged, beautiful and fascinating area, climbing the mountains, crossing the Drangajokull and exploring the valleys, corries and lakes. It didn't matter that some expeditions spun out to twenty hours, for being only thirty miles south of the Arctic Circle, darkness never fell. On that first brilliant day we climbed the mountain Skardsoxl, pushing our way through low birch scrub and bilberries to an extensive high plateau of shattered lava. Long tongues of snow then gave way to a precarious ridge of lava slivers stacked up crazily in towers. Just below the snow was a patch of steep, soggy, waterlogged ground: obviously its stability was finely balanced because as we walked over it, its equilibrium was disturbed and several mudslides started. We felt guilty at our intrusion: natural erosion was fast enough without our help.

From the summit we gazed north across the Arctic Ocean to find that the polar pack-ice had been driven south to within two miles of the shore. As far as the eye could see, gleaming ice extended to distant horizons. A few individual floes had broken away and were nudging the coast itself, and it was even possible that a polar bear or two might have landed – not for the first time in Iceland.

How lucky we were. This was the nearest that the ice had approached Iceland for thirty years, and being a devotee of Bill Tilman's voyages in *Mischief* and *Sea Breeze* when he had numerous encounters with pack-ice in the Denmark Straits, I was hypnotised and elated by this astonishing vista. The ice which hugs the east coast of Greenland, Spitzbergen and Ellesmere Island has inspired exploration and endeavour throughout history, and has led to many triumphs and disasters graphically described by Peary, Nanson and Gino Watkins.

South of Skardsoxl the vast white dome of the Drangajokull dominates the scene, while dozens of lesser peaks rise up in all directions.

Later we moved across to the shattered crest of Hattarfell, which reminded us of the black Cuillin ridge on Skye. It had been a mountaineering day for the conoisseur, and as the sun began to sink we glissaded down the snow tongues to regain Hrafnsfjordur. Back at camp, mussels in sherry sauce was on the supper menu, and as the last rays of sun lit up the surrounding peaks, we concluded a memorable day with cigars and whisky.

The Drangajokull ice-cap sits squatly on the high ground south of Hrafnsfjordur like icing on a cake, and only three rock nunataks break the sweep of snow and ice which covers an area of about a hundred square miles. The top of the snow dome is Jokulbunga, and at 3,035ft it is the highest point in the Hornstrandir region and makes an obvious objective.

Our maps were the Icelandic Geodic Survey scale 1: 100,000, and they were far from accurate. This is not a criticism of the survey because mapping must be a nightmare in a country where rivers constantly change course and new islands appear off the coast at the drop of a hat, but the lack of any indication of cliffs was particularly tiresome. For instance, on our first attempt to climb out of the Hrafnsfjordur to gain the Drangajokull we were repulsed by a line of loose and vertical cliffs about 500ft high. We were forced to traverse west to find a broken and rather treacherous rock rib which led to the plateau snowfields.

The actual expedition to cross the ice-cap and visit the nunataks took twenty-two hours. The snow was soft and sugary and progress was slow; the sun beat down and we were stripped to T-shirts. But at 9pm the sun dipped, the temperature dropped and we put on jerseys and duvets. The ice-cap was suffused in a pink glow as we plodded across the wastes and witnessed a magnificent sunset. Yet hardly had the sun finally disappeared below the horizon and a weird gloaming descended, than it reappeared over a distant ridge to cheer our descent to the north and the long walk back through Skoradalur.

After the unexpected and unforgettable experience of seeing the polar ice sheet, the north coast drew us like a magnet. On another day we descended a wide river valley running north to a deserted settlement at Furufjordur. Red phalarope, whimbrel and snipe rose at our approach, and a ruined building had been adopted by a family of foxes; we watched with delight as the cubs played amongst the chaos of boulders and ancient timbers. We were surprised to find the wild northern shore littered with massive, bleached logs. These logs are carried to north-west Iceland from the great forests of Siberia by favourable ocean currents. The collection and subsequent sale of these logs for firewood, fence posts and construction (for there are no trees in Iceland) by this isolated community allowed them to eke out a precarious living.

From the high mountainous country inland, long frost-shattered ridges run north, producing a succession of bays with storm beaches of shingle. Behind these shingle banks green meadows of coarse grass run up into wide corries until they meet moraines, boulder fields and snow. Without exception these corries carry swift rivers of meltwater, some up to three feet deep and requiring the use of safety ropes, while they provide habitat for arctic skuas, snow buntings, gyr falcons, sea eagles and whooper swans. To traverse this magnificent coastline is a daunting task. Sometimes at low tide it is possible to work round the headlands at sea level, the black basalt cliffs towering overhead, ledges providing nest sites for fulmars, guillemots and razorbills. I remember one notable occasion when the tide was rising and our way ahead appeared blocked by a sheer rock face; in the nick of time someone found a tunnel through the rock and we scrambled through to the safety of a bay on the far side. When it becomes necessary to climb a ridge to gain access to an inlet, much sweat is involved. Rarely less than 1,000ft of loose, treacherous scree must be negotiated, and this is usually followed by some snow climbing. Unstable, crumbly rock is a major hazard in Iceland.

Our north-coast camps were unique and uplifting experiences. We will never forget sitting on the shore at midnight beside a driftwood fire, a slight chill in the still air and the sweet smell of burning pine logs in our nostrils. A marvellous greenish light would be reflected on the Arctic Ocean, while the distant line of clouds slowly turned pink and then deepened to a fiery red. In the foreground the ubiquitous eider ducks slowly swam in and out of the off-shore rocks, the gentle females often leading flotillas of a dozen or more chicks, keeping them in line with their musical 'oo-ah' calls.

Boat charter in Iceland is very expensive and we couldn't afford the luxury of a return voyage to Bolungarvik. However, every four days or so the ferry boat *Flagranes* links the remote farm at Baeir, on the north side of Isafjordardjup, with Isafjordur itself. Thus when we had eaten down our food to manageable quantities, we set out on the two-day march to Baeir. Unfortunately the weather broke and we had torrential rain for the entire journey, first crossing the wide flood plains of Leirufjordur with water swirling up to our thighs, and then on the bleak, exposed plateau further south. The temperature was -2°, and the sleet was freezing where it fell. This was a return to the Iceland of old!

Contrary to popular belief there are no mosquitoes or midges in north-west Iceland, which makes the Hornstrandir an attractive proposition when compared with Arctic Scandinavia or north-west Scotland. Iceland has much to offer the adventurous traveller. The stark scenery of the interior, with its lava deserts and snowfields, is well documented, but the rich, alpine-like valleys and the interlinking of the mountains and the sea in the far north-west are a revelation.

Opposite: Descending the moraines of the Leksyr glacier in Svanetia, an inaccessible and hidden kingdom deep in the Caucasus

Pages 98–9 (main picture) Nearing the top of the Biafo glacier where it is hemmed in by spectacular peaks in the Karakoram; *(inset top)* The extraordinary Priut Hut, now destroyed by fire, on the slopes of Mount Elbrus; *(inset below)* Snow Lake in the Karakoram, first explored by Tilman and Shipton in 1937

Above: Walking into the Titcomb Basin in the remote and beautiful Wind River Mountains of Wyoming on the approach to Gannett Peak

Below: The Cirque of the Towers in the Southern Wind Rivers. We climbed the face of Pingora, the peak on the right

Left: Zig-zagging across the lower reaches of the Biafo glacier to avoid crevasses

On the Horntalerjoch in the Stubai Alps

Above: In the Zillertal Alps looking towards the Schrammacher

Below: A sparkling morning on the summit of the Fluchtkogel in the Otztal Alps

Left: A family ascent of the Ruderhofspitz in the Stubai Alps

Above: Crater Lake in the Yukon; one of the many beautiful lakes passed whilst backpacking the Chilkoot Trail

Below: In 1898 100,000 prospectors crossed over the notorious Chilkoot Pass on their way to the goldfields of the Klondike. Discarded equipment still litters the ground throughout the trail

The tranquil beauty of Lyngen Fjord in Arctic Norway is seen here on a still summer's evening

Below: The village of Rougon sprawls on a steep hillside overlooking the Verdon Gorge (*bottom*) in Haute Provence. Towering walls of vertical limestone overhang the trail through the spectacular gorge

The bleak beauty of the Hornstrandir Peninsula of north-west Iceland where the arctic pack ice approaches close to the shore
Inset: Flowers bravely bloom in the short summer of north-west Iceland

Charles Morton on the summit ridge of Kolahoi

Overleaf: Kolahoi. This superb peak was climbed by members of the Ampleforth College expedition in 1977, the first ever school expedition to the Himalayas from Britain

STRUGGLE AND STRIFE

'We watched hypnotized as the massive rock, the size of a double decker bus, slowly topped over.'

From Elation to Nightmare in the Stubai Alps

Mountain lovers thrill to Innsbruck, gateway city to the Tyrol, whence frequent transport will speed them into the Lechtal, Stubai, Zillertal, Otztal, Karwendal, Silvretta and Vorarlberg. There is an excellent Italian restaurant beside the Innbrucke, near the old part of Innsbruck, where you can sit out with a bottle of wine on a soft summer evening, watching the swallows skimming the milky glacier water of the river Inn as it gurgles under the bridge. As the shadows lengthen and the bustle of the city dies away, you can hear the chiming of bells from a score of clocks. By late August darkness is descending early, and the lights of the chalets on the Hafelekar Spitze twinkle down from seemingly impossible heights. `

At the end of an Alpine holiday the beauty of Innsbruck's ancient streets, its narrow Gothic houses and Baroque palaces, the comfort of its *pensions*, the quality of its restaurants and the peace of its parks, gardens, squares and churches make it the perfect complement to one's strenuous activities in the mountains. I am not alone in finding satisfaction in contrasts. Too much ease and indulgence makes us hanker, eventually, for the primitive life of the mountains. Likewise, after a few weeks of rigorous exercise, hardship and danger we are eager for another dose of luxury: a hot bath, a meal eaten with a knife and fork rather than a spoon, a good book and some Schubert.

On a recent holiday in the Tyrol we met an English family who had sandwiched a week in the mountains between cultural weeks in Salzburg and Venice. Talking to them reminded me of one of my early Alpine seasons, in 1960, when, with Roger Putnam and Alan Wedgwood, we pre-booked seats at the Salzburg Festival for a performance of *The Magic Flute*. The Opera House insisted on the wearing of suits, and so for three weeks we carried suits in our rucksacks while climbing in the Dolomites and the Bernina. Eventually we donned the crumpled garments, passed the scrutiny of the doorman, and enjoyed a truly memorable performance.

When our youngest son reached double figures we could wait no longer: we put away the bucket and spades and planned a modest walking holiday in the Alps. We chose Austria, caught the Calais to Innsbruck express, and had the holiday of our lives. For the next eight years, at popular request, we returned every year.

The mountains of the Tyrol are considerably lower than those of the Pennine Alps, rising to a maximum of 12,162ft with the Gross Glockner, but the huts are more numerous, less crowded and the weather is certainly better. Of the principal mountain groups we started with the Stubai because of its accessibility and charm, and the ideal combination of snow- and rock-work.

For nearly a hundred years a network of huts has been been strung out across the Tyrol for the convenience of walkers and climbers. The huts are solid constructions of stone and timber, and they are built in prominent positions on rocky spurs high above the valleys. Clearly marked paths link the huts, and even in misty weather route-finding is no problem. The paths contour steep hillsides and boulder fields, they cross high cols where new peaks and glaciers burst into view, yet you are never far from a reassuring marker cairn or red-blazed boulder. Hut dues include a small levy for path maintenance, and it is the responsibility of each hut warden to repair eroded sections on his patch. A whole range of mountains can be traversed without ever having to descend into the valley.

The mountain walker finds this to be the great attraction of the Tyrol, and the height of the huts (between about 6,800 and 8,200ft) and the network of paths over the cols allow great flexibility in route planning. To begin with, when you are unfit and not yet acclimatised, you can give yourself easy days of three to four hours' walking; later on you can walk two stages in one day, and climb a peak on the day saved.

The huts offer a choice of sleeping accommodation. We took our own sheet sleeping bags and settled for the communal, but cheap, *Matratzenlager* where mattresses, pillows and blankets are provided, the blankets being conveniently marked *Fuss Ende* (foot end) and *Kopf Ende* (head end). However, if you can't stand the snoring of your bedfellows, beds with clean sheets and duvets are available in smaller rooms for a supplementary charge. No one is ever turned away from a hut and we have found it quite unnecessary to prebook.

Hut kitchens provide varied menus including soup, *wienerschnitzl*, sausages, pasta, salads and *apfelstrudel*. In addition they have to provide a climber's high calorie meal called *Bergsteigeressen* which is cheap and nourishing. Another cheap favourite with my family is *Tiroler grostl mit spiegelei und salat*, a potato and meat hash with fried eggs and salad. Although tea and coffee is expensive, it is quite acceptable practice to bring your own instant coffee and tea bags, as boiling water (*teewasser*) can be purchased cheaply. Basic food for breakfast and lunch, such as bread, butter, jam, cheese, salami and chocolate, can be bought at most huts.

The horrific 2am call is unheard of in the Tyrol, and even for a long day involving a major peak, a 5.30am start is early enough. For a mere hut-to-hut walk, 9am is adequate and by mid-afternoon you should be at your destination, sitting on the hut terrace soaking up the sun, with a carafe of local wine at your elbow. With some physical exercise behind you, indulgence is all the more enjoyable.

The bugbear of the mountain walker is the rucksack. When the midday sun beats down and the path winds steeply up to the col, the last thing you need is a heavy pack. You should not, however, economise on safety gear, because ice-axes, crampons and rope might be needed for even the smallest glacier crossings, and conditions can change dramatically. We learned this to our cost as you shall hear later. On several occasions we have met parties without sufficient equipment, who have been forced to descend into the valley and make long detours to reach the next hut because of mildly crevassed glaciers across their path.

Most of the mountains have easy ways to the top and if you have some climbing gear with you it should be possible, even with a family party, to bag some peaks. With a flexible itinerary you can stay several nights at any hut which particularly appeals, climb a peak or two, and then proceed on your journey.

One year we planned to walk right across the Stubai range from the Brenner Pass to the Otztal valley, taking ten days and staying in a different mountain hut each night. My youngest daughter, Lucy, had just returned in a shocked state from a school expedition to the Svartisan glacier in Arctic Norway, where the leader had been killed in a crevasse accident before her very eyes. Thus we decided to have a totally relaxing holiday in the Alps: no dawn starts, no major summits, no steep glaciers and positively no crevasses; just ten days' walking through a familiar and well loved range of mountains. To reduce weight we left crampons at home, but we did carry ice-axes and a lightweight rope.

During the first seven days of our traverse the hot southern sun blazed down from a blue sky and we dawdled along the paths, stopping to watch marmots playing amongst the boulders, to admire myriads of colourful butterflies on the flowers and to feed the friendly floppy-eared sheep with crusts. Although the season was too late for gentians and azaleas, the campanulas, scabious and saxifrages were exceptionally fine.

For friendliness, comfort and lack of crowds (even in the *Matratzenlager*) the huts that lead you into the heart of the Stubai from the east are unsurpassed: the Bremer, timber-clad but firmly perched on a rock shoulder beneath the Simminger glacier and the sharp rock summit of the Feuerstein; the Nurnberger set in the middle of an amphitheatre of rock peaks; the Sulzenau, recently destroyed by an avalanche off the north face of the Sulzenaukogel but now rebuilt and modernised; and the Dresdner, doubling up as mountain hut and cafeteria for the summer skiers on the Schaufel glacier. Finally there is the Neue Regensburger, at the centre of a dramatic horseshoe of mountains dominated by the Ruderhofspitze, and certainly the most spotless of the Stubai huts, it always serves delicious meals, and the traditional Franz-Senn. With its smoke-darkened wood panelling and aura of the nineteenth century, its stature is akin to the great Berliner hut of the Zillertal alps. In such huts friends are easily made with other walkers and climbers, and spontaneous folk singing by Austrian hill lovers often provides entertainment after supper in the Gastube.

On the second day of our Stubai traverse we climbed to the Simmingjochl, from where the Wilder Freiger burst into view. Normally the glaciers and snowfields on this lovely peak are piled up like a cornet of whipped ice cream, but this year the scene was grey, not white: poor snowfall in the winter, followed by a hot early summer, had melted the snow from the glaciers and exposed crevasse-ridden grey ice. This observation was reinforced a few days later when crossing the high Grawagrubin-nieder, which has a small glacier on the Regensburger side. This is normally a steepish snowfield of about 500ft, but on this occasion the top section was bare ice requiring some step cutting. It later transpired that the previous day an English party of twelve, with no rope and only two axes between them, had taken over two hours to negotiate this glacier.

The Franz-Senn hut is situated at the north end of the vast Alpeiner glacier which is surrounded by the great peaks of the Ruderhofspitze, Schrankogel and Lusenser Fernerkogel, all of which we had climbed with the children on previous occasions. However, the Stubai mountains extend much further to the north-west in a series of rock peaks, many comfortably exceeding 9,850ft and having their own glaciers, paths and huts. This was to be new ground for us, and our expectancy was high.

It was a long and hot crossing of the Horntalerjoch between the Franz-Senn and the Lusens valley to the north to reach the lonely Westfalen Haus, tucked under the Grubenwand at 7,457ft. We were the only guests that night, showing the relative unpopularity of the north-west Stubai. It was the last day of the hot spell, and out on the terrace in the broiling sun, the thermometer read 42°C.

But next morning a strong wind was blowing and storm clouds were gathering. Spots of icy rain began to fall soon after we left the hut, and by the time we reached the Zischagen-Scharte, at 9,632ft, curtains of rain were driving over the col. A hundred feet of horribly loose scree and rubble led to the edge of the Zischgen glacier which was bare ice. It was a different story from the moderate Grawagrubin glacier, and we had to use the rope for security and cut steps along the bergschrund lip until we found a bridge. With mist now swirling and visibility poor, the rain had turned to sleet and the grey ice was wet and slippery.

Beyond the bergschrund the convex glacier continued down into the mist and the slope ever steepened. There was no alternative but to descend carefully, cutting steps the entire time, in the hope that the visibility would improve and the angle ease. We had no ice-screws for belays, and a slip by any one of the family would have spelt disaster, but everyone kept their heads remarkably. After two hours we had descended 600ft and could see rocks at the bottom of the ice sheet. It was almost dark, save for constant flashes of lightning, while ear-splitting booms of thunder made communication difficult. Half-way down we had been badly unnerved by the rumble and crash of falling rocks close by from the Grutenwand, and not being able to see anything, we wondered whether we were to be swept by a stone avalanche; but the debris fell elsewhere.

By the time that we had descended the glacier it was blowing a full-scale Alpine blizzard and the snow was building up by the minute. Trying to find the path in the white-out, with iced-up faces and eyes, became something of a nightmare, because the comfortable red marks on the rocks were hidden under the snow. We were becoming seriously chilled, and it was absolutely essential to lose height as quickly as possible to alleviate the arctic conditions. Slidy new snow on steep traverse lines was an additional hazard, and it was thanks to the keen eyes of the children that we maintained roughly the correct route down the valley. At long last the Neue Pfortzeimer hut reared up on its plinth above the stream, and looking like snowmen, we burst through the door to find the big stove alight; soon we were luxuriating in dry clothes and quaffing Gluhwein.

By next morning the mountains were transformed, and six to eight inches of fresh snow lay on the path over the Gleirschioch to the Gubener hut. More snow fell that afternoon and evening, and so it was with some relief that we strode down the valley from the Gubener to the village of Umhausen in the Otztal valley.

The Stubai, scene of so many carefree and relaxed holidays, had stung us at last. It was a salutary reminder that the temperature can drop 40° overnight and transform a mountain walk into a serious expedition requiring experience and proper equipment.

An Epic in Knoydart

The Rough Bounds of Knoydart in the West Highlands of Scotland are aptly named. This wild, remote and mountainous peninsula, bounded by the fjord-like Loch Nevis and Loch Hourn, have witnessed many adventures, but none more serious than the life and death epic which befell us on our first visit many years ago.

A sizeable chunk of the Knoydart estate is now owned by the John Muir Trust who are striving to maintain it in its natural state; they want no development whatsoever, save some planting of natural woodlands in Coire Dhorrcail on the northern flanks of Ladhar Bheinn. Yet in 1982 it was under threat from the Ministry of Defence who wanted to buy it as a military training ground, and only vehement opposition from conservation organisations prevented the purchase. The 52,000 acre Knoydart estate had been put on the market by the owner, Major Nigel Chamberlayne-Macdonald, and it was finally bought by Philip Rhodes, a property developer from Surrey.

At the time of writing it has just been announced that the part of Knoydart that is not owned by the John Muir Trust has been purchased by the Knoydart Foundation, a partnership of half a dozen interested organisations, which hope to inject much needed investment into the infrastructure of Inverie, the tiny community on the south side of the peninsula. Knoydart deserves some care and attention for it has suffered grievously in the past. In 1854 the coastal strip of

Knoydart supported a crofting population of over six hundred, but savage evictions by factor Alexander Grant, acting under the orders of the owner, Mrs Macdonell, cleared the land for Cheviot sheep.

In the centre of Knoydart lies the mountain of Ladhar Bheinn, one of my very favourite mountains in all Scotland. Deep, cliff-girt corries descend from a sharp summit ridge, and its perfect combination of grandeur and remoteness, together with the close presence of the sea, exemplify the unique magic of the hills of the Western Highlands. No roads run into Knoydart, but the settlement at Inverie can be reached several times a week by public ferry from Mallaig. The approach from the north, however, involves a seven-mile walk along the south shore of Loch Hourn, from the road-head at Kinlochhourn, to Barrisdale Bay which is the best centre for exploration of the peninsula.

It was a bright and sunny morning in mid-March when Trisha and I, with our friends Alan and Janet, set off with heavy loads from Kinlochhourn for several days' Munro-bagging in Knoydart. The switchback path to Barrisdale passes ancient cottages at Runival and Skiary. In the last century the Reverend A.E. Robertson, the first Munroist, passed this way and visited Skiary, but criticised the dirt and the bad whisky. Several stretches of this path hug the very edge of the loch itself, and we peered down into the clear, green depths to see the waving weed, limpet-encrusted rocks and sea urchins. In other parts we passed under gnarled Caledonian pines where our feet were cushioned by thick layers of cones. At Barrisdale we camped on a spit of grass on the far side of the burn and cooked supper over a driftwood fire. The evening sun lit up the surrounding hills and Ben Sgritheall north of Loch Hourn; deer grazed nearby, and the place was enchanting and still.

The next day was warm and the sun shone from a cloudless sky. We traversed Ladhar Bheinn, returning to camp by mid-afternoon. The summit ridge had been sharp and snowy, and our eyes had been drawn to the great sweep of the Hebrides and down to the blue water of Loch Hourn. Back in camp Alan and Janet bathed in the loch; it really was summer weather. After tea we shouldered our packs and struck up Glen Unndalain towards Luinne Bheinn. We found an idyllic campsite by a stream on a platform of grass at the 2,200ft level, with a view down the glen to Loch Hourn and the west. That evening there was a tremendous sunset reflecting the hills in the loch; even late at night the western sky was alight with a greenish glow. We were startled by a falling star, which looked so near that it seemed it must hit us. After supper we breached the whisky.

The weather held as we tackled wild and rugged country to climb Luinne Bheinn and Meall Buidhe, and then descended to sea level again at Carnoch on the shores of Loch Nevis. Here we basked in the sun and brewed up before attempting the 2,500ft steep ascent to the south-west ridge of Sgurr na Ciche. A pair of golden eagles paid us a fleeting visit. The climb was hot and exhausting, and we made a detour to drink at a waterfall where we disturbed a herd of deer. On the ridge the weather was looking ominous so we camped for the night. Mist swirled around, but we had occasional glimpses of the sharp summit of Sgurr na Ciche only 1,000ft above us.

Life was at its very best. We finished off the whisky and had a last round of liar dice, and only an easy day lay between us and the car and our pre-booked dinner at the Tomdoun Hotel. It was with a clear conscience that we polished off our last main meal and settled down to sleep.

We woke early to the sound of rain and wind buffeting

the tents. There was no question of riding out the storm, it was imperative that we got moving fast, so we forewent breakfast, bundled up our already sodden equipment and continued up the ridge of Sgurr na Ciche in thick mist. The gale was increasing every minute, the temperature had plummeted, the rocks were verglassed and dangerous, and several times we were forced to find alternative routes. It was difficult to look ahead with our faces covered by gloved hands as protection from the driving sleet.

Quite suddenly we arrived at the summit trig point, and here we held a council of war behind a rock. Our next Munro was two miles away, but according to our map virtually *en route* to the car – so we decided to press on. It took two hours to gain the col 600ft below the summit of Sgurr nan Coireachan, and the traverse was a nightmare: horizontal sleet driven by an 80mph gale pounded us the whole way and we were soaked and frozen. However, we fought our way to the summit of the mountain, much of the time on hands and knees, crawling from rock to rock and hanging on for grim death with numbed fingers. Conversation was impossible. It was this col that was crossed by Bonnie Prince Charlie at midnight on 19 July 1746.

After dropping down from the summit the wind eased somewhat, but the rain poured down unabated. While crossing the Allt a' Choire Reidh Trisha fell into the whitewater and was completely submerged, but it made little difference to her bedraggled state – and for once, humour was lacking. Then to our astonishment we arrived at Loch Quoich-side. This, we discovered, was because our ancient map did not show the new dam and the resulting two- or three-mile westward extension of the loch. To reach the causeway at the west end of Loch Quoich we had either to negotiate exhausting moraines, or to wade knee-deep through mud and ooze by the water's edge. With our leaden packs we chose the latter.

At 1.30pm, after wading waist-deep through a burn, we reached a good track leading along the north side of the loch in the direction of the car. This was the old shooting path – but it had been made before the loch level was raised, and so at frequent intervals it would disappear into the loch and we would have steep, trackless hillside to traverse instead.

The rain was incessant. None of us has seen rain like it before or since: it swept down in curtains and the hillsides were white with water. In spite of our desperately slow progress, by 3pm we were only four miles from the Kinlochhourn road – and then came up against what seemed to be an insurmountable obstacle: as we rounded a hummock we could see the Amhain Cosaidh burn ahead, and it had become a foaming, roaring torrent fully fifty metres across, hurtling into Loch Quoich. It reminded me of photographs I had seen of the Dudh Khosi river flowing down through Nepal from the Everest Base camp area. The top branches of trees were sticking out of the water in places – and beyond, tantalisingly, we could see our path continuing.

Our only possible course of action was to strike up Glen Cosaidh alongside the burn in the hope that the flow would lessen, and thus allow us to effect a crossing. Some hope! The glen above was turned into a lake and beyond that the water swept on. The rain never eased, our packs bore us down and we were nearly exhausted. I had pins and needles shooting up my arms and legs and my hands were numb and useless. Our last supplies of gingerbread had sufficed for breakfast and lunch some hours before.

By now the minor burns flowing down into the main stream had become major obstacles and often entailed wading up to our waists. At 6pm we were several miles up the corrie and the burn divided. The mountainside became steeper, but the branched burn was still unfordable, thundering down in a cloud of spray. A stag swam across ahead of us with just its antlers visible above the foam.

At 7pm, safeguarded by the rope, Alan managed to cross the nearest strand. Janet followed, but was swept away, only to be 'played' to the bank by Alan. They advised us not to follow, so we staggered on up the corrie. Alan and Janet recrossed over to Trisha and myself and we decided to camp where we were as it was nearly dark. Somehow we got a tent up in the gale. Pegs were useless in the soggy, saturated ground and we needed to put huge boulders on the guys. Even so the guy ropes were snapping at intervals like cotton. We lay exhausted in our sodden bags knowing that once the tent went our plight would be desperate indeed.

It was a hellish night, and only Janet slept at all. Water was entering the tent all the time and we were shivering uncontrollably. However, by morning the wind and rain had eased and we squeezed out our dripping clothes and surveyed the watery scene. Although we were desperately hungry and weak we managed to cross both branches of the burn and eventually reached the track again. All of us suffered from raw rubbed thighs and feet from our wet clothing and our hands were peeling, but the lost dinner was made up for twofold later that day in Fort William.

In retrospect, I think it was extremely fortunate that this incident took place years ago when we were very young, fit and strong. Equipment in those days was rudimentary, with cotton anoraks and thin nylon cagoules, and it was generally accepted that if it rained heavily you just got wet. Before the Quoich dam was built there was a rain gauge at Kinlochquoich which recorded the highest annual rainfall anywhere in Britain, at a staggering 159in. Indeed, Professor Gordon Manley in his book *Climate and the British Scene* reckons that the rainfall in the high glens west of Loch Quoich could average over 200in per annum. Luckily, our horrendous experience on that final day of our first visit to Knoydart did not put me off this unique area. I have returned many times, at all seasons, to climb Ladhar Bheinn and the other peaks, and to enjoy the glorious views down the lengths of Loch Nevis and Loch Hourn to Skye, Rhum and the distant hills of the Outer Hebrides.

One of my most memorable visits to Knoydart ignored the hills entirely. It was early November and I caught the post-boat from Mallaig to Inverie, stepping ashore on a sparkling morning with Ladhar Bheinn and the distant Cuillin gleaming white with the first snow of the winter. I spent four days, with a small tent, walking round the coast from Inverie to Barrisdale, exploring the bays and inlets and marvelling at the rugged beauty of this lonesome corner of Britain. To my delight I discovered that several crofts had been renovated and were the homes of thriving families. One mother told me disarmingly that most of the inhabitants were 1960s' drop-outs who, although now approaching middle age, so loved the area that they could never think of leaving. Most parents had obtained approval from the Education Authority to teach their own children and I was impressed by the natural, confident, direct approach of the children I met. In one cottage power was provided by a wind generator, in another by a small hydro-electric plant set in the tumbling burn. Incongruously a ten-year-old boy was playing on a computer in the kitchen.

Life on Knoydart is hard. Most of the men in the remote parts earn a living by prawning or diving for clams. Families keep a few sheep and chickens, and the women spin wool and knit. With no telephone and the nearest neighbour perhaps three hours walk away, life can be lonely. One young mother told me she saw about five visitors a year. Every few months they would cross Loch Hourn to Glenelg and drive sixty-eight miles to Inverness for a mammoth shop at the supermarket.

Evidence of the depopulation of Knoydart could be seen everywhere. A large ruined church stood gaunt by the shore at Sandaig, a church which once attracted a congregation of over 400 every Sunday. Likewise the sheltered and picturesque bay and village of Airor is now overgrown and inhabited only by a lone fisherman. However, it was a sense of beauty rather than decay which struck me about Knoydart, for there are few stretches of coastline in Britain still completely free from chalets, caravans and car parks. I watched an otter slipping down the beach into the sea, seals basked on islets off-shore, herds of red deer observed me from a respectful distance, while buzzards and a golden eagle soared overhead to investigate my intrusion into their territory.

Where the peninsula runs back eastwards, alongside Loch Hourn, any vestige of a path disappears, cliffs plunge straight down into the sea, and I was forced to climb over 1,000ft up steep hillsides on an inland detour. However, I could descend again, through ancient deciduous woods, to the shore at delectable hidden coves inhabited only by oyster catchers, although parallel furrows and grassy banks indicated lazy-bedding and wall building in a bygone era.

At Barrisdale there is a shooting lodge with a farm attached, supplied by boat from Arnisdale across Loch Hourn. Smoke was coming out of a cottage chimney and dogs barked, but I saw nobody and pressed on up the excellent path leading over the Mam Barrisdale pass to Inverie and the Mallaig ferry.

Very Severely Frightened

'Very severely frightened on rock?' I exclaimed disbelievingly to Geoff's (the editor of *High* magazine) question. 'Of course I was, nearly all the time.'

Most of my rock climbing was done in the 1950s and 1960s when the sport was very different from that of today. Although climbing had progressed some way from the hemp rope, shoulder belay era, most equipment was rudimentary. We used awkward cable-laid white nylon rope but, traditionally, our waist bands were several turns of hemp cord secured by a reef knot. Harnesses and helmets did not exist, suspect ex-WD karabiners were still around, and nuts were obtained from breakers' yards and threaded onto nylon line.

I learned to climb in heavy boots nailed with clinkers, muggers and tricounis; but then I discovered Robert Lawrie's Alpine boots with Vibram soles. You had to go to his workshop in London to be fitted out, and the boots gave wonderful friction on classic VSs such as Munich Climb, Belle Vue Bastion and Nose Direct. Later came Kleterschuhe of soft, light suede leather and rather bendy Vibram-type soles. I never did buy PAs: these were for the top climbers only, the Extremely Severe operators like Peter Crew. In my circle of friends it was frowned on to wear PAs for any but the hardest climbs, and the climber who wrote in the log book in Ynys Ettws that he had worn gumboots for an ascent of Crackstone Rib received universal acclaim.

In those days the maxim was 'a leader never falls': if he

did, he could expect to be killed or severely injured. Run outs of 50 or 60ft with no intermediate protection at all were commonplace, and the subsequent exposure was horrendous. Unprotected climbs such as Diagonal, Javelin Buttress and Central Buttress on Avon Gorge required nerves of steel and left you a quaking wreck.

At university, in the OUMC, there was constant pressure to push your standard higher. This arose from tradition, a legacy from pre-war days when Oxbridge climbers thought themselves to be among the country's best and, in recognition of this, the Presidents of the OUMC and CUMC were ex-officio members of the Climbers' Club Committee. When I went up to Oxford as a freshman in 1958 the recent death toll of Oxford climbers was appalling, with fatal accidents having occurred on the British hills and outcrops, the Alps, the Himalaya and the Radcliffe Camera.

Then there was peer pressure. Most weekends a convoy of motorbikes, scooters and ramshackle open-topped cars (there was no MOT test and a conveyance could be bought for £30) would proceed to North Wales via the pubs of Worcestershire and Salop. We would sleep in Helyg, Ynys Ettws or Cwm Glas or bivvy under the Llanberis boulders and drink in the Pen y Gwryd on the Saturday night.

This was the generation of Colin Mortlock, Peter Hutchinson, John Cole, Kim Meldrum, Nigel Rogers, Roger Putnam, Alan Wedgwood, Colin Taylor, John Burrows and Alan Heppenstall, when regular Monday night meetings were held in the Cobra, in St Ebbs, Oxford, and when, over eye-wateringly hot curries, stories would be swapped about the weekend's epics, and plans laid for the future. But all good things come to an end, and two incidents in particular radically changed my aspirations to become an ambitious rock climber.

Mur y Niwl on Craig yr Ysfa, in the Carneddau, was always a great favourite with its heart-stopping reverse mantleshelf over a gaping abyss, but no other routes had been made up the sheer wall to the right. Then in 1959, Wharton and Isles put up Agrippa, 280ft, HVS, which soon gained a reputation for seriousness and severity.

The following year Nigel Rogers and I roped up at the bottom of Agrippa and tossed a coin for the lead. I won, and started up the first pitch of 50ft to a ledge; there was almost no protection, although after about 30ft I casually looped a runner over a rounded knuckle of rock. The last 5ft to the stance were vertical, but my outstreched fingers were just inches short of the ledge. I was getting worried, and seriously thought of descending to better holds for a rest before my strength ran out when I spied a piton below the ledge. Without clipping in I put a finger in the ring and pulled up to reach the jug-handle holds above. But I had not tested the piton, it was loose, and as I pulled outwards rather than downwards it popped out and I flew head first down towards the screes.

I remember thinking rather sadly: 'That's it! That's the end for you, Richard!' when, with a terrific jerk, I came to rest upside-down, one hand just touching the scree, looking into the face of Nigel who had been pulled clear of the ground. Nigel lowered me to the screes with my left forefinger still hooked into the piton (I still have it today), and we shook the main climbing rope. At the first tremor the runner slipped off the knuckle of rock and slid down the rope. One of the three strands of the runner had broken, and the karabiner was bent and twisted. My hand which had just hit the rocks was cut and bruised and I spent the afternoon getting it X-rayed at Bangor hospital; luckily all was clear.

Later that night in Ynys Ettws, when I was still shaken and upset, Colin Taylor said: 'After a fall like that you must go straight back onto the rock or you'll lose your nerve.' Thus, next morning, having already lost my nerve, I reluctantly followed Colin up the Snowdon railway and down to Cloggy for an ascent of Great Slab.

'Provided you don't fall off the first pitch, where there is no protection for the second man, and pendulum out over the overhang, the climb is a doddle,' said Colin. In the event I need not have worried, for once back on the rock I regained some confidence and found little trouble with the crux.

Great Slab is a 600ft climb with ever-increasing exposure but ever-decreasing difficulties. The last three pitches consist of a long slanting traverse across the top of the slab to reach easy ground. I was perched in a tiny and very exposed niche, belayed rather inadequately by a single sling. Colin, a great traditionalist, was wearing moleskin breeches, a coloured handkerchief tied round his neck, and a deerstalker. I could tell he was enjoying himself by the arias from Rigoletto which echoed round the cwm.

Half-way along the traverse I saw Colin deviate from the route and begin to climb straight up to the top of the crag: 'I think I can see a feasible direct finish to the route,' he shouted. 'It would be a first ascent, I'll have a go.' Colin was already a good 80ft away from me with no intervening runners and I was nervous, my hands were wet with sweat, my head was starting to spin and the screes looked a long, long way down.

Colin moved up further, there was little rope left and I could see his bulging calf muscles as he stood on tiny holds. Then I saw his legs begin to shake, the singing stopped. 'This is very, very dicey,' he shouted; 'I hope you've got a good belay because I could peel at any moment.' I glanced sideways at the single sling and down the never-ending sweep of rock to Llyn Du'r Arddu, and shuddered: 'No, I haven't. For God's sake be careful. Come down.' I yelled. 'Easier said than done,' croaked Colin.

At that moment I made a decision, a pact with myself: 'If I survive this one I'll never get into the same predicament again. I'll give up heroics. I won't seek further massive injections of adrenalin from rock climbing. I'll step back from this madness. Honestly.'

Colin inched his way back to the correct route, fixed a bomb-proof belay and brought me across. I was sick with relief as we coiled the rope at the top of the crag and began the long walk back, each of us deep in his own thoughts. 'I'm sure there is a direct finish, I'll have to come back for another look,' said Colin. But my resolution held. 'That's your lot. To the brink twice in one weekend. Never again,' I swore.

Colin did not return to the direct finish to Great Slab. After a few more very active climbing years he was tragically killed when a rock ledge on which he was standing, collapsed on the South Face of the Obergabelhorn. He is buried in Zermatt.

I shall always remember my third Alpine season, when I was climbing with a novice OUMC party on the Allalinhorn in the Swiss Alps. I was carefully descending the razor-sharp south ridge, just below the summit, on a crest of fresh snow overlying hard ice. I had cut steps into the ice for our crampons and was roped to my climbing partner, Angie, who missed a step and started to slide headlong down the face towards the glacier many thousands of feet below. Without thinking I threw myself down the other side of the ridge to arrest her fall. When we came to rest we gingerly cut steps back to the summit and returned to the hut by the easiest way.

The rest of the party, sitting on the summit rocks, were very frightened indeed at the near accident that they had witnessed. I was physically sick at the mental strain.

No climber can look back and honestly say that he or she was never frightened. Climbing is a dangerous sport, with many objective dangers and unsuspecting hazards round every corner. It is rather like the months immediately following the passing of your driving test when you are much more likely to have an accident. The early days of your climbing career, when you are at your most impetuous, are the most risky.

Schoolboys on Kolahoi

We watched hypnotised as the massive rock, the size of a double-decker bus, slowly toppled over, slid down a band of snow, accelerated and then smashed to pieces, the debris sweeping down the central couloir and finally coming to rest on the glacier 2,000ft below. We were belayed on a rib of rock to the right of the couloir 200ft away, but the sulphurous fumes drifted up into our nostrils. The knot in my stomach tightened and I sighed with relief; I suppose at that time we should have turned back, after all we were only a school party and I had Charles, Simon and Patrick in my care, sixth formers aged only seventeen and eighteen. But another three or four rope lengths would see us to the summit ridge, and after eighteen months of planning and intensive training we could not admit defeat; besides which I would have had a mutiny on my hands.

We were climbing the south face of Kolahoi, a beautiful pyramid of rock and the highest peak in the Kashmir valley area at 17,933ft. Our party of thirteen was from Ampleforth College in Yorkshire and we had the distinction of being the first-ever party from a British school to climb in the Himalaya. I had two assistant leaders, a doctor and nine boys, chosen from over sixty applications from the the school. Who says that the spirit of adventure is no longer present in the younger generation?

Base camp was on the moraines below the northern glacier snout of Kolahoi, two days' walk up the idyllic Lidder valley from Pahalgam. The valley, described by some as the most beautiful on earth, was ablaze with flowers, including eidelweiss and gentians, and we saw marmots, monkeys, water buffaloes and strange horned sheep. The birds included eagles, kites, vultures, kingfishers, humming birds and hoopoes. We had acclimatised for six days and had managed to find a route that avoided the main icefall by ascending the east glacier. Camp 1 was at 12,470ft on the lower slopes of the east glacier, and camp 2 was tucked under the long east ridge of Kolahoi at 14,436ft. The entire expedition had carried loads to establish and equip camps 1 and 2, but my hopes of putting two small tents at the very bottom of the south face had had to be abandoned, because the snowfield at the base of the cliffs was littered with avalanche debris and recently fallen stones. Since there was no safe place for a camp I had decided to launch the assault from camp 2.

From our reconnaissance the previous day I had underestimated the height of the south face. Climbing in two ropes of two, Charles and myself and Simon with Patrick, it took fifteen long rock pitches to reach the summit ridge. The south face was exposed to the sun's rays from dawn, and although we rose at 3am and started up the rocks at 7am, the stones had already begun to fall.

I don't think any of us slept that night, and at intervals we listened in awe to the sound of avalanches roaring down the north face of Kolahoi. It was with great relief that we heard the Brrr of the alarm clock at 3am. We cooked porridge and tea from the warmth of our sleeping bags, and then emerged into the cold to strap on crampons and rope up. The glacier was frozen hard and a mess tin tobogganed away down the slope. The stars gave enough light for us to see Kolahoi looming above as we cramponned up the snow in silence. Soon after

5am the sun burst over the horizon and we came to life. It was a golden dawn, and the Himalaya were spread out to the east as far as the eye could see from Ladakh to Kishtwar. 'If we get no further it will have all been worth while just to experience the sun rising over the Himalaya,' I said to myself.

We had felt pleased with ourselves as we perched on the lower ledges of rock above the bergschrund and took off our crampons. In spite of two and a half hours cramponing up to a height of about 15,900ft we had hardly noticed the altitude. As soon as we started rock climbing, however, and began using hands and arms as well as legs, we suffered the well documented symptoms of rasping breath and tight chests. There were times when we just had to bury our heads in our arms and heave and pant for several moments before being able to continue. The climbing was totally absorbing and required our full attention, and we were hardly conscious of the stones winging down over our heads or the magnificent panorama of peaks coming into view behind neighbouring Bur Dalau and Buttress Peak. Along with many British parties abroad we felt at home on rock in spite of the horrible looseness, for most of our training had been done on Yorkshire outcrops and in North Wales. We were all competent to lead up to Hard Severe at least, and we preferred to find routes up smooth slabs of rock which, although steeper, were at least sound.

There were plenty of placements for nut runners and we were entirely engrossed in the climbing, but time was slipping by. It was 11am when we completed the final (hardest) pitch at grade IV and paused on the summit ridge for some biscuits. The exposure was monumental; 6,500ft down the sheer north face we could just make out the base camp tents. Charles announced he was going to be sick, the half-cooked porridge for breakfast hadn't agreed with him.

The true summit was a snow cornice 650ft along the ridge, and again I seriously contemplated a retreat, but decided to continue just a little further. The first obstacle was a nasty overhanging gendarme 30ft high. We managed to descend a pitch down the south face and traverse across a gully of rotten snow to by-pass the gendarme, but the climbing was distinctly tricky and I was extremely worried. Slivers of rock were piled up at crazy angles and nothing could be trusted. Dislodged rocks would crash down on either side and bound down to the glaciers in a most unnerving way.

At 1.30pm, after six pitches along the ridge, we assembled at the last rock belay before the snow-cap. Individually, and safeguarded by the rope, we kicked steps to the top of the cornice and planted a small Union Jack (after all, it was 1997 and Jubilee Year!) but were far too exhausted and shattered to feel much elation. Monsoon clouds had built up in the north and we were denied distant views of Nanga Parbat and K2. To the south-east, however, we could clearly see the giant Nun Kun massif only forty miles away.

We all knew that we now faced one of the most testing descents of our lives, and headaches and sickness were pushed to one side as we turned our backs on Kolahoi's snow-cap. We were far behind schedule, and foremost in our minds was the thought of the return along the knife edge and then down the unending and loose south face. It is to the great credit of the boys that without delay we rechecked the gear and climbed down steadily for six hours non-stop until we reached the glacier. No one put a foot wrong. The first down on each rope left running belays to protect the last man. In general we preferred to climb down rather than abseil since it would have been more time-consuming to have found secure abseil points or cracks for pitons, although we did abseil the last pitch before the glacier. Dashing down the glacier in a rope of four and jumping crevasses in near darkness we reached camp 2 at 8.30pm.

Unfortunately there was no welcome for us at camp 2 for we had made our climb two days earlier than expected. The main party was down at base camp enjoying goat curry and duty-free whisky. Wearily we melted snow for tea and forced down leathery chuppaties and jam.

I had cut two days off our planned schedule for several reasons. Firstly, the weather had been fine for four days running and I did not think the spell could last. Secondly, we were so excited and mentally geared up for the climb that no one was sleeping and physically we were deteriorating at a great rate. Thirdly, the food situation at camp 2 was desperate. We had not brought any staple food from the UK and had not been able to buy any English-type tinned food in Kashmir. The rations at camp 2 comprised three-day-old chuppaties cooked at base camp by Ram our Indian cook, porridge, biscuits and Kendal Mint Cake. Nutri-nuggets of concentrated artificial protein, bought in Srinagar, were inedible unless curried, and our pressure cooker was at base camp so we couldn't cook rice. This was a major planning hiccup, for I knew well that an army marches on its stomach and growing boys need large meals at regular intervals, but we had confidently been informed that lightweight convenience food could be bought in Srinagar.

There was no question of mounting a second assault. None of the other boys had sufficient expertise, the objective dangers were too high, and anyway the weather broke the following day and we had a thoroughly unpleasant, and rather dangerous descent to camp 1 because gaping crevasses had opened up across the route. I was expecting a great deal of disappointment from the boys when I announced my decision, but in fact they all confessed to being extremely relieved.

It had been a team effort throughout. The other boys had load-carried and established camp 2 while we sunbathed at camp 1. Our chances of success would be raised if we were nursed as far as possible, I told them! The route from camp 1 to camp 2 was 2,000ft of steep, crevassed ice and this tested everyone's technique to the limit, particularly when carrying heavy loads. The week we had spent snow- and ice-climbing on Lochnagar in the Cairngorms back in March was barely adequate. We did have two crevasse incidents, but nothing serious.

The first ascent of Kolahoi was in 1911 by Neve and Mason who climbed a snow couloir to one side of the south face. We had hoped originally to climb the mountain by this couloir but we could not identify it. Hunt and Brotherton had climbed the south face in 1935 via the Central Couloir and the rocks to one side of it. This was the couloir in which we witnessed the rock avalanche. In 1977 there was far less snow than usual, which forced us to take a rock route all the way. The long east ridge has also been climbed in its entirety, but the north-west and south-west ridges and the stupendous north face await first ascents.

Later on in India we were privileged to meet Colonel Kumar (just back from Kangchenjunga) and Major Ahluwalia (of the 1965 Everest expedition) who told us we were only the second party to have climbed Kolahoi since 1970, three different Indian expeditions having failed on the mountain.

At the conception of the expedition I was worried about the attitude of the climbing establishment to taking schoolboys to a big mountain. Everyone I spoke to, however, was extremely encouraging and we received much useful help and advice both in this country and in India. In particular I must mention Lord Hunt, our official adviser, and the Winston Churchill Memorial Trust for giving me a Fellowship as leader of the expedition.

We got a tremendous amount out of the expedition. None of us had been to the Himalaya before, and we were able to experience at first hand the joys and tribulations that such a trip had to offer. There was no bitterness, envy, back-biting or jockeying for the lead, and the boys were always cheerful and co-operative. Volunteers for load-carrying were always forthcoming, and in many other ways a school expedition scores over an adult team of ambitious and sometimes selfish climbers. But there are disadvantages: because of their limited experience one has constantly to be on the look-out for careless belays, loose rock, balled-up crampons and other safety points that can be taken for granted with adults. On the face proper, though, we were climbing as equals and the three boys realised that their lives depended on their own ability. When they left school Charles and Simon went on to become extremely keen and competent climbers in their own right, and both led major expeditions from their respective universities.

India itself provided another unforgettable experience for us. The time spent in the foothills and in Srinagar, on our overland jouney from Kashmir to Delhi and in Delhi itself was as eventful as our time in the mountains – but that is another story.

THE HEBRIDES

'Boreray and the stacks loomed up into the clouds, while thousands of gannets wheeled and screamed overhead.'

Failure and Success on
the Cuillin Ridge Traverse

Whenever I need to give my morale a boost I re-read some of the old guidebooks where the authors don't mince their words in describing and grading climbs. Thus George Abraham in *British Mountain Climbs* grades as 'Exceptionally Severe Courses' old favourites such as Great Gully on Craig Yr Ysfa, Monolith Crack, and B route on Gimmer Crag. Likewise Central Buttress, Scafell, now graded a modest 5b, was the hardest climb in Britain for thirty years after its first ascent in 1914 (Trevor Jones, Cumbrian Rock). Yet these climbs, which seemed so hard and committing forty years ago, are nowadays knocked off with disdain by precocious teenagers.

W.H. Murray fired much of my early enthusiasm for the hills, and I can remember with clarity my first trip to Skye in 1959, when we hitched up and climbed Cioch Direct and Crack of Doom, described glowingly by Murray as the best rock climb in the Cuillin. At that time Murray's *Mountaineering in Scotland* was one of the few books describing the hills and climbs of Scotland, and any recommendation from Murray could be relied upon. Nowadays you couldn't get away with such a statement: it would provoke numerous letters to magazine editors. I am afraid that Tom Patey was right when he wrote that a man's ability and achievements must only be measured against the yard-stick of his contemporaries.

However, there is one mountaineering route which I am

sure all guidebook authors, since 1911, would unanimously agree is the finest in the British Isles: the Cuillin Ridge Traverse, first described in the *SMCJ* of October 1911 by L.G. Shadbolt. Over the years I had various attempts at the traverse only to fail ingloriously, and I was beginning to feel like Chris Bonington in 1985: over fifty years old, time running out, but still wanting to climb Everest. How well I recall one such ignominious failure. The whole mad scheme was mooted one cold March evening in the bar of the Feathers Inn, Helmsley. The conversation turned to long mountaineering days in the British hills and, inevitably, the Cuillin Ridge Traverse. A few pints later the party of seven was agreed, conviviality rather than expertise being the over-riding factor, and a training programme was suggested.

Tilman would have approved the simplicity of the plan which could have been written on the back of a postage stamp, let alone an envelope: a party of five would leave Glen Brittle at midnight, ready for a 3am start from Gars Bheinn at the end of the ridge; a support party of two would carry water and food up to the ridge for a rendezvous at Bealach Coire na Banachdich; and everyone would celebrate later that evening in the bar of the Sligachan Hotel.

The first inkling that all might not go smoothly arose at Fort William when we ran into a belt of heavy rain which extended across the entire Western Highlands. Dutch courage re-emerged in the bar at Sligachan, but Glen Brittle at midnight was pitch black and very wet indeed. The long-suffering inhabitants of the Glen Brittle Memorial Hut informed us that the ridge had only been clear of mist for three hours during the previous week. At 6am, however, the rain had stopped and the clouds appeared to be lifting. By 7.30 we were off; the support was not feeling confident of making

Bealach Coire na Banachdich, and so joined the main party.

It is a long way to Gars Bheinn at the south end of the Cuillin Ridge, and I made the tiresome mistake of crossing Coires Lagan, a'Ghrunnda and Laogh at far too high a level which meant a six-mile, ankle-wrenching traverse of wet, slippery grass, heather and stones, and the negotiation of numerous ravines. The final 1,500ft to the summit of Gars Bheinn consists of loose boulders and scree set at the angle of limiting friction. As the mist thickened and drizzle set in I could sense a certain silent hostility emanating from my colleagues. We became strung out, each in his own private hell, when a cry came from below: 'My legs are wracked with cramp, I can't continue, I'm going back.' It was our secret weapon, our rock-climbing ace who had climbed Cenotaph Corner and was to have led the Thearlaich-Dubh Gap and Naismith's Route on the Bhasteir Tooth. He turned about to begin a four-hour limp back to Glen Brittle, cursing the Cuillin and dreaming of gentle strolls to the cliffs of Tremadog, the Avon Gorge and Bosigran.

By the time we reached the pointed summit of Gars Bheinn, four hours had elapsed and we glanced with envy at the numerous bivouac sites which lie dotted around. In our exhausted state, some of the flat ledges surrounded by sheltered walls of boulders looked positively inviting. Martin fumbled with his new and expensive SLR camera, and let it slip – and we listened with horror as it bounded down the cliffs towards Loch Coruisk, nearly 3,000ft below, with a shattering of glass. We did not retrieve it: time was pressing and we had far to go.

As we wound our way slowly along the easy ridges leading to Sgurr nan Eag the rain stopped and the clouds began to roll back, giving us enticing views of the ridge ahead and the ground below. Like a peep show the Isle of Soay, the Sgurr of Eigg, Canna, Hallival and Askival on Rhum, Sgurr Dearg, Sgurr nan Gillean and Blaven came successively into view, wreathed in mists like mountains from the Lost World.

A break for late lunch was called on Sgurr Dubh na Da Bheinn, and we lounged on the summit rocks for thirty minutes while John and Paul, our two Munro baggers, made the deviation to collect Sgurr Dubh Mor. At this point Murphy's Law (when everything seems to be going well, you find you have overlooked something) made its first strike of the day: on delving into my rucksack I discovered that I had left the lunch behind on the kitchen table, and three litres of water were no substitute for a large box of jam sandwiches. However, the party's attentions were firmly fixed on the exposed rock pitches leading up to the Thearlaich-Dubh Gap, which effectively blocks the way ahead to Sgurr Alasdair.

Three of the party, sensibly realising that, as second on the rope, an ascent of Downbeat at Peak Scar was inadequate preparation for this exposed rock section of the Cuillin, traversed the scree at the head of Cor' a' Ghrunnda to reach Sgurr Sgumain, hoping to meet up with the rest of us on Sgurr Alasdair. A few minutes later John, about to make a committing move, 200ft above the scree, started muttering about his responsibilities as husband and father and his inadequate life insurance, and retreated to join the Sgumain party.

Paul and I abseiled into the Thearlaich-Dubh Gap and gazed up at the polished chimney and V-groove running up the north side. The actual climb is easier than it looks, a few bomb-proof runners take care of the exposure, but when I was sitting at the top, enjoying the sunshine and pulling up the rucksacks, Murphy struck again: a rucksack, tied on to the end of the rope, became stuck fast in the chimney. It would move neither up nor down and was out of reach of Paul's hand from below. What to do? I moved my belay to the edge of the drop and tried to lower a loop of rope to Paul, but all I did was to tangle the rope round some jammed blocks until it looked like a crocheted dishcloth. After half-an-hour of shouting and shaking the rope the situation was becoming desperate.

I was about to suggest in strong terms that Paul should climb unroped, twenty feet to the apex of the chimney to free the rucksack; Paul sensed my mood and had a two-word answer ready on his lips, but we were both spared embarrassment by the knitting suddenly becoming unravelled. Paul grasped the loop of rope and pulled the rucksack free. He then tied the rucksack to the middle of the rope, thus allowing him to guide its ascent from below; an obvious solution that we should have thought of from the start.

Our minor trauma had delayed us further, but Paul soon joined me above the Gap and we hastened on to Sgurr Alasdair. But where were the others? It transpired that they had met a nasty rock step on the Sgumain-Alasdair ridge, described in the guidebook as a *mauvais pas* but which they had read as *pas mauvais*. The section was beyond them, and they had slunk down to the glen.

It was now 5pm and Sgurr nan Gillean looked no nearer. Clouds were racing in from the west and we had no food. Sadly this was the end of the great Cuillin Traverse attempt, and a few hours later curtains of rain were driving down the glen, a river of muddy water was running down the side of the road and the clouds were so low that their ragged edges brushed the waves on the loch.

Returning to the Cuillin a few years later I tried a new ploy. Gars Bheinn is the bugbear; its horrendous 2,000ft of loose scree exhausts you before you even leave the summit for Sgurr nan Gillean at the far end of the ridge. But with a bivvy you can rest and recover, and then leave next morning at first light. As we were formulating our plans in the Glen Brittle Memorial Hut the temporary warden, Tim Winter, and his climbing partner John, asked if they could join us. Now Tim is small of stature but he has an iron will, the strength of Goliath, he knows every rock in the Cuillin and, as Rob suggested, is cast from the very gabbro itself. Confidence grew, and when our friends Sandra and Keith selflessly offered to bivouac with us and then carry down the sleeping bags and surplus equipment in the morning, there was no way we could wriggle out of the attempt.

In the early hours a wet mist cloaked the ridge, but was mostly burnt off later by the rising sun. Wreaths of light cloud kept the temperature down, but the TD Gap at 4am was wet, cold and greasy. We offered Tim the lead. I found it quite diabolical; I jammed and thrutched and panted, and somehow forced myself up the appalling groove to lie exhausted and retching on the rocks above. An easy escape down the Alasdair Stone Shoot lay ahead, and Richard, the youngest member of the party and on his first visit to Skye, decided to take it: 'I'm only twenty-three and will have many other chances to do the ridge,' he said. This shook me, and I thought to myself, 'You're fifty-two and won't have another chance.' I agreed to continue.

Throughout the long day Tim led us expertly over every fantastic pinnacle and crest of the Cuillin Ridge. The direct route up the 200ft abutment of An Stac was a revelation to me since most parties traverse the screes below. Moderate climbing up An Stac on sound rock, poised between heaven and earth with Loch Coruisk shimmering far below, was a tonic and finally dispersed the early morning nausea. By the time we reached the Inaccessible Pinnacle the rock had dried out completely and climbing became sheer joy. However, we were shocked and dismayed to see red arrows painted on the first of Bidein Druim nan Ramh's three peaks to indicate the way up. This is an act of vandalism which must surely be deplored by all British climbers.

Earlier in the week, on a day of rain and wind, we had climbed Bruach na Frithe by the easy north ridge and Mike had buried a two litre flask of water near the cairn. Now he unearthed it and the cool nectar revived and refreshed us and saved a 200ft descent to the spring in upper Fionn Choire. Finally, at 4.30pm we wriggled through the 'window' and shook hands on the pointed summit of Sgurr nan Gillean. I was close to tears, not so much for having fulfilled a life's ambition, but because of the friendship and support of my companions who had encouraged and helped me in a thousand different ways during that unforgettable day.

And the final verdict? Oh yes, the commentators are absolutely right: by any standards the Cuillin Ridge Traverse stands head and shoulders above anything else in Britain.

Andy Hyslop and the Cuillin Ridge Record

As dawn broke on the 7 August 1994, Andy Hyslop picked his way through the myriad primitive bivouac shelters of stones at the extreme southern end of the Cuillin Ridge, and hailed the summit cairn on Gars Bheinn. Behind lay a 350-mile drive from Ambleside, a few hours sleep in the back of the car, and the exhausting toil up rough moorland, loose boulders and scree from Glen Brittle. Ahead lay the famous ridge, only seven miles long but involving 13,000ft of ascent, the most formidable day's mountaineering in the British Isles which was first traversed by McLaren and Shadbolt in 1911 in a time of 12 hours 18 minutes.

With a backward glance at the morning light shimmering on the Sound between the islands of Soay and Rhum, Andy set off for the next summit, Sgurr nan Eag. He was wearing ETA fell running shoes specially fitted with Stealth soles, and on his back he carried a Camel Pack filled with two litres of a fructose-based drink: 3 hours, 32 minutes and 15 seconds later he arrived on top of Sgurr nan Gillean, having beaten the ridge record (which he had already established ten weeks previously) by 35 seconds. There was no support party, no one to shake Andy's hand on Sgurr nan Gillean, and no champagne; so having noted the time, he trotted back down to Glen Brittle and commenced the long drive home.

The first serious attempt to achieve a fast time over the ridge was in the spring of 1967 when Eric Beard (Beardie) recorded 4 hours and 9 minutes. It is thought that some of the technical sections were roped before Beardie's arrival, and it is not certain that Sgurr Dubh Mor was included; nevertheless it was a magnificent time and thought by many to be insurmountable. Sadly we may never know the full details because Beardie was tragically killed soon after.

I first met Andy Hyslop in the Glen Brittle Memorial Hut when I was having one of my futile attempts on the ridge and Andy was carrying out a recce prior to an attempt on Beardie's record. The weather was poor, but he learned enough about the route to mount a record attempt the following May, when he successfully achieved 4 hours, 4 minutes and 19 seconds for the south to north traverse. He reached the In Pin in 1 hour and 38 minutes.

Two years later the team of Stott and Davies lowered the

record to 3 hours, 49 minutes and 30 seconds, having been two minutes slower to the In Pin than Andy. This record stood until June 1990, when Martin Moran raced across in 3 hours and 33 minutes. Andy realised that more recces would be necessary if he were to have a chance of regaining the Blue Riband, and he made two visits to Skye in October 1993 to make notes; but he was dogged by bad weather on both occasions. However, in May 1994, he made his second serious attempt on the record. At the In Pin he was five minutes ahead of Moran's schedule, but by Am Bastier he was just one minute behind. A storming ascent of the west ridge of Sgurr nan Gillean placed him on the summit just thirty seconds inside the record. As we have seen, Andy improved on this time later in the year.

What sort of mountaineer is capable of such feats, and what drives him forward? To find some of the answers I tracked down Andy at the Rock + Run shop in Ambleside, one of three such shops that he manages with a business partner. Over lunch Andy told me a little about the challenges which, throughout his life, he has loved to face. Now in his mid-thirties he has spent twenty years seeking adventure, and he has resisted the tedium and predictability of a humdrum life which it is all too easy to slip into. A mountain enthusiast since early life in Brampton, Cumbria, he started hill walking in the Lake District and then, at sixteen, became a self-taught rock climber developing his talents to a prodigious degree. In the Alps, Andy climbed many of the classic routes such as the Walker Spur and the Central Pillar of Freney. He received acclaim for a new direct start to The Shroud on the Grandes Jorasses and for daring clmbs in the Karakoram and Peru with Jon Tinker.

Most unusually Andy combined climbing with fell running

where he also had many notable successes: winning the Capricorn Elite course in the Galloway Uplands in atrocious conditions, coming fifth in the Karrimor Elite Two-Day Mountain Marathon and coming second in the Saunders Two-Day Lakeland Mountain Marathon. He is a member of the Bob Graham Club, having completed the round in 19 hours and 19 minutes. Between fell running, managing three shops and climbing to E6 standard, Andy has found time to climb in the US, particularly in Arizona and New Mexico. And recently he succeeded in another self-imposed challenge: to climb the Nose of El Capitan inside twenty-four hours.

By now I had some inkling of what it takes to traverse the Cuillin Ridge in three-and-a-half hours: fell-running ability to national standard, and supreme confidence on rock so you can solo rock climb in running shoes in complete safety. In addition you must believe in yourself and be motivated to an extraordinary degree. Many people, I know, think that running across the Cuillin is the height of madness: it is a needlessly dangerous and pointless pursuit, they say. If you go slowly you can savour to the full the unique environment. But the mountains are there for our enjoyment, and who are we to say how they should be used? Andy Hyslop and his companions have my utmost repect.

Celebrations on the Cioch

We had to laugh. The invitation was preposterous: a fiftieth birthday luncheon party, in black tie, on the Cioch, Sron na Ciche, Cuillin of Skye: RSVP The Countess of Cromartie.

The party was for John Mackenzie the eccentric earl, clan chief, explosives expert, guidebook writer, pioneering climber of new routes on remote crags in the North-West Highlands and doughty fighter for free access to the hills, who was active behind the scenes during the negotiations for the Letterewe Accord. What could be more appropriate for John than a party on the Cioch, which was christened by John Mackenzie the Cuillin guide, after he and Collie had made its first ascent in 1906? The Cioch is an amazing geological freak, a pinnacle which protrudes from the cliff face half-way up the 1,000ft crag of Sron na Ciche at a height of 2,300ft.

Inspection of our diary showed that we could make it to Skye, but there would be no leeway. The prospect was 900 miles of driving in two days for just one day in the Cuillin, quite probably in atrocious weather. Ah well, didn't Mick Fowler do the equivalent from London, weekend after weekend? We'd go for it.

For mid-June the weather was unseasonal, with heavy icy rain in Yorkshire and fresh snow on Ben Nevis. But as we drove through Kintail, the western sky was bright, and from Sligachan the Cuillin Ridge was almost clear with only a few clouds lingering in the high corries. John's wife, Janet, had arranged accommodation at Bracadale, fittingly overlooking the tiny church and graveyard where two simple headstones, set side by side, mark the resting places of John Mackenzie and Norman Collie. As we walked down to pay homage to these giants of Cuillin exploration the late evening sun was lighting up the green hillsides emphasising the furrows of the old lazy beds, the gorse and broom were a startling yellow and the gabbro of the Cuillin Ridge was glowing pink. Could it be that the weather would hold?

The next morning in bright sunshine and cold wind we plodded up the excellent path, constructed by Pathcraft Ltd, which leads from the Glen Brittle campsite up into Coire Lagan. It had been nearly forty years since I had climbed on Sron na Ciche and the huge cliff looked steeper and more intimidating than ever. John and his climbing partner Graham Cullen tackled Petronella and met the rest of us on the terrace below the Cioch Great Slab. We took the East Gully variant route and then climbed the Cioch via the right-angled corner on the west side of the slab. Trisha and I were very much the riff-raff of the party, and in our bendy Brasher boots, found the climb sufficiently hard. However, we were expertly marshalled and advised by Blyth Wright, late of Glenmore Lodge and now co-ordinator of the avalanche advisory and investigation service in Scotland, who was entirely unruffled and reassuring.

Eventually eighteen people were assembled and belayed on the top of the Cioch. In spite of the biting wind, dinner jackets, kilts, highland regalia and off-the-shoulder ball gowns were donned in preparation for a sumptuous banquet. An important, though rather quiet guest who had lost his appetite, was Sir Hugh Munro himself: Robin Campbell had carried up his life-sized effigy, and had also in fact carried him to the summits of the Inaccessible Pinnacle, Carn Ealar and Carn Cloich-mhuillin to ensure that he was qualified to attend the dinner, for those three summits were the only ones he had failed to climb in his lifetime. I had last seen Sir Hugh at the Munro Centenary dinner in Edinburgh in 1991.

The tiny perch which is the top of the Cioch is extremely exposed, yet somehow Janet produced a vase of fresh flowers, spread out a white table cloth and served, on a silver salver, a magnificent meal of quails, eggs, smoked salmon, chicken, rice, salad, strawberries and cream, champagne and coffee. A cake with fifty candles was produced. Not often can the corrie have echoed to the sound of popping champagne corks and the strains of 'Happy Birthday To You'.

Paul Brian, writing of the Cioch in *Classic Rock*, would certainly have approved. He says, 'The summit of the Cioch is a fabulous place! Surely it is the finest luncheon place in the country. Apart from the exhilarating situation, the place reeks of history. The flat surface seems to have been designed for the concave bottles of Bouvier bottles and tapping out Meershaum pipes. How garish and tasteless are our coloured ropes and Mars Bars.'

As the sun moved round on to Sron na Ciche we basked in a little warmth and delighted in our position. Ant-like figures could be seen crawling up the long east ridge of the Inaccessible Pinnacle on Sgurr Dearg, and a party were just finishing the top pitch of Integrity, but it was out to the west and north that our eyes were drawn. The truncated cones of MacLeod's Tables were prominent, Canna floated on the bluest of seas, while in the Outer Hebrides we could identify the entire string of islands: Barra Head, Mingulay, Barra, Eriskay, South Uist, Benbecula and North Uist.

The afternoon was far advanced before we turned to the

problem of the descent. Sir Hugh was well wrapped up and snugly ensconsed on a pack frame on Robin's back, so *he* had no worries. It was not easy climbing back down from the Cioch itself to the narrow neck at the top of the Great Slab, but once there, Blyth and a 200ft rope made life very much easier and we were soon all safely back on the terrace. John, Graham and Ken Crocket climbed the Upper Buttress via Wallwork's Route while the rest of us ambled slowly down the Sgumain screes to Glen Brittle, wondering what mad scheme John will think up for his sixtieth birthday.

The Isle of Colonsay

The white shell sand of the bay was bounded by dunes and marram grass, interspersed with weathered rocks covered in yellow lichen. It was a still and sunny early morning, the only sounds being the crump of waves on the shore and the occasional piping of oyster catchers. As we sat on the machair overlooking this idyllic scene an otter swam slowly across the bay and scrambled over the rocks before disappearing amongst the reefs. His long wet body glistened in the sun and his hair was a rich russet colour. Our early rising had rewarded us and we made our way back across the island for breakfast in high spirits.

It was early April on the Hebridean island of Colonsay, which is rarely visited by walkers but is clearly seen from the more popular hills on Jura. Looking west from the summit of Beinn an Oir in the Paps of Jura, across nine miles of ocean, the low outline of the Isle of Colonsay is conspicuous for the waves creaming over its rocky coastline and the sun highlighting the strands of its numerous bays. Colonsay and Oronsay are really two islands joined by a seaweedy strand which is exposed at low tide. Together the islands measure only ten miles by two miles, with the highest point, Carnan Eoin (470ft) on the north side of Colonsay, but they contain such a wealth of natural history, fascinating archaeological remains and rugged landscape features that they provide the perfect venue for a walking holiday. Low-lying and standing out far to the west, Colonsay gets the best of the weather, and we enjoyed many perfect summer days while clouds boiled over the hills of Islay and Jura to the east and Mull to the north.

Three times a week the Cal Mac ferry from Oban docks at Scalascaig pier on the east side of Colonsay. Here is situated the post office and store, a café and the hotel which, on ceilidh or quiz nights, attracts many of the one hundred or so inhabitants of the island. There are a few holiday cottages and farms, but no industry, and even the magnificent Colonsay House (home of the absentee landlord, Lord Strathcona) and its once world-renowned gardens have an air of decay and neglect. The house dates from 1722 and was constructed from stones taken from nearby Kiloran Abbey, founded by St Colomba. It is situated in the middle of the island and you are free to walk through the extensive woodland gardens admiring the rhododendrons, azaleas, magnolias, cherries, figs, peaches, palm trees and water lilies on the ornamental ponds. Spring arrives early on Colonsay, and we found many trees and shrubs in flower, with primroses and violets in the hedgerows and cowslips on the roadside verges.

Emerging from the gardens it is only a short distance to the wild west coast and majestic Kiloran Bay. Atlantic rollers break on half a mile of golden sand framed by rocky headlands, and the scene is reminiscent of Sutherland's Sandwood Bay or some of the equally spectacular bays of the Outer Hebrides. On our visit, Kiloran Bay was empty and lonesome, save for a few ringed plovers strutting about the high-tide mark, and it induced a feeling of melancholy that I last felt at Harris Bay on the Isle of Rhum. The grave of a Viking warrior, dating from 850AD, was found at Kiloran Bay, while Neolithic remains have been discovered in rock caves in the north and south headlands.

A steep little climb up the heather and rocks takes you to

the highest point on the island, Carnan Eoin, a superb view-point for the north of Colonsay and across the Firth of Lorn to Iona. An additional bonus for us was the sight of choughs and a golden eagle. A scramble down the north side of Carn Eoin leads to a farm track running further north to Balnahard, another exquisite strand backed by dunes which runs into a green, translucent sea. We followed the coast round, over cliff tops carpeted with sea pinks, to Colonsay's extreme northerly point where a colony of fulmars were noisily contesting nest sites on the rocky ledges. Looking north-east we could clearly see the disturbed water from the notorious tide-race that sweeps through the Sound of Corrievreckan between the north of Jura and the island of Scarba.

Every corner of Colonsay is packed with interest. Inland from the rugged and desolate coastline lie shallow, reedy lakes and wide expanses of grazing which prove most popular with migrating geese. We saw white-fronted, greylag, Canada and barnacle geese, little grebe, teal, shellduck, golden eye, eider and three kinds of diver: great northern, black-throated and red-throated. Colonsay has recorded 150 birds from the British list, and we saw about half that number during our brief stay.

No walker who visits Colonsay should leave without an expedition to Oronsay. This island can be reached on foot via the strand, about one-and-a-half hours each side of low tide, although you must be prepared for wet feet because the strand never completely dries out. Having sloshed across, a Land Rover track leads south-west for a mile to the ancient priory and its adjacent farm which, sadly, was built with stones filched from the priory. It is said that St Columba landed on Oronsay in the sixth century on his way from Ireland to Iona, and some masonry on the site does date from that time.

The ruined priory that stands today dates from the thirteenth century and is one of Scotland's most glorious ecclesiastical monuments. A Celtic carved cross stands 12ft high outside the priory, and the cloisters have magnificent arches, pillars and tracery. Thirty carved tombstones from the fifteenth century are on display, and the setting, on an exposed peninsula with an open sea, rocky coastline and off-shore skerries where Atlantic grey seals breed, is vastly superior to Iona with its thronging coach parties and ice cream parlours. Oronsay Priory is entirely uncommercial and you may wander around the ruins at will. From a base at Scalascaig, the walker can easily reach any part of Colonsay or Oronsay. It is remarkable that such a small island offers a distillation of all that is best in the Hebrides as a whole.

High Living on
the Isle of Rhum

Perhaps we read too much about epics in the mountains, desperate struggles against the elements, enforced bivouacs, privation and suffering. If you like this sort of thing, give this chapter a miss because here I am going to report on a short break spent in the lap of luxury, and in Edwardian splendour, at the fabulous Kinloch Castle on the island of Rhum.

The Cuillin of Rhum have long been a favourite haunt of mine. I first visited the island nearly thirty years ago, crossing from Mallaig in Bruce Watt's fishing boat with half a dozen members of the school mountaineering club. A row of stinking fish were strung out to dry between the masts, the sea was rough and I was horribly sick. It was the November half term, and we camped at the tiny settlement of Kinloch in foul weather and climbed the principal peaks. But a prolonged storm delayed our departure for three extra days which we spent in the leaky boathouse, watching with awe the white horses in the mouth of Loch Scresort. Contact with home was via radio telephone (Rhum I) and my wife was having to deal with an irate headmaster, who demanded I got the boys off the island at all costs because of impending Oxbridge entrance examinations and the annual Sedbergh rugger match: the hooker was in my party. He never did make the game.

A few years later the Mountain Bothies Association renovated Dibidil bothy, which stands isolated above the shore five miles south of Kinloch. This bothy misses five-star rating only because there is no driftwood for the fire; it is also plagued by rats, and I still remember the scream of anguish as one entered my friend Paul's sleeping bag in the middle of the night. Rats apart, Dibidil is vastly preferable to wet tents at Kinloch. At that time Caledonian MacBraynes were using the ancient converted minesweeper, the *Loch Arkaig*, for the Small Isles' run, a boat which later hit a rock and sank.

Rhum continued to fascinate me, and Trisha and I returned to Dibidil with four small children. With huge rucksacks the undulating and boggy path from Kinloch was exhausting; the rain was incessant and snow fell to 1,500ft, and we seemed to spend the whole time traipsing a further two miles to the wood at the inlet of Papadil to keep the fire going. Papadil is one of the most lonesome, wild and beautiful places in the British Isles. A proud pinnacle of rock guards a shallow inlet of the sea, above which sits a tranquil loch and a small ruined shooting lodge built by George Bullough of Kinloch Castle. Sadly the roof has now collapsed and rhododendrons have all but smothered the ruins, yet on my first visit to Rhum we found wicker chairs, panelled walls and dinner plates bearing the Bullough family crest: bull's heads and bees (for industry).

John Bullough, son of a very rich Lancashire industrialist, bought Rhum in 1887 as a sporting estate and his son, George, gave instructions to the London firm, Leeming and Leeming, to build a grand shooting lodge at Loch Scresort. Rose-coloured sandstone was to be shipped from the Isle of Arran, and no expense was to be spared. Kinloch Castle was finished in 1902, and legend has it that the Lancashire workmen were paid a shilling a day extra to wear the kilt. The Bulloughs would visit Rhum in their luxurious steam yacht,

Rhouma, and give extravagant house parties in Kinloch Castle. Guests were offered stalking, fishing, shooting, yachting, bowls, golf and billiards; they could dance in the ballroom, listen to synthetic music from the mechanical orchestrion, or stroll in the palatial gardens, observing turtles and alligators in an ornamental pool.

The internal decorations were opulent and sumptuous and contained many art treasures and trophies from George's travels around the world in *Rhouma*. At the time of the Boer War, George Bullough lent *Rhouma* to the government as a hospital ship for wounded officers; he was knighted for his patriotism. In fact Sir George was not only a playboy, he was also a conservationist who planted many thousands of trees of various species; his wood on Rhum is now one of the most important in the Hebrides.

In 1975 the Nature Conservancy Council acquired Rhum as a nature reserve, and the original contents of Kinloch Castle were donated by Lady Monica Bullough. The castle is now run as a hotel by Scottish Natural Heritage, who offer accommodation on two levels: self-catering hostel-type accommodation in the old servants' quarters, or the 'full works' which includes use of the magnificent castle with all its delights and facilities, together with cordon bleu cooking with meals served in the splendid dining room lit by chandeliers, which overlooks the lawns and Loch Scresort. Thus on a wintry February day in Glen Coe, when comforts were noticeably lacking and the memories of hot summer weather in the Wind River Mountains were fading fast, a party of eight of us booked three nights of extravagant luxury in Kinloch Castle.

We went over by ferry, and were intrigued to see that in these days of belt-tightening, Cal Mac have come up with the brilliant plan of cutting their large ferry boats in two. Thus the Small Isles' ferry, always the Cinderella of their operations, is now worked by the top-heavy *Lochmor* – it is not obvious whether this is the prow or the stern of the original boat, but it successfully transported us to Rhum. Here we disembarked with our suitcases and walked up the drive to Kinloch Castle with some embarrassment.

Bad weather is not so depressing when you are staying in luxurious accommodation; thus next morning, full of porridge, Mallaig kippers, toast and a monumental fry-up, we struck up the Dubh Coire in thin drizzle and some discomfort, but with great cheerfulness. The huge grey bulk of Hallival loomed up out of the mist and we crossed the boulder-strewn, wind-scoured plateau to its north, delighted to find purple mountain saxifrage bravely flowering, even in the first week of April. The turf on Hallival is riddled with the burrows of Manx shearwaters; these beautiful birds which skim through the troughs of the waves, come in to Hallival and Askival by night to nest in vast numbers. As many as 120,000 pairs breed on Rhum, over half the total population of the species. We saw one miserable specimen flapping feebly outside its burrow, and thought it might have been oiled in Shetland from the *Braer* disaster; however the SNH warden told us that these birds are pathetic on land, and can only take off from the sea or from steep cliffs. The parents leave the fledglings to make their own way down the hillside to reach the sea.

The wind and rain threatened to pluck us off the sharp north ridge of Askival, which steepened to near vertical at the notorious Askival pinnacle. A rift in the cloud momentarily revealed wet, overhanging buttresses of rock, while slabs and walls towered above us into the mist. The rock was greasy and our fingers cold. We had no rope, but Alan and Jane produced flasks of Cointreau and Lagavulin to give us courage for the ascent; it is barely 'Mod' standard under good conditions, but caused not a little heart-fluttering on this occasion.

How civilised it was to return wet and tired from the wild and remote Rhum Cuillin to Edwardian comforts: tea, log fires, a drying room – and the most extraordinary baths we had ever seen: giant Victorian slipper baths with six taps to control water jets that come at you with great force from every conceivable angle. There is also a wave-maker, and this forerunner of the modern jacuzzi caused much hilarity. Drinks followed with mein host in Highland regalia, accompanied by a medley from *La Bohème* on the orchestrion built originally for Queen Victoria. After dinner there was snooker on a superb Burroughs and Watts full-sized table, before bed in four-posters.

It is incongruous to live in such surroundings on a nature reserve on a remote Hebridean island, and SNH must feel some unease at its ownership. However, Kinloch Castle must be preserved and SNH are able to run the hotel on their terms. The National Trust would be reluctant to take over the castle because of the drain it would place on their resources.

During the night, heavy wind-driven rain set in, so in the morning we togged up and walked the seven miles to Harris Bay on the west coast. *En route* we passed one of Rhum's least successful experiments, an attempt by Lord Salisbury, in the middle of the nineteenth century, to dam the Kilmory river and re-route the water into the Kinloch river; by these means it was hoped that the Kinloch river would attract salmon. But the dam was not properly underpinned and it was swept away within two days of completion.

At Harris, with waves pounding the off-shore reefs,

stands the Bullough family mausoleum built in the style of a Greek temple. We ate our sandwiches in the shelter of Lady Monica's marble tomb where she was laid to rest in 1967, having lived to the age of ninety-eight. A herd of wild goats grazed nearby, with long, shaggy coats, curved horns and beards that trailed the ground. Old lazybeds abounded above the raised beach, for Harris was once a sizeable crofting community: 450 people lived and worked on Rhum before the clearances in the nineteenth century.

Today Rhum is a working island, with many on-going projects including a research group on deer, sponsored by Cambridge University and led by the indefatigable Fiona Guinness who has worked on the island for many years. There is also some forestry, deer management, a little cattle farming and a small school. Visitors must obtain prior permission from the SNH warden at the White House, Rhum, as there are a few restrictions on access. There is camping at Kinloch, two open bothies are available at Dibidil and at Guirdil, a cottage offers bed and breakfast, there is also hostel accommodation, and of course, the incomparable Kinloch Castle hotel.

To follow the Cuillin ridge of Rhum you must climb Barkeval, Hallival, Askival, Trollval, Ainshval, Sgurr nan Gillean and Ruinsival, and this makes a long mountain traverse; even so, it is inferior in length and difficulty to the Skye ridge. However, the proximity of the sea is a great bonus to Rhum, as is the fact that there are so few other climbers. The names of the hills are mainly Norse rather than Gaelic, and were given to the distinctive mountains by the Vikings to aid navigation.

My mind goes back to a brilliant autumn day of high wind and bright sunshine. We sat wiping our streaming eyes beside the cairn on the mountain of Orval in the extreme west of Rhum overlooking Bloodstone Hill, Schooner Point and Wreck Bay. A few prawners were checking their creels off the coast, the Cuillin of Skye were dusted with early snow, and south of Canna, waves were breaking over the tiny islets of Oigh-sgeir and Umaolo. These islets are owned by Canna, and farmers graze four and just one sheep on them respectively. How we felt for that lone sheep on Umaolo…

A Landlubber Visits
St Kilda

Back in the 1950s, as a schoolboy in the south of England, I hitch-hiked to the Isle of Skye with one of my brothers to climb in the Cuillin. Our final lift, from Shiel Bridge to Sligachan, was with Dame Flora MacLeod of MacLeod in her chauffeur-driven Rolls Royce, and she kindly shared her picnic lunch of smoked-salmon sandwiches and a bottle of wine with us. During a week of blazing hot weather we explored the ridges and corries, swam in deep pools in the burns and climbed a number of easier rock routes until our fingers were rubbed raw from the coarse gabbro. But that holiday gave me a love of the Hebrides which has enriched my life ever since.

Together with our four small children, my wife and I headed for Scotland's western seaboard every year, staying in primitive bothies on Rhum and Handa Island and camping on Tanera Beag and Priest Island in the Summer Islands group in the mouth of Loch Broom. Those were the days before the RSPB bought Priest Island and, inspired by Fraser Darling's classic books *Island Years* and *Island Farm*, we managed to cadge a lift to this remote outpost on an Ullapool prawner for a four-night stay that gave us a real adventure. Surely there is no finer experience on earth than to lie back on springy machair in warm sunshine, a light breeze carrying the aroma of heather and bog myrtle, and the only sounds the crump of waves breaking on a rocky shore and the cry of sea birds?

One summer our travels took us to Barra, and we climbed to the summit of Heaval, the little hill above Castlebay. I remember gazing to the west, eyes streaming in the cold wind, and catching my first glimpse of the dark silhouette of St Kilda on the far horizon. The islands appeared as mere pinpricks in the ocean, but the seed had been sown and to visit them became a life-long ambition.

Many years passed, until one day I spotted an advertisement offering Hebridean cruises. It was time for action. I booked the boat, obtained permission for a short visit to St Kilda from the National Trust for Scotland in Edinburgh, and phoned a few friends. 'Just twenty-four hours cruising from Oban to St Kilda, a few nights' camping on the main island of Hirta and a short diversion on the way back to visit the Flannans and the Monach Isles. The holiday of a lifetime.' I soon filled the twelve berths available on the *Falls of Laura*.

The day for departure arrived and we chugged out of Oban harbour full of expectation but slightly worried by dark clouds in the west, a freshening breeze and a poor forecast. Rounding Ardnamurchan Point we were rolling horribly in the swell, and the skipper confessed: 'Ah well, you see, she was built for the River Medway. I daren't take her across the Minch in these conditions.' Thus it was that we spent the night in the sheltered harbour on Canna and limped round to Portree the next day in a force 8 gale. On the third day, during a brief lull, we crossed the Minch to Lochmaddy and finally, on the fourth day, attempted to dash through the Sound of Harris and across forty miles of wild ocean to St Kilda.

There was a lumpy sea, the huge green waves were crested with foam, and seasickness took its toll. But as the stacks approached, excitement mounted, and we lined the rails to marvel at the jagged black rock of Boreray thrusting almost vertically out of the waves, its dripping towers and buttresses rising dizzily to over 1,000ft – perhaps the most thrilling sight in Britain. Rounding Boreray to the north, first Stac an Armin and then Stac Lee rise up like sharks' teeth. The 600ft cliffs of these amazing stacks appear to be covered by white guano, but on closer acquaintance you can see that every ledge and crevice holds a gannet: the air is thick with them, like gnats on a summer evening. Nest sites are contested vociferously, and the gannets dive into the waves with their wings swept back for maximum streamlining while others glide and swoop, riding the updraughts for sheer pleasure. St Kilda is the largest gannetry in the Northern Hemisphere, and we felt totally alienated and humbled in this most hostile environment.

In our sheer exhilaration we had forgotten the weather, which had now taken a turn for the worse. The wind was gusting to gale force, and we bucked over an angry sea to the comparative shelter of Village Bay on Hirta and tied up to a mooring buoy some way off shore. For thirty-six hours we were pounded by storm-force winds with gusts of 65 knots. Curtains of spray swept across the bay and columns of spume were driven through the narrow passage between Hirta and the 576ft high island of Dun which makes up the southern arm of the bay. Rainbows danced through the racing vortexes of spray and the menacing roar of the wind and the breakers was beyond our experience. It became possible to understand why the St Kildans were deafened for days following a severe winter storm.

Only a few hundred metres away stretched Main Street, Village Bay, with its line of stone cottages, but frustratingly there was no way we could land. Several large stern trawlers from the east coast came into the bay to shelter, as well as a naval vessel; the latter made a foolhardy attempt to make a landing using a heavy Zodiac inflatable with outboard engine, but no sooner had it been launched than a squall picked it up and tossed it aside like a fallen leaf, throwing the occupants into the sea. They were rescued by the prompt action of one of the fishing boats. On our second day in Village Bay the wind dropped a couple of notches and we braced ourselves for a nightmarish return voyage to Harris. However, the knots on the mooring ropes had been drawn so tight by the buffeting that they were jammed solid. 'Get me an axe,' shouted the skipper; 'We'll have to chop ourselves clear.' After a few lusty blows we sprang away like a cork from a bottle and our journey commenced.

Basically I am a landlubber, and I found it a terrifying experience to be in a small boat miles from land in a rough sea, particularly when the engine conked out. 'It's dirty diesel, I half suspected it when I filled up,' cursed the skipper as he rolled up his sleeves and started to dismantle the filters. Meanwhile the *Falls of Laura* had slewed sideways across the gigantic waves and was listing badly. I sat shivering in the deckhouse with my life-jacket on, waiting with resignation for Davy Jones' Locker. Eventually the engines spluttered into life and we were able to proceed through the sound of Harris to the Minch, although the fault reoccurred at regular intervals. With the weather deteriorating again we pleaded to be put ashore at Mallaig, rather than attempt to round Ardnamurchan Point. Never did we enjoy more the scenic railway journey from Mallaig to Oban.

Ever since our failed epic, now ten years ago, St Kilda had never left my mind; but time is a great healer and the 'never again' resolution weakened. A new route was the answer: a dependable Caledonian MacBrayne's ferry to the Isle of Harris, a fast motor boat, a weather window – and St Kilda here we come. Thus it was that we sat drinking wine on the deck of the m.v. *Eilean Na Hearadh* as she slid out of Drinishader on the Isle of Harris. It was a velvet evening in early July, the water was mirror calm and even at midnight the sky was glowing. This time our party was only five strong because the NTS had drastically reduced the number of visitors allowed on St Kilda. Moreover the *Eilean Na Hearadh* is a powerful 60ft boat with twin Volvo diesels, and this time we had utmost confidence in her seaworthiness and in her young owner, Roddy Campbell.

As dawn broke, Boreray and the stacks loomed up into the clouds even more dramatically than I had remembered, while thousands of gannets wheeled and screamed overhead. Shags stood in lines on the lower ledges, holding out their wings to dry. St Kilda at last: I felt elated and emotional as the dingy approached the landing stage on Hirta – although tripping over a rope on the seaweed- and barnacle-encrusted slipway brought me down to earth again.

More books have been written about St Kilda and its fascinating history than any other island in Britain, and I had devoured them all avidly; my favourite is a *Voyage to St Kilda* written in 1697 by Martin Martin. Now I was experiencing St Kilda at first hand, and I walked down Main Street, Village Bay in a daze – the street where all the grown-up males would meet every day of the week except Sunday to form a 'parliament' which would discuss current issues and make decisions. In thin mist and drizzle I visited the factor's house, the feather store, the schoolroom and the church where the St Kildans were subjected to three services with lengthy blood-and-thunder sermons every Sunday.

The resident warden directed us to camp in a small, elevated enclosure near the factor's house. It gave us a panoramic view over Village Bay, and from this high vantage point we could watch minke whales through the telescope; but it was exposed to the elements, and we squeezed into a nearby cleit to do the cooking. Cleits are igloo-shaped constructions made of boulders and roofed with turf where the St Kildans dried and stored their staple foods of fulmars, puffins and gannets. Wind whistles through chinks in the walls – but on this most inhospitable of islands any form of shelter is welcome.

Soay sheep roamed at will amongst the cleits, the ruined cottages and, of course, our tents. Many of the Village Bay sheep had been tagged to help the on-going research into this strange herd of small goat-like sheep with coarse brown wool that is thought to have been a unique, intact breed for thousands of years. Elsewhere the sheep are so wild that it is impossible to approach them closely. It is said that when sheep dogs were brought to St Kilda to round up the Soay sheep, it was the sheep that rounded up the dogs. It wasn't long, too, before we saw with delight the two sub-species of animal that are unique to St Kilda: the wren and the fieldmouse. The wrens flitted in and out of the holes in the cleits, cottages and walls, and the plump fieldmice soon found our crumbs on the floor of our cleit and provided an amusing diversion at mealtimes.

We savoured every minute of our week on St Kilda: memorable picnics on the cliffs of Mullach Bi, mesmerised by the puffins darting hither and thither from their burrows in the turf, their short wings beating furiously, while great skuas (bonxies) sat menacingly on vantage points choosing their prey; early mornings up at the Gap between Oiseval and Conachair to see wreaths of cloud pluming off Boreray and the stacks with the blue expanse of ocean tossed by white horses; and a walk along the north-west headland of the Cambir with the grass bright with flowers and the ancient grey granite rocks bearded with lichens of different hue, while waves crashed against the impregnable fortress of the off-shore island of Soay. Conachair, at 1,397ft, is the highest point on Hirta from where you can look east across the ocean to the faint outline of the hills on Harris and South Uist, while stupendous cliffs fall away below your feet. Fulmars and kittiwakes nest in profusion on the cliff ledges, and large numbers of these birds glide by, effortlessly riding the thermals.

Perhaps the most exciting occasion was when we located the natural arch that runs through the the eastern headland of Gleann Mor. After much searching and peering over the cliffs, Trisha announced, 'I can see a ramp running down from the cliff top to sea level.' This turned out to be the key, and we scrambled down to the mouth of the great cavern whose arched roof perfectly framed Boreray and the stacks. It was low tide and we edged our way across slimy, sloping rocks with seals bobbing in the boiling surf just below our feet, to emerge into daylight the other side of the promontory.

Evenings were spent happily in the Puff Inn, a small bar run by the army. Only a very few army personnel are now stationed on St Kilda, because most of the maintenance of the radar installations is carried out by civilian contractors. Amongst other interesting companions was a working party of archaeologists who were excavating ancient field boundaries; when we were there they were ecstatic at finding a stone axe-head possibly 5,000 years old. Also on the island were the Soay sheep researchers, and a few intrepid yachtsmen and women.

As the *Eilean Na Hearadh* powered into Village Bay for the return trip our hearts were heavy. But the sea was calm, and with the wind and tide in our favour, Roddy Campbell made West Loch Tarbert in a mere six-and-a-half hours.

WILD CAMPING IN BRITAIN

*'I continued to walk up into the hills for several miles with just
curlews, larks, plovers and wheatears for company'*

Cairngorm Traverse

The back window of my car carries a 'Save the Cairngorms' sticker, and a question I am often asked is: 'What are you saving them from?' So I launch into the usual diatribe against further ski developments, the funicular railway, overgrazing by sheep and deer, bulldozed tracks, path erosion and afforestation with foreign species. But unless the questioner knows this unique area, these are merely empty phrases.

The vast majority of visitors to the Cairngorms stay around the honey-pots: the craft shops of Coylumbridge, Loch Morlich, the Ptarmigan restaurant and perhaps an ascent of the steps to the summit of Cairn Gorm. Yet to appreciate the region's true quality, and the reasons why it is a potential Heritage Site, it is necessary to walk a long way from the centres of communication. In fact the Cairngorms are ideally suitable for implementation of the 'long walk in' principle which has been so effectively applied in wilderness areas in the USA. Keep cars and roads well away from the mountains and encourage visitors to walk. Backpacking, using a minimum impact approach, is by far the best way of exploring the Cairngorms.

Many years ago I traversed the Cairngorms roughly east–west from Feshiebridge to Cock Bridge, climbing as many mountains as possible and carrying just food and bivouac gear. But this was very strenuous, and here I shall describe a much more leisurely expedition of four days which my wife and I completed over Easter. We carried a well proven tent, delicious food and spare clothes; we kept to the shelter of the glens, and because we were not exhausted every night, could thoroughly enjoy delectable campsites.

Unless you are entirely dependent on local transport, one of the disadvantages of backpacking expeditions is the difficulty of returning to the car at the finish. This particular expedition, however, starts from Blair Atholl station and finishes at Aviemore from where Scotrail will return you speedily to the starting point. The sylvan glens and gently rolling hills of Perthshire can give a false sense of security to the backpacker setting out on this expedition. Conditions can be severe, because the route goes into the heart of the Cairngorms, it can involve the fording of swift rivers, and it reaches a height of 2,733ft at the summit of the Lairig Ghru where snow lies deep until late spring. Check your equipment before setting out, and carry a reserve of food in case you become storm-bound in your tent for a day.

The walk starts in style as you leave Blair Atholl station. Cross the A9 trunk road, pass confidently through the massive, decorated wrought-iron gates and march along an avenue of limes to Blair Castle, home of the tenth Duke of Atholl. The Duke is the only subject of the British Crown who is entitled to keep a private army: he has a corps of thirty men, employed for ceremonial purposes. The splendid and imposing white-harled castle dates from the thirteenth century, although the present castellations were built in 1869. It has a long and fascinating history, and was the last castle in Britain to have suffered a siege, in 1746. Mary, Queen of Scots was once entertained at a hunt at the castle during which 360 red deer and five wolves were killed.

Beyond the castle you pass the estate cottages at Old Blair, and then take the narrow tree-lined road which runs uphill, keeping some way above the river Tilt. This road is to the right (east) of the Glen Banvie road that leads over the hills to Glen Bruar. An alternative, and equally pleasant start to the walk, is to take the minor road from Blair Atholl to Old Bridge of Tilt and continue to Fenderbridge and Kincraigie. At this point you are high above the river Tilt which runs through a well wooded glen, but you gradually descend to Gilbert's Bridge, meeting the alternative track from Old Blair three miles upriver from Blair Atholl.

From this point on, the river Tilt is your constant companion, and the glen, although not fashionable or popular with walkers, represents the best of the Scottish romantic tradition. The lively river foams over a bed of boulders with swirling eddies and deep amber pools, or thunders through ravines overhung with willow, rowan, birch and alder. When, in early spring, the sun shines from a clear blue sky and sparkles on the snow-capped hills, when the burns are brimming with meltwater and the tips of the willows are tinged with green, then Glen Tilt is peerless.

The road crosses to the north bank of the river Tilt at Marble Lodge, but if you have expectations of a grand edifice you will be disappointed, for the lodge is merely a low grey cottage. Marble was found in Glen Tilt in the early nineteenth century and this is probably the origin of the name.

On the south side of the glen, slopes of grass and heather, interspersed with broken crags, rise to the massive bulk of Beinn a' Ghlo: this is classed as three separate Munros and will be your companion for seven miles until you reach the Tarf. A fourth Munro, Carn a' Chlamain, lies two miles to the north. This is deer forest *par excellence* and I shall never forget the sight of a huge herd, well over a hundred strong, moving gracefully over the snow on the plateau of Beinn a' Ghlo's principal peak, Carn nan Gabhar.

Forest Lodge, which is inhabited throughout the year, is a substantial house with outbuildings set amongst trees, and it marks the end of the first stage of the walk. The preliminaries are over, the Land Rover track is almost at an end, and henceforth you must rely solely on your wits and the provisions and equipment that you are carrying. The Cairngorms are wild and unforgiving, and they do not take prisoners. Trisha and I had not left Blair Atholl until mid-afternoon, and by the time we reached Forest Lodge the light was fading, the wind was rising and we were looking eagerly for a campsite. About a mile beyond the lodge we found the ideal spot on level springy turf beside the river, slipped our rucksacks off our aching shoulders and erected the tent, placing boulders on the pegs and valances.

Confident that the tent was secure, we could enjoy the shaking of the fly-sheet in the wind and the straining of the guys. We had decided to carry extra fuel and plenty of tea bags in spite of the weight; there is nothing more luxurious than sipping a mug of tea while lying snug in a down sleeping bag – and nothing worse than having to stint on hot food when the gas cylinder is running out. Good sites are less easy to find as you proceed north because the glen becomes more enclosed, with a narrow path cut out of the hillside and the river running through a deep defile below. But, if you made an early start, you could easily continue to the river Tarf where excellent campsites abound.

The first sight of the river Tarf is a high point on this expedition: as you round a shoulder of hillside the Tarf can be seen bounding down a rocky amphitheatre, ringed with trees, in three giant steps before joining the Tilt. The Tarf is spanned by a suspension bridge built in 1886 as a memorial to Francis Bedford, who drowned at this spot when he was only eighteen years old. Soon after the Falls of Tarf the river makes an abrupt turn to the east and disappears up a deep ravine. The path divides: to the right it can be seen snaking up the hillside on its way to Fealar Lodge, which rivals Carnmore as the most remote house in Britain. The path to Deeside follows the Allt Garbh Buidhe for two miles until the watershed is reached at 1,600ft.

The landscape now opens out, giving expansive views north to Ben Macdui and Carn a'Mhaim, and we enjoyed a brief spell of sunshine as we lunched amongst the ruins of Bynack Lodge. Although the lodge is now a mere skeleton and offers scant shelter, it is surrounded by a few decayed pine trees and its situation is splendid; it carries an aura of bygone days. The momentary warmth of the sun had stimulated thousands of frogs to feverish croaking. At first we thought the noise was a chainsaw at work in a distant forest, but then we noticed copulatory thrashings in every pool, with one wretched female receiving the close attentions of no less than seven males in an obscene ball of intertwined froggery.

Before reaching the river Dee at White Bridge it is necessary to cross two sizeable tributaries, the Bynack and Geldie burns. Since both were in spate with meltwater, we considered it prudent to keep to the east bank and cross the Geldie downstream of its confluence with the Bynack by means of a bridge, clearly shown on my 10s 6d Cairngorms Tourist Map, published in 1967. Two miles later we were not unduly surprised to find no bridge in existence, only the ancient abutments.

The river was wide and swift, but the alternative was a seven-mile round detour via Linn of Dee. River crossings are one of the principal hazards for walkers in the mountains, and in these conditions, the Geldie was a serious proposition but just viable. With Trisha boldly in the lead, and with our ice-axes as a third leg, we inched across seeking firm purchase on the bouldery bed for our boots, as the current tried to sweep us downstream. Concentration and determination were essential, and the shock of the icy water was secondary. Thoroughly relieved we sat on the far bank and wrung out our socks, then crossed the Dee at White Bridge (which is not white but wooden) and headed north towards the Devil's Point.

In the heart of the high Cairngorms the winter was still very much in evidence, with almost complete snow cover on Monadh Mor, Cairn Toul and in the upper reaches of Braeriach's Garbh Choire, but we found a magnificent camp-site on a patch of coarse grass beside the Dee near the mouth of Coire Geusachan and under the dripping black boiler plates of the Devil's Point. The main Lairig Ghru path comes in from glen Luibeg near Corrour Bothy, which is damp and unfriendly and not worth crossing the river to visit, and at once the quality of the walk diminishes. Columns of heavily laden backpackers appear, the path is muddy and suffering from erosion, and we shivered as an icy wind swept down from the top of the pass. With ragged clouds wreathing the tops the mountains appeared cruel and intimidating, and it was a relief to pass the mysterious Pools of Dee, set amidst a chaos of rocks at the top of the pass at 2,733ft, and to start the descent towards Rothiemurchus.

A prominent hump of moraine just beyond Creag an Leth-choin (Lurcher's Crag) marks the site of the old Sinclair Memorial Hut, removed entirely in 1991 following severe erosion and vandalism. A path branches off here and runs below the northern corries of Cairn Lochan and Cairn Gorm to the ski-lift car park.

Rothiemurchus Forest is a delight at any time of the year, and even the slight warmth of an early spring afternoon is enough to raise the sweet aroma of Caledonian pines. Secluded campsites, well away from the path, can be found on the upper fringes of the forest. After a hard day backpacking through the Lairig Ghru we found it blissful to lie back on a soft bed of pine needles, cooking a leisurely supper outside the tent and admiring the ancient, twisted trees which had bent and soughed in the breeze for over three hundred years.

The knowledge that Aviemore and the train back to Blair Atholl were a mere five gentle miles away was a recipe for a sound night's sleep. A four-day schedule for this expedition is ample and puts no real pressure on the walker, but it is no less enjoyable or adventurous for that.

At Peace in the Cheviots

Being alone in the mountains can be a most beneficial luxury, and even an indulgence when you only have to consider yourself and your own immediate needs. In my job as a school teacher I find that a few days by myself in a remote mountain area acts as a tonic and a stimulus and restores my sanity. Furthermore, however well you get on with your companions in the hills, life is a compromise: the selection of the objective, the campsite, the speed of walking, where to have lunch, what time to have supper, which side of the tent to sleep on, what time to get up, and so on and so forth. Even a few days alone can give you a slight sense of the exhilaration felt by solo round-the-world sailors, or by Reinhold Messner on his fantastic lone ascents of Everest and the Eiger, climbs which might not have been achieved if he had been concerned for the safety and well-being of others on the rope. The rolling Cheviot Hills on the Scottish Border provide ideal country for solo walking and wild camping, for the hills are seamed by deep hidden valleys with tumbling streams and grassy banks, where you can pitch a small tent with impunity and sheep will be your only companions.

At Whitsun the Breamish valley, which runs deep into the Cheviot hills from the east, was a riot of colour. After recent rain the meadows were lush green and bright with buttercups, the hawthorn overhanging the road was in full bloom and pervading the air with a sweet aroma, while a luxuriant growth of bright yellow gorse and broom lined the river bank.

Leaving the car at the new National Park Information Centre near Ingram, I walked along the private road to Linhope House which is set amongst exotic trees and rhododendrons. Here the Linhope burn joins the river Breamish, and half a mile above the house, it plunges in a cascade of white water over a 60ft step of brown porphyritic rock into a deep black pool overhung by trees and moss-covered rocks. The falls, known as Linhope Spout, are popular with picnickers, but the Breamish valley west of Linhope is wild and lonely and rarely visited.

The Breamish is a considerable river, rising in the mainly smooth and rounded hills south of the Cheviot itself and sparkling merrily down its bouldery bed through an increasingly narrow valley. The rough road up the valley stops at the exceptionally remote farmsteads of Low and High Bleakhope, surely two of the most isolated farms in England, but I continued to walk up into the hills for several miles with just curlews, larks, plovers and wheatears for company. At 6pm, with the sun still high in the sky and fleecy clouds drifting slowly by, I pitched the tent on a grassy platform above a tributary beck, and lay back enjoying the warmth of an early summer evening. A leisurely brew was followed by a prolonged supper, and I read outside until the light faded and the dew began to fall. Tension was slipping away and I slept deeply.

But the heavenly weather of that memorable day could not last, and low cloud, drizzle and a cold wind greeted me next morning. No matter, with anorak hood up I plodded slowly up to the Border Ridge. Before being engulfed in the swirling mist I looked over the vast area of forestry below Bloodybush Edge which had been planted in 1974. How vividly I remembered the Karrimor Two Day Mountain

Marathon held in the Cheviots that year when, at 8pm and by torchlight, we climbed in and out of the deep, water-filled drainage furrows because we were too exhausted to jump over them. When we finally made camp all the best sites had been taken and we pitched the tent on a saturated bed of reeds.

Quite suddenly, near Auchope Cairn, I came upon a well used path constructed of huge stone slabs laid carefully over the black peat bog. This was the Pennine Way, and five minutes later a stout wooden sign pointed to 'Cheviot Summit'. Grateful that I could dispense with the compass I followed the path to the gaunt trig pillar marking Cheviot's summit. The pillar is raised on a broad concrete plinth which is surrounded by the most evil black bog I have seen outside Bleaklow or Black Hill. I have always found the summit of Cheviot to be a great disappointment and unworthy of such an attractive range of hills. Unfortunately the stone slabs do not continue along the descent path to Langleeford and the going is atrocious. However, the weather was improving and I soon emerged below the clouds into bright sunshine with views east to the Northumbrian coast and the Farne Islands.

With no predetermined route to follow, or schedule to keep, I took a long lunch break at an idyllic spot beside the Harthope burn, watching cloud shadows moving across the hillsides. A steady climb through coarse grass, heather, bilberry and cloudberry then brought me to the col between Comb Fell and Hedgehope Hill, with entrancing views down the wild valley of the Standrop burn to the distant rounded and barren Cushat Law.

Fortunately the army were not using the enormous 26,000 hectare Otterburn artillery range to the west of Hedgehope Hill on this particular day, and all was peace and quiet. On many previous visits gunfire has echoed around the valleys, and the crump of exploding shells has made the hills tremble. Now, disturbingly, the army wants to put in many more miles of tarmac road so that they can bring in 45-tonne tracked A5-90 self-propelled guns. These plans are being strenuously resisted by the Northumberland National Park.

My second night's camp was also beside a remote and secluded mountain stream where I could enjoy watching a pair of dippers and a heron. The sound of a shepherd whistling to his dog floated up the valley and the sheep moved restlessly, but soon even this faded away.

At 5am next morning the sunshine was streaming into the tent and I lazily stretched out an arm and put the kettle on the stove. Later my boots left a trail across the dewy grass as I made my way down the valley to Linhope Spout and the river Breamish. The real world was beckoning, but I was returning with renewed spirit.

The following year, after a depressingly long and cold spring, I eagerly anticipated the Whit weekend and a chance to escape to the hills by myself for a few days. The Lake District and the Yorkshire Dales would be thronged with holiday visitors, I argued, thus I decided on a return to the Cheviots. Having explored the river Breamish the previous year I would head further west to Upper Coquetdale.

The clouds were clinging to the hillsides and the rain was teeming down as I set off from Byrness along a grassy ride through an extensive forestry plantation. I had intended to camp high up on the Border Ridge to allow extensive views north to the Eildon Hills and the Lammermuirs, but in the atrocious conditions, I was glad of the shelter provided by the Lodgepole pines. However, readers will know that the quickest way to get wet feet is to walk through long wet grass, and similarly, pushing through soaking wet branches forces water through even the heaviest weight GoreTex anorak.

Eventually, when the cold and wet had penetrated right through to my skin, I decided to camp at the next clearing; but then I spied a low stone hut half hidden by trees: fortuitously I had stumbled on a bothy, recently restored by the Mountain Bothies Association. It was unoccupied, dry, possessed a few sticks of furniture and, most important of all, held an ample supply of dry wood. Within moments I had stripped off my wet clothes, lit the fire and put on the kettle.

Later I cooked a leisurely supper and read my book, enjoying the sweet smell of burning pine logs as my clothes dried on the rack and the rain drummed on the corrugated iron roof. Thank you, MBA, for saving me a wet tent, a cold midgy night and having to suffer the agony of donning wet clothes in the morning. But one question: why do you provide bothy books which, in my experience, are used by some visitors for writing obscene graffiti and showing off their deplorable humour and one-upmanship?

By morning the rain had moved away and I soon broke out of the trees onto the Border Ridge. Gaps appeared in the clouds, the sun emerged and I followed the Pennine Way track to Coquet Head and thence down to Chew Green Roman Camp. I had the hills to myself save for a herd of eight feral goats with long shaggy coats, the nannies' mottled grey and the young billies' black. The leader of the herd was a massive and magnificent billy with a beard trailing to his knees and long curved horns.

Chew Green is a fascinating archaeological site in a dramatic setting on the southern shoulder of Brownhart Law (itself the site of a Roman signal station) above the river Coquet. It is just outside the danger area of the Redesdale artillery range which encompasses so much of the southern

Cheviots, thus it is accessible at all times. Thankfully there is no commercialisation of Chew Green: no fences, visitors' centre, leaflets, toilets or telephones. The Roman Camp was built by Agricola in the first century AD beside Dere Street, which runs from Corbridge to Trimontium (Melrose) and on to Crammond on the Firth of Forth. Although the camp is now completely overgrown and just grazed by Scottish Blackface and Cheviot sheep, the walls, ramparts and ditches are clearly visible. Chew Green was a marching camp built to accommodate a legion; it was excavated by Sir Ian Richmond in 1936. Much later Chew Green was a mediaeval settlement, and in the eighteenth century, a well known meeting place and shelter for cattle drovers. Hundreds of thousands of Scottish cattle crossed the border annually to be sold at the more lucrative markets of Northern England.

In the bright afternoon sunshine I followed the broad line of Dere Street, back up to the Border Ridge heading north-east towards Lamb Hill. The air was pure and sharp and the white clouds moved quickly across the great vault of blue sky. Away in the distance rose the mighty bulk of Cheviot, still carrying extensive patches of snow. A succession of beautiful and enticing valleys run north from this stretch of the Border Ridge: the valleys of the Capehope Burn, Heatherhope Burn and the Hindhope Burn, all of which drain into the Kale Water, thence the river Tweed. The valleys are overlooked by prominent hillocks such as Hownam, Blackbrough, Whitestone and Heathercope, all of which carry Iron Age forts.

Just below Lamb Hill, on Yearning Saddle, stands a wooden emergency shelter. An eyesore, undoubtedly, but a possible life-saver in bad weather for exhausted Pennine Way walkers attempting the last, long and bleak leg of twenty-seven miles between Byrness and Kirk Yetholm. An elderly couple, each with an arm-band reading 'Voluntary Warden', approached the shelter and produced a hammer and a 6in nail from their rucksacks to secure a loose board. They had walked up from the Coquet Valley just to do the job, and I was impressed by their devotion.

Shadows were beginning to lengthen as I made my way south to the crystal-clear and swiftly running Blind Burn which led me down into Coquetdale. This was Cheviot country at its most enchanting: close-cropped grass dotted with lambs, rock outcrops, gorse, broom, countless meadow flowers and the sound of rushing water. I camped beside the river Coquet on a still warm evening and, lying outside on my Thermarest as the light faded, listening to the curlews and peewits, I was reluctant to get into the tent.

Next morning the clouds were down again and a cold wind was blowing. To my disappointment the red danger flags were flying and army lorries were rumbling along the Alwinton to Chew Green road, cutting off my short-cut route back to the car. With a sigh I resigned myself to a long trudge back to the A 68, and as it began to spit with rain, I quickened my step and put up my anorak hood.

Wild Camping at the Falls of Glomach

It was a grey morning in late October, with clouds over the Kintail hills, as we emerged from the Cluanie Inn and drove west to Kyle of Lochalsh. The season was over; the leaves on the larch, birch and sycamore trees beside Loch Duich were a rich autumn gold, and the burns were foaming after near-record rainfall. But the area was a hive of activity: at Balmacara a TV film crew had set up headquarters for recording a second series of *Hamish Macbeth*, which is set in Plockton, while police cars, vintage cars, ancient MacBrayne's buses and luxury coaches were heading for Kyle and the opening of the new Skye Bridge.

The official ceremony was low key and was boycotted by Charles Kennedy MP and many local inhabitants who were unhappy at the high tolls that were to be charged; but a crowd of about two hundred had assembled to hear the opening address by the Scottish Secretary, Malcolm Forsyth, and to witness the cutting of the ribbon by a child from Kyle primary school. A thin drizzle was carried on the wind, the distant Cuillin rose into the mist, white horses rode across the sound, a pipe band played and the huge arched bridge of white concrete was stark against a leaden sky. The conditions for the occasion were typical and entirely appropriate. In front of us two plain-clothed policemen accosted a young man with pony tail and leather jacket. They frisked him and removed several eggs from his pockets which they smashed on the ground before leading him away. Apart from this incident the opening was peaceful.

Later in the afternoon we packed our rucksacks and set off along the six-mile-long path from Morvich to the Falls of Glomach. Following repairs by the National Trust for Scotland, this path is well drained, and the route through Strath Croe, the forest of Dorusduain and over Bealach na Sroine is always interesting – with the autumn colours and gushing burns it was a delight. The Falls of Glomach themselves invite superlatives. W.H. Murray describes them as the most spectacular falls in Britain, and I agree that the combination of height, volume of water and the grandeur of the surroundings are unsurpassed. The fall of Eas a' Chual Aluinn in Sutherland is higher, but the flow there is feeble and the actual vertical drop disappointing: it is more of a cascade. The considerable river, Allt a' Ghlomaich, is fed from many tributaries rising at the head of Glen Affric and on the Munros of Beinn Fhada, A' Ghlas-bheinn and Sgurr nan Ceathreamhnan. The water plunges 80ft to the top of a buttress, whence it rebounds 220ft into a deep pool; a further 50ft fall then takes it to the bottom of a steep-sided and well vegetated gorge.

After a quick peep over the lip of the gorge we erected the tent just as the rain began in earnest. Throughout the evening and night it lashed the tent, the guy ropes strained and the walls cracked and flapped in the gale-force gusts of wind. By first light the river was in full spate, a foaming torrent lapping the banks, while the roar of the falls made conversation difficult. At ten o'clock a brief weather window appeared, the clouds parted and the sun shone. Rainbows spanned the Glomach gorge, which was filled with spray, while the rich colours of the birch, rowan and moor grass provided the perfect background. But within minutes clouds and heavy rain returned, and we picked our way down the steep and narrow path that descends the west side of the gorge. Such was the power of the falls that we ignored the soaking spray and the rain, and marvelled at the thundering water which made the ground tremble. The top buttress was almost submerged, while below, the tongues of water had coalesced to give a single wall of brown foam. We stood in awe on a tiny ledge, mesmerised by the spectacle.

Further down the gorge we found difficulty in crossing the tributary stream, Allt na Laoidhre, but eventually reached Glen Elchaig, where there is a memorial bridge to the first Munroist, A.E. Robertson. However, it was not a day to be out for long and the relentless rain soon drove us back uphill to our tiny tent. Even so, such a day made us appreciate Britain's varied climate. The rain and wind finally washed away the last remnants of dust and disease from our summer's Karakoram trek, and we were fully content to sit snugly in our weatherproof tent with rain drumming on the flysheet and the kettle hissing on the stove.

Years ago, in the 1950s, before the Black's Mountain tents became available, the only mountain tent on the market was the heavy Meade, with a sleeve entrance, made by Benjamin Edginton. Unfortunately the Meade had no flysheet, moreover it was designed for high altitude and not for the Scottish Highlands, and in wet weather it was a cardinal sin to touch the walls. Once the surface tension was broken the water would drip steadily through the fabric and slosh around the built-in groundsheet. Camping in the hills invariably led to a complete soaking.

In the early hours of the following morning the wind dropped and the rain ceased. Many herds of deer had been driven to lower ground, and the air was filled with the roaring of stags. This was unnerving, for we could imagine them attacking the tent to prove their courage and to show off to their admiring herds of hinds. Dawn brought clear blue skies, a stiff breeze, a myriad sparkling burns streaming down from the heights, and bright sunshine. We struck camp and walked up Glenn Gaorsaic, a little visited but charming glen set between A' Ghlas-bheinn and Sgurr nan Ceathreamhnan and overlooked by Beinn Fhada. The hillsides were teeming with deer, and a buzzard paid us a brief visit, but we saw no other people.

Beallach an Sgairne provided a magnificent view east across Loch a' Bhealaich to the Affric hills, and we resolved to camp the night on a grassy belvedere, but even as we unrolled the tent, the weather changed abruptly; clouds raced in, a strong wind tore over the pass and the sky darkened. The gusts were so fierce that Trisha and I were unable to erect the tent, and at times it was even difficult to stand. As the first spots of rain began to fall, we turned westwards and hastened down Gleann Choinneachain to Loch Duich and more sheltered ground.

Backpacking Through Flowerdale

How often have mountain walkers gazed west from the great giants of Torridon: Beinn Alligin, Liathach and Beinn Eighe? They command the prospect of a desolate area that appears flat and boggy, criss-crossed by rivulets and patterned by a mosaic of tiny lochans. A bleak and watery world, not unlike Coigach to the north, yet the quality of the landscape is transformed by several superb individual peaks which rear up from the sandstone bedrock to a height of nearly 3,000ft. Baosbheinn, Beinn an Eoin and Beinn Dearg all have fine ridges linking their principal summits which throw down steep, gully-seamed shoulders enclosing wild corries and dark lochans.

This is the Flowerdale Forest, a delightful name for a unique and rarely visited area of Wester Ross which is difficult of access and primeval in nature. I shall never forget the view of Flowerdale from Beinn Eighe's Coire Mhic Fhearchair one sparkling March day when the peaks were plastered with snow, the sun glinted on the ice-covered lochans, and Loch na h-Oidhche reflected the arctic blue of the sky. The scene was so beautiful that it made a greater impression on me than Coire Mhic Fhearchair's famous triple buttresses themselves.

Other craggy peaks – Beinn a'Chearcaill, Meall a'Ghiughais and Ruadh-stac Beag (an offshoot of Beinn Eighe) – lie on the southern edge of the Flowerdale Forest. These hills provide outstanding viewpoints for insights into the hidden corries of Beinn Dearg, Liathach and Beinn Eighe, as well as north across Loch Maree to the intimidating silhouette of An Teallach, twenty miles away across the Great Wilderness.

The huge tract of mountainous country which extends eighteen miles north–south from Little Loch Broom to Loch Maree, and twenty miles east–west from the Fannichs to Poolewe, is popularly known as the Great Wilderness. It includes the vast deer forests of Kinlochewe, Letterewe, Fisherfield, Dundonnell and Strathnasheallag. Great Wilderness was the name given to this area by Chris Brasher in an article in *The Observer* some years ago, and the name has stuck. Fortunately the area has not yet suffered from the ravages of afforestation, and there is a bare minimum of scarring from bulldozed tracks, for generations of sportsmen have approached the hills by boat using Loch Maree, Loch a'Bhraoin, the Fionn Loch and Loch na Sealga for their access. Apart from a few cottages on the periphery there is no permanent habitation within the boundaries of the Great Wilderness.

The land is predominantly rocky, and with glaciers having gouged out deep corries and hollows, there is an abundance of lonely lochs. A complex mixture of rocks from a very long series of geological eras has led to a wide variety of mountain features: sharply serrated ridges, soaring cliffs of gneiss, sandstone terraces, plateaus of shattered quartzite and grassy glens. Thus the Great Wilderness is a Mecca for the hill walker and mountaineer, a priceless reserve for wildlife and flora, and a fascinating relic of the old Highlands which has changed little since the retreat of the ice sheet nearly 10,000 years ago.

It is possible to traverse the Flowerdale Forest, the northern corries of Beinn Eighe and the Great Wilderness in a four-day backpacking expedition. Trisha and I did this marvellous trip a few years ago, and the grandeur of the mountains is still etched on our minds. An added bonus is that towards the end of the second day the route passes through the village of Kinlochewe, which can provide hotel, B & B or bunkhouse accommodation, hot baths and fresh supplies. The walk starts from Am Feur Loch on the Gairloch to Loch Maree road and takes the excellent stalkers' path which runs south to Loch na h-Oidhche (Loch of the Night). At first the path winds up grassy hillocks to a beallach, but then it descends to the lively Abhainn a'Gharbh Choire which rushes down its stony bed from the loch in a series of falls and cascades.

A boathouse at the north end of Loch na h-Oidhche can provide some shelter if the weather is bad. On our crossing the wind was roaring down the glen in great buffets, catching us unawares and driving us off the path into the bog. We lunched in the boathouse while spiralling columns of spray raced down the loch and dashed against the corrugated iron roof. This northern end of Loch na h-Oidhche provides a view rivalling the Coruisk basin in the Cuillin of Skye. The loch runs between the long whalebacks of Baosbheinn and Beinn an Eoin; beyond the head of the loch, the dark buttresses on Beinn Dearg rise to 2,997ft. Peeping round the end of Carn na Feola, Beinn Dearg's eastern summit, can be seen the stupendous pinnacles and corries of Liathach and the grey quartzite towers of Beinn Eighe's Coire Mhic Fhearchair.

Pick your way across the chaos of boulders on the east side of the loch, under the steep slopes of Beinn An Eoin, to reach the tiny locked bothy of Poca Buidhe which merges into the rocks above the shore. Poca Buidhe marks the end of the path, and from there you must find your own way through the myriad lochans, shallow pools, clumps of coarse grass and peat hags. In places, however, the underlying sandstone has been scoured smooth by glacial action, making progress much easier.

In wet weather the numerous burns which drain the northern corries of Beinn Dearg could be troublesome, for saturation is the norm for this spongy ground which is the source of two magnificent rivers draining into Loch Maree. The Talladale river is black and deep for much of its length until, two miles above the Loch Maree Hotel, it plunges down a deep wooded gorge that is picturesque with ancient Caledonian pines and birch trees. The Grudie river is more lively and it, too, is bounded by stands of relic pines in its lower reaches. In the 1980s, run-of-river hydro schemes were proposed for both the Grudie and Talladale rivers. Shocked and angry, the conservation bodies in Britain united in vehement opposition to the plans which, thankfully, were soon dropped.

In spite of the difficult nature of the predominantly bouldery hillsides we found no shortage of delectable campsites beside the burn under the south shoulder of Beinn a'Chearcaill.

The second day starts with more rough ground as you traverse under Beinn Eighe's Ruadh-stac Mor and the monolithic off-shoot, Ruadh-stac Beag, whose only line of weakness is the rocky south ridge. However, at the base of Meall a' Ghiubhais, you pick up an excellent cairned track of quartzite stones, maintained by workers from the Beinn Eighe National Nature Reserve, which descends to the Visitor Centre near Kinlochewe where there are good facilities and a campsite.

No one can fail to feel excitement and anticipation as they leave Kinlochewe for the Great Wilderness. Having crossed the river at Incheril and walked under the vegetated cliffs overlooking the Abhainn Bruachaig to the cottages at Heights of Kinlochewe, there is no further habitation until Dundonnell. As you climb Gleann na Muice *en route* to Lochan Fada the Land Rover track peters out on the east side of the river. Find a convenient rock to provide shelter for lunch, and gaze across the loch to the fortress of Slioch and the long line of severe cliffs on Beinn Lair. The northern end of Lochan Fada is surrounded by towering mountains of bare rock, and is one of the most awesome and lonely corners of mainland Britain; but there is no track along the lochside, and that particular visit should be left for another occasion.

Tighten your laces for the trackless section north-east up heather and coarse grass to Beallach na Croise, and then down into the upper reaches of Gleann an Nid. This is yet another wonderfully wild and remote spot, enclosed by the crags of Tom an Fhiodha and the steep grassy slopes of Beinn Bheag. On our expedition the clouds rolled back for the very first time, exposing the cockscomb of An Teallach filling the view north, while more black teeth emerging from the snow marked the sensational east ridge of Mullach Coire Mhic Fhearchair leading to Sgurr Dubh.

Near Loch an Nid our route meets the good stalkers' path from Loch a'Bhraoin; this passes the ruined cottages of Lochivraon and Feinasheen, and continues northwards above the eastern shore. There are plenty of ideal campsites hereabouts, either south of the loch where piles of stones and a tumbledown wall indicate an old crofting settlement, or below the loch itself. The former site lies at the base of vast sheets of glistening quartzite slabs which descend from Sgurr Ban, while the latter site is below a fine waterfall where the exit burn from Loch an Nid spills over the tip of the basin. Trisha and I have camped at both these sites, and they are exquisitely located: for instance, on the east side of Glen an Nid, the hillside consists of sandstone cliffs descending from Creag Rainich with tree-lined terraces; herds of deer graze the terraces, ravens nest on the cliffs, the piping of oyster catchers drifts up the glen, and dippers bob on the boulders in the river bed.

The fourth and final day of this expedition starts with a gentle walk north beside the Abhainn Loch an Nid on an excellent path, giving close-up views of the excessively steep slopes of grass and scree which descend southwards from the summit ridge of An Teallach. They give no inkling of the stupendous cliffs and corries which fall away to the north side of An Teallach and give this mountain its reputation. The line of west-facing cliffs on Creag Rainich continues to tower above the path, and several interesting chasms can be seen in the rocks. Stands of remnant birch and holly trees struggle for survival on the steep ground, which sheep and deer find difficult to graze.

Just before you meet the Land Rover track to Achneigie you must ford the considerable tributary burn that crosses the path from the east. The Eas Ban waterfall can be seen foaming down a rock step at the head of a wooded glen. In wet weather this burn will be difficult and dangerous to cross, and the use of a safety rope will be imperative.

Achneigie is a locked cottage set amongst trees and served by a track coming in over the hills from Corrie Hallie. Just one mile further west lies the cottage of Shenavall, a five-star bothy maintained by the Mountain Bothies Association. Not only is Shenavall dry and comfortable but it looks straight across Strath na Sealga to Beinn Dearg Mhor, the shapeliest Corbett of them all and a peak that is not infrequently mistaken for An Teallach. (Corbetts are separate mountains in

Scotland with a height of between 2,500 and 3,000ft.)

If time allows, it is worth making the short detour to Shenavall. Sit beside the lone rowan tree outside the cottage, eat your lunch and enjoy the view down Loch na Sealga and south towards six of the remotest Munros in Scotland: Ruadh Stac Mor, A'Mhaighdean, Beinn Tarsuinn, Mullach Coire Mhic Fhearchair, Sgurr Ban and Beinn a'Chlaidheimh. This marathon walk from Shenavall is known as the 'round-of-the-six' and is rapidly becoming a classic. Straight across Strath na Sealga you can see the low cottage of Larachantivore, which is kept locked and is used by the estate in the stalking season. A few years ago Larachantivore was the scene of a tragedy when two gillies were repairing an outboard motor inside a wooden shed. The petrol exploded and the two men were burned to death.

From Shenavall a steep and boggy path runs up a gully beside the cottage, crosses the shoulder of Sail Liath and joins the Achneigie track at a cairn near Loch Coire Chaorachain. If you have not detoured to Shenavall, this point is reached by keeping on the track from Achneigie and zigzagging up the hillside.

Descend north down Gleann Chaorachain, cross the outflow from the loch by means of stepping stones, and meet the A832 at Corrie Hallie, just three miles south of Dundonnell where there is an extremely comfortable and hospitable hotel that welcomes walkers. In spring this last stretch of the journey is sheer delight as the track passes through woods of birch, hazel and alder with bluebells, violets, wood anemones and wild roses. A river runs through a gorge beside the path, while deep heather and slabs of red sandstone run up to the base of the pinnacles and buttresses of An Teallach's Coire an Lochan. A fitting end to a magnificent walk.

Winter in Wester Ross

At 3pm the sun sank behind the shoulder of Slioch and the frost tightened its grip on the glen. There was no wind, and the mirror surface of Lochan Fada reflected the snow-covered surrounding peaks, while fingers of ice crept out from the shore. To our delight, a tiny crescent-shaped bay of fine shingle was backed by a patch of level ground which would just take our Phoenix Phunnel tent. Under the snow the grass was frozen hard and it took Trisha and me a long time to erect the tent to our satisfaction: boulders, prised from the frozen shore with ice-axes, were placed on the vallance and on those pegs which stubbornly refused to enter the ground. You learn from bitter experience that it is well worth spending an extra ten minutes erecting a tent properly in the evening, however tired you feel, rather than spend twenty minutes making repairs by torchlight in a blizzard in the middle of the night.

By 4pm the sun had left the tops of A'Mhaighdean, Beinn Tarsuinn and Mullach Coire Mhic Fhearchair, the moon had risen, our kettle and water bottles were full, and we retired for the night. Our final view was the sight of two hinds and two young deer standing on a ridge behind the tent, silhouetted against the last bright patch of sky to the south, and watching us intently.

Wild camping is harsh but rewarding, and in a Scottish winter in clear weather it provides an experience to be savoured. The lack of midges and horse flies, the sharp, crystal-clear air, the icily pure water, the unique light blue sky which fades to green and crimson as the sun sets, and above all the quietness. The severe frost had silenced the normally rushing burns beside Lochan Fada, the waterfalls and cascades were mere grey streaks of ice on the cliffs, the sheep were wintering on lower ground, the divers and waders had long since departed to the coast and estuaries, and by late November the rut was all but over and only the occasional roar of a stag echoed round the hills.

There is now a brand-new and spacious car park at Incheril, near Kinlochewe in Ross-shire, for those wishing to walk and climb in the Great Wilderness. As we laced up our boots we were shocked by the intensity of the cold. Leaving behind a damp and mild Yorkshire, the bright sun sparkling on the frost feathers and fresh snow as we drove through Strath Bran to Achnasheen had been an exhilarating and unexpected treat. But had we brought enough winter gear with us? To save weight we had left our heavy Rab goosedown sleeping bags behind and decided to make do with light three-seasons bags.

The track from Incheril to the Heights of Kinlochewe runs through a deep glen which sees no sun in the winter, thus the ground was iron hard and the puddles thickly covered in ice. To the south the Creag Dhubh summit of Beinn Eighe rose peerlessly into an azure sky, cloudless save for the occasional vapour trail from an aircraft. But once we had turned north into Gleann na Muice we left the shade, entered a fairyland of sparkling frost and enjoyed a hint of warmth, although there were few signs of thaw.

It had been a wet autumn in Wester Ross and the freeze had been sudden. Thus the path, which doubles as a stream bed when necessary, was now a ribbon of smooth ice and far too treacherous to walk on. We hugged the verges or deviated into the heather to find purchase for our boots and it was difficult to establish a rhythm. However, the extensive areas of bog were now rock solid, and the fluffy powder snow covering the heather just brushed off as we passed and our feet remained dry. The overhanging edges of the peat hags were curtained with icicles, and single blades of grass beside the burns became thick columns of ice where spray had frozen.

Small herds of stags were grazing the hillside just above the path, and we watched them for a while through the binoculars. Their coats were thick and they looked fit and strong and very much in their element for the winter was only just beginning. The remote Munro of A'Mhaighdean looked deceptively near, rising boldly at the far end of Lochan Fada, but winter days are so short that we knew it might prove to be an unattainable target for the next day.

It was a struggle to remove gaiters and boots with iced-up zips and laces like wire hawsers, and our boots steamed for a short while in the mouth of the tent before freezing solid. But the new Coleman self-sealing propane/butane mix gas cylinders were outstanding, delivering great heat to the kettle at high pressure. For once spilt tea inside the tent was no problem, for within minutes the puddle had solidified and could be lifted en block from the groundsheet.

Such nights are rare in Britain, and they are both beautiful and awe-inspiring. Although the moon soon disappeared over the horizon the stars were as bright and as sharp as needles and gave out a surprising amount of light. Our noses filled with ice spicules after a few breaths outside the tent and we soon snuggled into our sleeping bags; I wore three pairs of socks and Trisha wore anorak, hat and gloves. On exceptionally cold nights I find it best to curl into a ball right inside my

Above: An evening view, from a high camp in the hills, to Loch Hourn in Knoydart. The following day a ferocious storm left us fighting for survival

Below: A dusting of early winter snow on Ben Aden; looking north over the hills of Knoydart

The author on the Red Cuillin of Skye, with
the Black Cuillin ridge stretched out behind,
after a night of heavy snow

Above: One of the gems on the Isle of Colonsay is the majestic white sand bay of Kiloran

Below: Rhum, the jewel of the Inner Hebrides, is seen here across the Sound of Sleat from Arisaig

Above: Boreray and the Stacks seen here on a rare benign day from the summit of Conachair on Hirta, the largest island in the St Kilda group

Below: Puffins on Hirta. About 300,000 pairs, half the British population, breed on St Kilda and the turf on the cliff tops is riddled with their burrows (*Photo:* Lucy Gilbert)

Left: Looking from Hirta to the inaccessible island of Soay. The sea stacks in the sound are over 200ft high which gives some idea of the tremendous scale of the Soay cliffs

Above: The Falls of Glomach, Britain's grandest waterfall, an awe-inspiring sight as seen here in full spate after a night of heavy rain

Above: Winter backpacking in the Great Wilderness area between Loch Maree and Little Loch Broom

Below: A memorably cold camp on the shore of Lochan Fada, under the northern cliffs of Slioch

Above: The vast whaleback of An Riabhachan gleams white in the May sunshine when seen across Loch Calavie on the first day of the Across Scotland Challenge

Below: On a spring morning Glen Feshie, with its stands of ancient Caledonian pines, is peerless

Above: The Ptarmigan ridge of Ben Mor Coigach with squalls of hail driving down the mouth of Loch Broom

Below: In the heart of Coigach. A view north from Beinn an Eoin to Suilven (left) and Cul Mor (right)

Above: Merrick, at 2764ft the highest of the Galloway hills, rises above Loch Enoch

Below: A spring day on the Suilven ridge, looking north-east to Canisp (left) after a sudden storm has plastered the north face with fresh snow

Above: Driven in by a westerly gale rollers thunder onto the mile-wide Sandwood Bay, a magnificently wild and remote bay 6 miles south of Cape Wrath

Below: South of Sandwood Bay the cliffs have eroded to give pinnacles and sea stacks, as seen here from a ruined croft at Port Mor

Above: Ben Loyal and its numerous satellite peaks rises above the Kyle of Tongue in northern Sutherland
Below: On the undiscovered north-west ridge of An Teallach which leads over Sgurr Creag an Eich to Sgurr Fiona. The peak in the middle distance is Bidein a' Ghlas Thuill, the highest in the An Teallach massif

View south from An Teallach

Above: A typical winter scene at the head of Swaledale in the Yorkshire Dales

Below: A steam special crosses the massive Ribblehead Viaduct, a triumph of Victorian engineering which was completed in 1874 but cost many lives (*Photo*: Pete Shaw)

sleeping bag. In spite of a headache caused by stuffiness, such a cocoon minimises loss of body heat – any fingers or noses straying outside the bag soon become stiff and frozen.

In winter the hours of darkness are so long that you can usually catch up on some sleep; thus we spent sixteen hours inside our sleeping bags in an unsuccessful attempt to keep warm. It was not until 9am that we fished out the stove for morning tea and discovered the kettle contained a solid block of ice. Hoar frost and small icicles covering the tent inner melted and dripped in the heat of the stove, but once the stove was extinguished the inner froze again to cardboard. There is no doubt that lightweight nylon tents are far colder than the trusty old cotton ones such as the Vango Force Ten and the Black's Mountain. Nevertheless our spirits were high, for the sun was shining and the winter scene was entrancing, although our lack of adequate sleeping bags would ensure a second sleepless night which was unthinkable. We were not on a character-building Outward Bound course, and the thought of a warm bed was irresistible.

In order to reach the Gleann Bianasdail path, which runs down to Loch Maree, it was necessary to cross the outflowing river from Lochan Fada (the Abhainn an Fhasaigh). This was the crux of the entire expedition, a crossing which is usually a boulder hop in summer but can be dangerous or even impossible in spate. We were lucky, for the cold snap had vastly decreased the river's flow and a line of boulders emerged above the water, although they were sheeted in ice and lethal to balance on. The trick was to find rocks just beneath the water level on which to place your boots, and using an ice-axe as a third leg, to balance your way across. A fall into the deep, swift, icy water would have been serious, but we managed to cross pretty well dry-shod.

It was fascinating to see the north slopes of Slioch under such wintry conditions. The path wound its way through sheets of ice, frozen cascades and banks of drifted powder snow. Any exposed sandstone slabs appeared a rich red in the slanting rays of the sun. But our eyes were drawn north across Lochan Fada to the Great Wilderness peaks of A' Mhaighdean, Ruadh Stac Mhor and Mullach Coire Mhic Fhearchair with the Fannichs gleaming beyond. It was so slippery underfoot that we were forced to descend slowly to the river bridge below the gorge on Loch Maree-side. Although it was 3pm we just had time to boil the kettle for tea and wind our way back to Kinlochewe before the light failed. An owl hooted in the woods of oak and alder beside the loch, the frost returned with a vengeance, the stars emerged, and smoke rose straight up into the sky from the cottage chimneys at Incheril as Wester Ross settled down to another winter's night.

Across Scotland Challenge

There were about a dozen large rucksacks propping up the wall of the Strathcarron Hotel, one of the official start points for the 1997 Great Outdoors Challenge. I couldn't resist the temptation to test their weight, and then turned away with a smile of satisfaction: yes, Trisha's and mine were considerably lighter. Then 'Steady on,' I told myself; 'The GOC is strictly non-competitive, and here you are assessing the opposition before you've even started. Relax, you're not on the Karrimor or the Saunders Mountain Marathons.'

We had two weeks to cross Scotland by whatever route we chose, provided that we hit the east coast between Arbroath and Peterhead and reported to GOC control at Montrose. The GOC (originally the Ultimate Challenge) is an annual event held in May; it started in 1980 and is nowadays heavily oversubscribed, for the limit on numbers is 300. Uniquely, the event is not a race; if there is a winning team it is the one which manages to devise the most enjoyable route. It was our first attempt at the challenge, and we had spent many hours on winter evenings planning a route through the Western Highlands to Loch Ness, across the Monadh Liath and through the Cairngorms to Braemar, and finally, over the Eastern Cairngorms to the rolling hills of Angus and the long glens running down to the coast. In all it was a distance of nearly 200 miles, for which we had allowed twelve days including a rest day, and involving a mixture of wild camping, and bed and breakfast accommodation.

Since the GOC started in 1980, we had read accounts by challengers of blisters, pulled muscles, blizzards (yes, even in May) and other trials and tribulations, and we had wondered how we would cope. With nearly two weeks walking through the Highlands in all weathers and on a tight schedule there would be no respite and no skulking in the tent on wet mornings. 'But think,' I said encouragingly to Trisha, 'of the Highlands in May with snow still covering the tops, burns brimming with meltwater, birch and alder trees coming into leaf, the morning air sharp, the midday sun warm – and no midges.'

From Strathcarron Station an ancient stalkers' track wound through the hills overlooking Loch Carron, the views unfolded to the west, patches of blue sky appeared, and the tensions and anxieties of normal life slipped away. This is what we had signed on for! After a couple of hours' walking we passed a party of four challengers lying in the heather nibbling biscuits and brewing tea on a Trangia stove. This impressed us; this was doing the GOC in style. No grinding out the miles hour after hour with heads down for this party – we nicknamed them the picnickers, and we met on several other occasions during the next few days.

Our own lunch break was taken an hour or two later at Bendronaig Lodge in idyllic conditions, which we were often to look back on with nostalgia in the days to come. We sat with our backs against the tiny bothy in glorious warm sunshine surrounded by the magnificent snow-covered Munros of Bidein a' Choire Sheasgaich and Lurg Mhor, enjoying the wide green strath and the small stand of Caledonian pines beside the lodge. If our electrolyte drinks and Power Bars did not match the hampers of the picnickers, at least our sacks were manageable.

The path zigzagged up to Loch Calavie, which was a shimmering jewel in the afternoon sunshine; the faintest breeze rippled the surface, waves lapped the shore and the loch was framed by the gleaming white giants of the East Benula Forest: Sgurr na Lapaich and An Riabhachan. Heading off now in a north-easterly direction we made for the south shore of Loch Monar. Several burns were difficult to cross, the path petered out leaving miles of punishing peat hags, and we were lashed by a sudden squall of icy rain. But at 6pm we were camped on the shore of Loch Monar near the immaculately kept Pait Lodge, which is only accessible by boat. The evening sun bathed in a pink glow the long ridge of hills, culminating in Maoile Lunndaidh, north of the loch, chaffinches sang in the trees, and as the tea water came to the boil, our spirits rose again.

The second day of the GOC brought us down to earth with a bump. Scottish weather being what it is, we awoke to rain pattering on the tent; then the trackless hills leading to the nearest path to Glen Strathfarrar proved to be exhausting, I slipped whilst crossing the Allt Riabhachan, got wet feet, was too tired to change my socks, and suffered blisters as a consequence. By this time the euphoria of the first day had evaporated and the extent of the task ahead had grown all too apparent. As we emerged from the mist into a wild and rough corrie on the south side of Meallan Buidhe we met three other teams of challengers, including the picnickers, and compared blisters and states of exhaustion. It seemed amazing that ten challengers should all meet together in a trackless waste in the middle of a remote wilderness.

Leaving the picnickers to brew up at the power station, we entered Glen Strathfarrar at Inchvuilt and were astonished at the scene. The new, foreign, absentee landowner had reseeded the wide water meadows beside the river, with the result that literally hundreds of deer were grazing there; furthermore Braulen Lodge had been extended and tennis courts built, and many miles of new fencing erected to encourage the regeneration of Caledonian pines. We were fascinated to watch two deer standing on their hind legs boxing each other with their front legs.

The lower part of the glen, east of Loch Beanacharan, is a National Nature Reserve and quite beautiful in the best Scottish tradition: forests of pine, birch scrub flourishing in the fenced areas and coming into leaf with a delicate shade of green, and a big foaming river of brown, peaty water. We watched a heron flap lazily from a deep pool, and a woodpecker was drumming in the trees. However, Strathfarrar is an exceptionally long glen, and it was evening before we asked at a stalker's cottage for permission to camp beside Loch Beanacharan. Permission was politely refused – but then, seeing how tired we were, the stalker relented, saying that he'd pretend he hadn't seen us.

On the fifth day of the GOC, Gordon Menzies' motor cruiser took us across Loch Ness from Drumnadrochit to Inverfarigaig. A stiff wind drove white horses over the surface, we had classic views of Urquart Castle, and the exhilarating crossing was an ideal start to what was to be a long and eventful day.

A minor road led through banks of primroses, violets and wood anemones to Errogie in the foothills of the Monadh Liath mountains, the next barrier to the east. After a stretch of rough hillside we descended to Dunmaglass Lodge, a huge, new white lodge not marked on the map, built in Scottish baronial style on a bare moraine half a mile from the original stone-built lodge which nestled cosily amongst trees. The sun came out but the wind was chill, and we sheltered behind a rock for our lunchtime brew. We could see the way ahead, up a rough Land Rover track climbing towards an enormous wind turbine erected on a hill overlooking Dunmaglass new lodge. Was this another example of foreign money being poured into Scottish estates, we wondered?

The Monadh Liath is characterised by vast, rounded, whale-backed hills of coarse heather and peat hags. Luckily for us the track ran deep into the hills before stopping abruptly and leaving a choice of routes over the ridge to the half-ruined cottage of Dalbeg beside the river Findhorn which conveniently bisects the range. We rounded a corner and found two cheerful smiling faces under floppy white sun-hats: they were Alec Cunningham and Robin Murdoch from Rannoch, aged seventy-six and seventy-seven respectively. Alec and Robin were experienced challengers with many crossings to their names, and were enjoying every minute of the walk. 'We're taking the full fourteen days, and we can't afford the luxury of a rest day or we wouldn't finish in time,' they laughed. We enjoyed their company enormously, and our paths crossed several times over the next few days.

By mid-afternoon the rain started in earnest and we followed a compass bearing over the watershed and down towards Dalbeg. Heavy rain falling on already saturated ground ran off in rivulets, and tiny streams soon became raging torrents. The Findhorn, laden with particles of peat and silt, was roaring down the glen. I was chilled to the bone, exhausted and shivering uncontrollably, and once the tent was up, I crawled into my sleeping bag and gratefully sipped a mug of tea. It was 6pm, and during the next three or four hours, as the rain increased in intensity, another seven parties arrived including, we were relieved to see, Alec and Robin.

Our tent was a new model from Terra Nova called a Solar. It weighed only 1.7kg, but it was an outstanding success, never letting in a drop of rain throughout the second-wettest GOC in eighteen years. Likewise our ultra-lightweight Micro Stove from Coleman, weighing only 158g, was fast, efficient and reliable.

The following morning was cold and sharp, but the sun was shining, the river was sparkling, the sky was blue, the hillsides were streaked with snow, oyster catchers were piping, deer were grazing in the corries and white mountain hares were scurrying up the hillside. In other words, it was the perfect Highland early spring morning and the Monadh Liath were at their best. Our route lay down the glen to the huge, grey stone Coignafearn Lodge, turned south beside the Etrick burn, and then climbed to the bealach under Carn Sgulain. This was another rough and trackless section, but it led to a popular rendezvous point, the bothy near the headwaters of the river Dulnain set deep in the heart of the Monadh Liath. And yes, cooking up a pasta lunch in the bothy were the picnickers! A Land Rover track runs south from this bothy, over the hills to Kingussie: three hours' hard walking to the Spey Valley, but with exciting views east to Glen Feshie and the Cairngorms, and south to Ben Alder, with the prospect of our long-anticipated rest day in the fleshpots of Kingussie.

In the event, although this rest day was a wonderful luxury, it caused a loss of momentum and a tightening of leg muscles, and on proceeding eastwards I limped my way through the forest to Glen Feshie with a painful, knotted calf. But no one could fail to be in high spirits in Glen Feshie on such a day, for the beauty of the scene transcended physical discomfort. Sunshine, sharp air, brightly coloured flowers, and stands of noble Caledonian pines with a lively river running through mountains still carrying winter snow, more than made up for some ugly bulldozed roads running over the hills, acts of sheer vandalism by the estate.

Before leaving Strathcarron we had agonised over the question of walking poles. Eventually I had decided to bring just one of my lightweight aluminium telescopic poles, and Trisha had opted to go without. That pole was a blessing for river crossings, providing the all-important third leg, and having crossed the troublesome burn I would throw it over for Trisha to use. It now came into its own in relieving my leg of strain and it got me through a sticky patch until my calf muscle relaxed again. In addition, the possession of a stout pole was reassuring when confronted by snarling dogs.

As the jaws of Glen Feshie began to close and the path climbed to higher ground we met two experienced and interesting challengers, Mary and John Allcock from Kendal. Absorbed in conversation we ticked off the miles with ease, delighting in the lively river overhung with pines, alder and rowan which was always beside us. At 5pm Mary and John camped on a splendid site of level grass beside the river, but with clouds massing, Trisha and I decided to continue, and although we slowed to a snail's pace, we crossed the dangerous river Eidart by the bridge upstream and almost reached Geldie Lodge. At 7.30 we had the tent up and a brew on in one of the most isolated spots in the Cairngorms. Before zipping up the tent entrance for the night we peered into the gloaming to watch a large herd of deer grazing close to the tent.

Next morning we packed up the tent in wind and rain. 'Thank goodness we put in those extra miles last night,' remarked Trisha, tightening her anorak hood. The rain swept down the glen as we doggedly struggled along the path to White Bridge, where we crossed the river Dee, and on to Linn of Dee. Passing the Youth Hostel at Muir of Inverey the warden beckoned us in and we sat dripping by the gas fire, drinking mugs of tea. A challenger with horribly blistered feet was sitting with his feet in a bowl of potassium permanganate solution in an attempt to harden the skin. The Braemar doctor had suggested he retire from the event but he was determined to continue, even if it meant a road route to the east coast. 'To cap it all,' he announced, 'I've just phoned my wife for sympathy, to be told she's in bed with suspected meningitis.' Later that day, in Braemar, we met a man whose wife had suffered a stroke on the GOC in Glen Affic, had recovered and entered again, only to slip and fracture her coccyx. Oh, they're hard characters these challengers.

Braemar was bursting with challengers that night. There was not a bed to be had for those that had not booked previously, and the bar at the Fife Arms was doing a roaring trade. The rain lashed down and the thunder rolled and we were thankful to have a roof over our heads. With a tight schedule we left Braemar next morning in incessant, torrential rain with thunder still booming overhead. One party reported a bolt of lightning singeing the heather beside the track to Loch Callater. Our boots were soon full of water and we became cold and bedraggled, although thankfully my RAB Downpour jacket kept out the rain magnificently. The jacket, which has a Pertex outer and a fully taped Permatex laminated dropliner, is light and beautifully soft (an ideal pillow at night) and I was able to test it thoroughly on the GOC.

Loch Callater was a dismal sight with clouds almost down to water level, the path was a river, and the roar of water from a thousand torrents coursing down the hillsides made conversation difficult. I had doubts about our ability to cross the Allt a' Chlaiginn at the head of the loch because it was hurtling down the mountainside in a welter of foam; however, on lower ground, the main stream braided and we managed to cross it channel by channel.

Route finding became difficult at the head of Loch Callater because of the mist and the fact that streams couldn't be identified from the map – indeed, there were streams everywhere, many posing problems to cross. Somehow we lost the faint path over Jock's Road, and together with two other challengers, Janice and Ray, blundered about for an hour or more on compass bearing with increasing desperation. At last Trisha spotted a fresh bootprint in the black peat, and minutes later a cairn loomed up. We were at 3,000ft, on the featureless plateau between Tolmount and Fafernie.

Eventually we emerged below the clouds into Glen Doll which was spectacular with waterfalls cascading down the black cliffs. Janice and Ray stopped at the Youth Hostel, and here we met Bill Robertson from Perth, the most experienced challenger of all, with seventeen crossings. The rain returned relentlessly for our last, endless four-mile plod to the inn at Milton of Clova where we could thankfully sink into hot baths of soft, peaty water. That day Aberdeen reported nearly 3in of rain.

Ragged clouds still clung to the hills next morning, and we decided on a longer, low-level route to Edzell. Glen Clova was a lake, with sheep marooned on islands of higher ground while floodwater swept by. We enjoyed the rolling, wooded hills of Angus, the kingcups by the streams, the tiny yellow pansies on the verges and the constant calling of the peewits and curlews. A combination of footpaths, forestry tracks and minor roads led us eastwards, but by the time we reached Edzell, at 7.30pm after twenty-eight miles walking, we were struggling badly. Trisha's calf was now tight and knotted, and my feet were bruised.

With heads down we walked through heavy rain next morning from Edzell to St Cyrus on the coast, but by 3pm we were drinking tea with Roger Smith and the headquarters team at the Park Hotel in Montrose. It had been an expedition of great contrasts; the constant rain had not really depressed us, for we knew well the vagaries of the Scottish climate, and the GOC had taken us to hitherto unknown corners of the Highlands; and it had also introduced us to some wonderfully friendly and entertaining characters who were united in a common cause. It is a unique event and one which we shall never forget.

MOUNTAINS AND MEMORIES

'We lingered long on Bidein a' Glas Thuill, reluctant to leave our perch with its taste of heaven.'

Ben Mor Coigach –
Mountain of Many Moods

Mountain walkers who have spent their Easter holidays in north-west Scotland in recent years will be highly sceptical of global warming. Daily snowfalls, sleet and a bitter wind have characterised the first half of April, and I have had to turn the diary back many years to read of warm spring sunshine, shirtsleeves, leisurely picnics on mountain tops, the children swimming at Gruinard Bay and muirburn (the burning of old heather to encourage the growth of new young shoots) restricting access to Sail Liath, *en route* to An Teallach. When we drew back the curtains, half-starved deer could be seen browsing in our Ullapool garden, and we puzzled as to how they managed to gain entry over the 8ft high fence. The mystery was soon solved: deer are intelligent beasts, and they negotiated the horizontally strung wires by twisting their heads this way and that so their antlers passed through the gap first, then with a wriggle their bodies and legs followed.

With a constant succession of squalls racing in from the west, fine spells were brief, and we restricted ourselves to familiar ground. At any time of the year Ben Mor Coigach provides spectacular mountain scenery, airy ridges, deep corries and unsurpassed views of the western seaboard – and all this from its modest height of 2,438ft, just 20ft more than Whernside in the Yorkshire Dales. The cliff-girt little peak of Cairn Conmheall is the western outlier of Ben Mor Coigach and it overlooks the narrow road running south of

Achiltibuie. Access was easy, the sun was actually shining and I planned to link Cairn Conmheall with the rock prow of Sgurr an Fhidhleir (the Fiddler) and return via Ben Mor's main summit, the Ptarmigan Ridge and Culnacraig.

All went well to the summit of Cairn Conmheall and I revelled in the cry of curlews, the rumble of surf on Horse Island and the distant outline of the Harris hills. But quite suddenly the light faded, black clouds rolled up, I was enveloped in thick mist and it started to snow. The map and compass were deep in the rucksack but I convinced myself I didn't need them, for an obvious ridge led up to the Fiddler where I knew every boulder, besides which the squall would be over in ten minutes.

One-and-a-half hours later, hood up and head down, face pinched and frozen and tramping through several inches of new snow, I became slightly anxious. Where was the Fiddler? Surely I was overdue. Then I spotted footsteps: another walker was on Ben Mor Coigach, and I would follow his or her tracks to the Fiddler. I relaxed again. However, after another half an hour's plod I emerged from the mist into a white world and realised I was back on Cairn Conmheall. I'd been following my own footsteps. 'You idiot, a day lost because you couldn't be bothered to check the compass. Will you never learn?' I said to myself as I slunk back to the car.

It is all too easy to get lost in the mountains either by sheer bad map reading, or by not referring to the compass, or by forgetting it or not trusting it. I doubt whether anyone who goes regularly into the hills can honestly say that they have never been lost. In bad weather it is all too easy to hasten to lower ground, trusting to one's sense of direction rather than fumbling for the compass with frozen fingers. But getting lost is always humiliating and often extremely inconvenient. I shall never forget descending north rather than south from the summit of Ben Cruachan: emerging out of the mist, we realised our mistake and returned to the summit where we reassessed the situation, and promptly descended the north ridge again.

As you drive north from Ullapool the mile-long summit ridge of Ben Mor Coigach can be seen rising steeply beyond Ardmair Bay, and its sandstone buttresses look dark and forbidding, especially when the sun sets and shadows lengthen. The effect is accentuated when you glance left to admire the Summer Isles in the mouth of Loch Broom silhouetted against a fiery sky. Behind this great wall of rock lies a complex mountain with satellite peaks rising above hidden glens, deep gullies and steep corries. Broken, vegetated cliffs and tiny lochans abound, and several days should be allowed to explore this mountain wilderness thoroughly; it has a rich and diverse flora and is a Grade I SSSI, administered by the Scottish Wildlife Trust.

The classic traverse of Ben Mor Coigach goes from the tiny crofting settlement of Culnacraig, at the road end beyond Achiltibuie, to Drumrunie at the junction of the Achiltibuie road with the A835. A rushing burn, the Allt nan Coisiche, cascades through a deep ravine about 300 yards above Culnacraig. From here you will traverse slopes of coarse grass and heather, making for the top of the ravine where the burn is easily crossed. Almost immediately you begin the delightful scramble up the sandstone abutment to reach Garbh Choireachan at the west end of the Ptarmigan Ridge.

If you keep to the steepest part of the nose you can enjoy magnificent scrambling over rough sandstone, with a fair degree of exposure as you look down to the grey waters of Loch Broom, the Summer Isles and the tiny, brightly painted prawners attending their creels. White-washed cottages are dotted along the coastline of Badentarbat Bay, while away to the south-west you can see the jagged outline of the Cuillin, the giants of Torridon and An Teallach. Eastwards rise the Beinn Dearg hills and remote Seana Bhraigh. There are few hills outside Skye and Rhum which combine coastal and mountain scenery so dramatically.

Ben Mor's main summit lies at the north-east end of the ridge, which is quite narrow in places with numerous gendarmes and towers of rock. Once again you can scramble over the crest, or take sandy sheep tracks to avoid all the difficulties. The main summit of Ben Mor is flat and not particularly distinguished, and you should traverse round the corrie edge, overlooking Lochan Tuath, to reach the broad ridge of Beinn Tarsuinn. A rough, but easy, descent of the open, tussocky hillside leads to the road junction at Drumrunie.

A splendid circular walk over Ben Mor Coigach, shorter than the traverse described above, can be completed comfortably from Culnacraig in an afternoon. The first section along the Ptarmigan Ridge to the cairn on Ben Mor is the same as before, but then you should descend northwards to the bealach under Sgurr an Fhidhleir. Follow the edge of the cliffs to the pointed summit of the Fiddler, whence you can gaze down dripping, boiler-plate slabs to Lochan Tuath 1,200ft below. The crags continue northwards for one kilometre to a group of rock turrets marking the end of the Beinn nan Caorach ridge. Here you should head south along the prominent ridge until you can make a rough descent to the road just north of Culnacraig.

An even shorter round (four hours), and perhaps the most rewarding day in Coigach, traverses the two principal peaks of Beinn an Eoin, Sgor Deas and Sgor Tuath, which lie just to the north of the Ben Mor massif. The approach is from the south end of Loch Lurgainn, crossing the saturated moorland to the base of Cioch Beinn an Eoin. A steep scramble over layered sandstone brings you to the top of the Cioch, with spectacular views north to Cul Beag, Cul Mor, Stac Pollaidh, Suilven and across Enard Bay to the Stoer Peninsula.

Smooth, glacier-scoured sandstone slabs littered with boulders characterise the ridge, which rises easily to the 2,027ft summit of Sgor Deas. Just below the summit, in a pocket of rock, lies an exquisite tear-drop lochan of clear water, while across the corrie the intimidating prow of the Fiddler thrusts upwards. Another lonely, wind-ruffled lochan is passed on the bealach under Sgor Tuath, whence a scramble up rocky bluffs and gullies takes you to the final summit block which is split by a 20ft deep fissure. Weathering has sculptured the rocky crest of the Sgor Tuath ridge into weird and wonderful shapes which mirror the pinnacles on Stac Pollaidh, seen prominently across Loch Lurgainn.

The descent from Sgor Tuath to Loch Lurgainn is very rough and boggy; the best route traverses the corrie on high ground, contouring close under the cliffs of Cioch Beinn an Eoin.

The Unique Challenge of
the Galloway Hills

The last fire engine was leaving Glen Trool as I drove into the Galloway Forest Park late in the afternoon. An errant spark had ignited the beds of dead bracken and deep, tangled tussocks of moor grass, as combustible as tinder after one of the driest Mays ever recorded in the Southern Uplands. One hundred acres of the Fell of Eschoncan were black and smoking, and at the height of the blaze, walkers returning from Merrick along the Buchan Burn path were lifted to safety by helicopter.

I rounded the massive Bruce's Stone, which commemorates the victory by King Robert the Bruce over the English in 1307, and passed through cool oakwoods to reach the traverse across Buchan Hill to the Gairland Burn. At Loch Neldricken the path peters out and I was left to find my own way to Loch Enoch across the roughest ground in Britain. Ten years had passed since I last visited the Galloway Hills, and time had dulled the memories of the appallingly deep, twisted and tangled moor grass and ankle-wrenching tussocks. Only the occasional blue heath milkwort emerged above the matted grass, which was bleached white after the long winter. It is hardly surprising that when one of the early Karrimor Two-Day Mountain Marathon events was held in the Galloway Hills, in dreadful weather, there were over 90 per cent retirements.

Rounding the western limb of Loch Neldricken I disturbed four greylag geese, which flew off with a tremendous commotion, before climbing easier heathery slopes above Loch Arron to reach Loch Enoch, one of my favourite spots amongst the British hills. The loch is an expansive sheet of water, dotted with islands, set between the steep grassy slopes of Merrick and the broken granite outcrops on Craignaw and Dungeon Hill. I pitched my small tent beside a sandy bay and cooked a leisurely supper outside. It was a warm, still evening with the sun flooding into the corries and sparkling on the loch. Sleep came easily, to the sound of lapping waves and the occasional bark of a fox.

The sun rose early but the tent remained in shadow, so leaving the condensation to dry, I climbed the steep east ridge of Merrick to the wind-scoured summit: at 8am I had the world to myself. I gazed south to Cairnsmore of Fleet, which inspired John Buchan to write *The Thirty-Nine Steps*, to Wigtown Bay, the Solway Firth and distant Lakeland where the hills still carried patches of snow. Merrick is the highest point of a group of mountains connected by ridges which together make the shape of a hand. The range is known as the Merrick–Shalloch–Rhinns, or 'Range of the Awful Hand'.

Back at Loch Enoch, with the tent now folded and in the rucksack, I headed for the magnificent granite hills of Dungeon Hill and Mullwharcher, passing the wreckage of a crashed plane in the black peat. Glaciation has produced cliffs, shallow lochans and broad plateaux of bare, scoured rock littered with erratic boulders. On Craignaw a vast flat slab of granite is speckled with round boulders, deposited when the ice sheet melted ten thousand years ago. It is known as the Devil's Bowling Green. The strange scar on the cliffs below is more recent: it is the place where an FIII fighter flew staight into the hillside and exploded.

The chunky granite hill of Mullwharcher, further north, was proposed as a possible site for the disposal of nuclear waste because the bedrock has not shifted or changed for millions of years. Luckily these proposals have now been abandoned. A tumbling stream led me down to the valley of the Gala Lane under Corserine and the Rhinns of Kells. Since my last visit the entire west side of the ridge had been planted with sitka spruce and lodgepole pine, and I made for a firebreak which would lead me up to the bare west spur of Corserine.

Corserine exemplified all that is most rewarding about hill-walking: a broad ridge of cropped grass rising above impenetrable forest, rough gritstone boulders, a herd of wild goats browsing the bilberry, and fleecy white clouds drifting overhead, driven by a fresh breeze. On a patch of boulder scree beneath the summit I put up a ptarmigan, the furthest south I have ever seen this attractive bird. This was a most unusual sighting which gave me a great lift; later I reported it to the county bird-recording officer, who told me that my sighting was the second in four years, and they were hoping that ptarmigan would breed in Galloway rather than just visit occasionally from the Isle of Arran.

To the north the ridge narrows and runs out to Carlin's Cairn, while the blue waters of Loch Doon, immortalised by Robert Burns in his poem *Ye Banks and Braes o' Bonie Doon*, stretch away towards Dalmellington. A simple white trig pillar marks the summit of Corserine, which gives splendid views west over the cliffs on Mullwharcher, Dungeon Hill and Craignaw to Merrick and the Ayrshire coast. On a previous visit, in clearer weather, I have seen the hills of Arran. As I walked south along the magnificent Rhinns of Kells ridge I could look back into the high south-east-facing corrie which was still packed with snow. The green forest blanket stretches in all directions as far as the eye can see, but planting stops at the 1,500ft level and walking is open and unimpeded on mainly springy turf with harebells and cotton grass.

Conscious that Glen Trool was now a long distance away, I left the Rhinns of Kells ridge at Meikle Millyea and descended to the tree-filled glen of the Curnelloch Burn, expecting to find a forest access road. This was a grave mistake, for not only was there no road or path whatsoever, there was no firebreak, either, which might have taken me to lower ground. Eventually, after several hours of utmost struggle down stream beds, and blundering about blindly through trees – at one stage following a herd of red deer – I was forced to climb back up above the tree level on Craigeazle to get my bearings.

Evening was well advanced when I hit the track near Black Water of Dee and turned off along the rough road running south of Loch Dee. In the failing light I put up the tent beside the White Laggan Burn and, bruised and blistered, retired to my sleeping bag to cook supper. Second round to the Galloway Hills. At 5am, at first light, a cold and blustery wind tugged at the tent. In rapidly deteriorating weather I struck camp and limped back to Glen Trool, arriving just after the heavens opened.

A Suilven Traverse

There is no doubt in my mind that the drive north from Ullapool, taking the A837 towards Durness, is the most scenic route in Britain. Almost at once the long wall of Beinn Mor Coigach dominates the skyline behind picturesque Ardmair Bay, while a glance over your shoulder will reveal the Summer Isles floating on the bluest of seas in the mouth of Loch Broom and the sandstone escarpment on Beinn Ghobhlach rising high above the curve of Annat Bay. Turning through 360°, the massive sugarloaf of Sail Mhor, the serrated ridge of An Teallach, the pointed summit of Sgurr Mor Fannich, and finally the rounded hills of the Beinn Dearg Forest, combine to produce a thrilling panorama.

Just beyond Cul Mor's twin peaks, as you descend gently to the crofting settlement of Elphin, Suilven bursts into view. At first you rub your eyes with disbelief at this monster whale-back rising isolated and inexorably steeply from a flattish landscape of Lewisian Gneiss, but its sublime shape grows on you over the years like a great work of art.

Suilven and its neighbours are sandstone mountains, the final detached relics of a vast mass of rock, fully 7,000ft thick, that once spread over most of north-west Scotland. This was the shore-line of a submerged continent, one of the first land masses in the world, and the parallel strata can clearly be seen picked out by the rays of the evening sun. Many of these hills (but not Suilven) are capped by a thin layer of grey Cambrian Quartzite which has helped to protect them from weathering. Suilven makes an obvious objective for the adventurous walker, but its remoteness deters the hordes and thus it has not suffered from the ravages of erosion seen on, for example, Stac Pollaidh.

Unless you are prepared to swim, a direct approach from the south is impossible because Suilven is guarded by Loch Veyatie and the Fionn Loch which interlink to form a ten-mile stretch of water. Again, a direct ascent of the western prow, Caisteal Liath (the Grey Castle), necessitates rock climbing: rearing above the fishing village of Lochinver, it looks most intimidating. This leaves us with ascents of the two loose, steep gullies which run down north and south from the lowest point of the ridge, Bealach Mor, or a scramble up the eastern summit of Meall Beag. The eastern approach is by far the most rewarding, for it involves a long walk across typically rough Sutherland moorland, some airy scrambling to reach Suilven's crest, and the negotiation of an exposed *mauvais pas*. Walkers who are nervous of steep rock or who suffer from vertigo should restrict their routes to the Bealach Mor gullies, for Suilven is a serious mountain, there are no escape routes, and help is far away. In spring, when the gullies are packed with hard, icy snow, it is essential to use ice-axes and crampons.

Just north of Elphin the road crosses the Ledmore river by a stone bridge. You can leave the car 50 yards beyond the bridge in a layby, which also marks the start of a stalkers' path running along the north shore of the Cam Loch. Early on a spring morning this loch is peerless. Small waders strut along the stony shore, gorse buds open in the sunshine, rowan and birch trees hang over the water from rocky bluffs and primroses peep shyly from sheltered nooks. On my last visit there wasn't a breath of wind, and Cul Mor was mirrored with astonishing clarity in the still water; kestrels played 'catch-me-if-you-can' above us, and a skein of honking geese flew past high in the sky.

As so often happens, the path is excellent to begin with, but soon deteriorates and becomes boggy and less distinct. After crossing the Loch a' Chroisg burn it leaves the Cam Loch and climbs north up the hillside, a few cairns helping you to locate its route through the heather and tussocks. All this time the superb eastern abutment of Suilven attracts the eye. It looks desperately distant but infinitely desirable, and motivation is no problem. At this stage leave the path and strike boldly uphill making for the broad shoulder of Meall na Braclaich; this brings you out of very thick and tangled heather onto slabs of smooth sandstone and erratics. You look down on watery wastes: the Cam Loch, Loch Veyatie and Loch Sionascaig with its tree-covered islands. Smaller, shallower lochans fill every hollow, and one bitter but sparkling March day we skimmed stones over the sheets of ice, revelling in the high-pitched zinging noise.

Seen head-on during the long approach march from Elphin, Suilven's east ridge has appeared daunting, but as you get closer, the angle seems to ease and your confidence grows. In fact you can scramble up almost anywhere; the spur is well supplied with good hand-holds and small ledges, and it provides a truly exhilarating climb. Pause awhile on the rounded summit of Meall Beag and enjoy the panoramic views extending from Foinaven, Arkle and Quinag to Ben More Assynt, Conival and Seana Bhraigh and due south to Stac Pollaidh and the Coigach hills. The view west along the ridge is effectively blocked by massive Meall Mheadhonach, Suilven's second-highest summit, which is not particularly easily climbed from any direction. Firstly you must step across a deep fissure in the sandstone strata, where the ridge narrows dramatically, and then you arrive above a sheer 100ft cliff with no apparent point of weakness. This, the *mauvais pas*, can be turned by descending rather steep rocks on the north side to gain a weak traverse line running west to the dark, dank bealach which is overhung by dripping crags. It is a relief to climb steeply up to Meall Mheadhonach by a loose, zigzag path.

Another scrambly descent is necessary to reach the broad grassy slopes running down to Bealach Mor. An old wall, still in remarkably good repair, runs across the ridge at this point and you can peer down the gully on the north side, your eventual route of descent from Suilven. One perfect spring day I cut steps up the frozen snow packing this gully to emerge into warm, bright sunshine where I surprised a pair of gleaming black ravens courageously mobbing a golden eagle that had entered their territory.

On now easily to the turf-covered dome of Caisteal Liath, 2,399ft, which looks over Lochinver, Ennard Bay and north to the island-dotted bay of Eddrachillis: this is a perfect example of the close affinity of mountains, wild coastline and seascape which characterises north-west Scotland. It is all too easy to dream the afternoon away on this most exquisite of Scottish peaks, but the toy-like boats in Lochinver harbour and the distant white line of breakers on the rocky shore bring home to you the task ahead. So it is back down to Bealach Mor and the unpleasantly loose gully which eventually leads to easy, if boggy ground above the west end of Loch na Gainimh.

A more rewarding alternative route of descent, but one which is longer and leads you not into Lochinver but to Inverkirkaig three miles to the south, takes the south scree slope from Bealach Mor. This runs down to a narrow path above the Fionn Loch and eventually to the tourist trail that winds up beside the foaming river Kirkaig from Inverkirkaig to the Kirkaig Falls. This impressive waterfall, which plunges into a deep, dark pool set romantically amidst crags and trees, makes an impasse for salmon which can often be seen leaping clear of the water in a vain attempt to proceed further upstream.

Returning now to the *voie normale*, a well constructed stalkers' path crosses the Abhainn na Craich Airigh by a wooden bridge and continues easily down the glen. At the ruined crofting settlement of Suileag another path runs north to meet the A837 at Little Assynt House, but you continue westwards over a few minor hillocks to Glencanisp Lodge. This beautiful stone house in the best Scottish tradition looks over the reedy Loch Druim Suardalain. In spring the approach path is bright with gorse, primroses, violets and buttercups and the woods resound to birdsong, while hundreds of daffodils surround the lawns. The right-of-way runs behind the house through luxuriant rhododendrons to meet the tarmaced private road to Lochinver.

A Loyal Toast

Many of Sutherland's mountains are underrated, and none more so than Ben Loyal which rises two miles south of the Kyle of Tongue on the north coast of Scotland. Ben Loyal makes Corbett's list of 2,500-footers by just 4ft, yet it has no need of any contrived statistic to enhance its stature: judged by many criteria it could be considered the perfect mountain. It divides the rough, harsh, quartzite mountains of the Reay Forest from the flat, saturated moorlands of eastern Sutherland's Flow Country. Its four shapely rock summits, rounded ridges, bold crags, smoothly sculptured corries, lochans, gorges and woods not only thrill the motorist to the far north-west, but provide the hill walker with a day of extravagant pleasures.

From the village of Tongue an unfenced road runs south off the A838 to Kinloch Lodge at the head of the Kyle of Tongue, and you can park at Ribigill farm under the wide northern slopes of Ben Loyal. When I went in late March, a few snow patches lingered on the seaward face of Sgor Chaonasaid, which rises in a craggy pyramid reminiscent of Buachaille Etive Mor. Clouds were racing across the sky, driven by a gale-force north-easterly which gusted over the bare moors, flattening the coarse grass and sending me reeling off the track. I shuddered with apprehension at the thought of the conditions on the summit ridges.

The rough path ends at the stone shieling of Cunside, and you are left to scramble up the ever-steepening heather and rocks on the east side of the rock face. By clambering up the bed of a gully I found temporary shelter from the tearing wind; but once I emerged on to the plateau I was all but plucked from my feet and dashed over the cliffs. The various summits of Ben Loyal are characterised by huge rock tors made of syenite, an igneous rock very similar to granite, and in normal conditions they would provide diverting scrambles. Today, however, it was a battle to make any progress against the wind which came roaring across the exposed tops, giving me just enough time to fall to my knees, grab a rock for security, and hang on for all I was worth.

A broad ridge runs around a high, hidden corrie containing a lochan, and the trig point is built on a vast rock castle on the southern lip. To my utmost surprise and delight I enjoyed an almost dead calm on the summit castle, and could open the Thermos in peace and comfort while the buffets of wind passed below. Only once before have I experienced this phenomenon, on the summit of Ben Lui, also in March. I have never been offered an explanation for this extraordinary quirk in the weather pattern.

Having climbed down from my perch to continue the traverse, the wind summoned up all its energy and battered me into submission. With face lashed by a loose anorak cord and eyes streaming so that I could hardly see, I headed down into the corrie to seek shelter. Here at last I could breathe again and take stock of my surroundings: Ben Hope rising white and majestic six miles to the west, the indented cliff-girt coastline of northern Scotland stretching to far horizons, and the blue outline of St John's Head on the Isle of Hoy. From below I could appreciate the magnificent 200ft sheer buttresses of clean rock falling from the western edge of Sgor a' Bhatein. The westernmost peak, Sgor a' Chleirich, boasts even more impressive west-facing cliffs fully 800ft high, described by R.J. Jolly in the 1970 *SMCJ* as having climbing potential equal to Carn Mor or the Shelter Stone Crag. Although several routes have been done on these cliffs, they remain largely unexploited.

Down in the corrie I stumbled upon the skeleton of a stag, its bones picked clean by the ravens and bleached white by the sun. It was laid out on the grass like a specimen for a zoology class, and I was attracted by the whitened skull carrying two magnificent antlers. What a splendid trophy they would make, I mused, and I could picture them decorating the wall of my garage. Unfortunately the antlers were fixed fast to the skull, and I didn't want to be burdened with that as well on the long walk out to Ribigill. Thus I seized the antlers, raised the skull above my head and and dashed it on a rock in an attempt to break it off. However, the skull smashed like a ripe melon and splattered my entire person with putrid grey matter.

The smell of sticky, clinging brains was sickening in the extreme and quite overpowering. I lurched, retching, to the nearest burn, and ignoring the crust of ice, buried my head and hands in the rushing water to wash off the putrifaction. But I was not entirely successful in this task, and felt extremely pathetic, sorry for myself and foolish as I walked through the birchwoods to the flat moorland, with the foulest of odours wafting from my rank clothes.

I had no stomach for lunch or tea, and even the late sun lighting up the corries and tors of Ben Loyal did little to cheer me up. Ah well, we live and learn.

JMT
Buy Sandwood Estate

The recent announcement that the John Muir Trust has bought the 11,000 acre Sandwood estate in Sutherland is wonderful news for all who value the wild and romantic places in Britain. The estate is the third purchase by the JMT since its foundation ten years ago, the other two being Ladhar Bheinn in Knoydart and Torrin on Skye. The purchase price of £100,000 was met from the Trust's own funds, plus substantial contributions from Scottish Natural Heritage and the National Heritage Memorial Fund.

Even more than the Ladhar Bheinn purchase, the knowledge that Sandwood will be preserved for the nation in its natural wild state fills me with elation. It is an inspired purchase for which chairman Nick Luard, director Terry Isles and trustee Nigel Hawkins must be congratulated, and hopefully it will do much to increase the membership of, and the flow of funds into, the JMT. A great deal of our priceless wild country has been desecrated by developers and unscrupulous landowners, and it is a relief to know that a growing number of prime sites are safe from their clutches for all time.

Over thirty years ago I was given a book entitled *On The Hills Of The North* by J. Hubert Walker. All the old favourites – Ben Loyal, Suilven, Ben Mor Coigach, Beinn Eighe, Applecross and so on – were lovingly described and accompanied by black and white photographs, but it was the photo of Sandwood Bay off the west coast of Sutherland which moved me most, and the picture of waves breaking on a broad strand against a backcloth of beetling cliffs and a towering rock stack rising off-shore has haunted me ever since. Since that date, literally dozens of visits to Sandwood Bay have confirmed it as one of the very special and most loved places in all Britain for myself and my family. We have camped there during heatwaves when our skin has been blistered, during storms of rain when the dunes carrying our tents became an island, and during plagues of midges.

The most dramatic visits have been when the on-shore wind has gusted to force 10, dashing the waves against the cliffs with a clap of thunder and sending columns of spray a hundred feet into the air; days when the fishing fleet has hastened back to Kinlochbervie harbour, pitching like corks and burying their prows in the white horses. On such days, down on the beach, the roar of the breakers is deafening and the sand is sucked up and dashed down with terrifying ferocity.

But on days of high summer, Sandwood Bay is benign and idyllic. You can sit on a bleached log at the high-water mark and watch the gannets diving for fish. Gannets, the most beautiful of all sea birds, plummet into the seething water, wings folded and their bodies perfectly streamlined at the point of impact, putting an Olympic diver to shame. Oyster catchers and ringed plovers probe the water's edge for morsels of food. A thin line of foam outlines the off-shore islets of Am Balg, sea thrift decorates the top of the cliffs overlooking the great stack of Am Buachaille (The Herdsman), and the sun glints on the white-washed Cape Wrath lighthouse, six miles away to the north.

You can enjoy the diverse bird life: fulmar petrels gliding past the red sandstone cliffs, the graceful kittiwakes, shrieking herring gulls and superior shags standing aloof in rows on the ledges of the rock skerries and holding out their wings to dry. Watch out for great skuas (nicknamed bonxies): huge, evil birds which will eat young birds and even new-born lambs, and will dive-bomb your head given the chance.

When the tide is out two more bays become accessible on the north side of Sandwood Bay, making an uninterrupted stretch of sand over a mile long, although two tiny tidal islands of bare rock break up the main beach. Winter storms can totally alter the character of the beach. Thousands of tons of sand may be shifted overnight, and I have seen shingle banks one year, only for them to be replaced by sandbars the following year. Sometimes a shallow lagoon forms between the dunes and Sandwood Loch, and quicksands may be a hazard, but spring tides frequently wash over the dunes themselves and then all is changed again. On one occasion the shifting sands exposed the remains of a crashed Spitfire, and we could clearly see the engine and propellor sticking out of the sand at low tide; a few weeks later it had been reburied.

Legends abound. A Spanish galleon, fleeing after the Armada débâcle, is said to have foundered off-shore and the remains, including treasure, are buried at Sandwood Bay. A mariner from the wreck haunts the remote Sandwood cottage overlooking Sandwood Loch. On wild nights visitors to the cottage have reported hearing knocking at the window and seeing a swarthy, bearded sailor wearing a cap, tunic with brass buttons and seaboots, and displaying long, gold earrings, peering into the room. Shepherds, tending their flocks on the rough pasture of the hinterland, have seen a mermaid sitting combing her hair on the tidal islands of the bay. But there is much more to Sandwood estate than Sandwood Bay. The area purchased by the JMT extends south to include the crofting townships of Oldshoremore, Blairmore and Sheigra.

One of Britain's most exciting coastal walks runs from Oldshoremore to Sandwood Bay and on to Cape Wrath. However, before leaving Oldshoremore, prospective walkers should check that both the minibus service to the Kyle of Durness and the Kyle ferry are running, or they will find themselves with an extra sixteen miles to walk at the end of an already very arduous day. Heading north out of Oldshoremore you pass several lonely sandy bays and coves. These early sections of the walk are in gentle surroundings and run across flowery cliff tops where the tiny communities of Droman, Balchrick and Sheigra extend walls and fences to the sea. From the highest ground the sheer cliff on Handa Island (a bird reserve of international importance administered by the Scottish Wildlife Trust) can be seen thrusting out into the sea to the south, while inland the unmistakable outlines of Foinaven, Arkle and Ben Stack are silhouetted against the sky.

At Port Mor there is a beach piled high with driftwood and jetsam. A roofless croft stands by the shore and a stack of rock, bearded with grey lichen, thrusts skywards, topped by an extraordinary ovoid stone covered with bright yellow lichen (*Xanthoria parietina*), like the egg of a giant prehistoric bird. Further on, as you draw level with the island group of Am Balg, one mile out to sea, the cliffs rise to 400ft, and if you peer over the edge you will see the famous pinnacle of Am Buachaille rising 220ft above the waves. It was first climbed in 1967 by Tom Patey's party, who crossed the boiling gulf between the shore and the base of the stack with the help of two ladders. Nowadays the ascent of Am Buachaille is often combined with that of Scotland's other two great rock stacks, The Old Man of Hoy on Orkney and The Old Man of Storr just down the Sutherland coast. Recently the JMT found a conservation-minded rock climber to remove the tangle of loose ropes and slings from Am Buachaille. North of Sandwood Bay we leave the Sandwood estate, but the walk on to Cape Wrath continues in the same vein. I shall not describe it here, but will leave it to the reader to discover and provide his or her own superlatives.

The geographical remoteness of Sandwood Bay, coupled with the fact that a minimum of four miles must be walked from the nearest car park, should ensure that the JMT will be able to realise their management objectives for the estate. On many occasions throughout the year the JMT organise voluntary working parties on their estates. The tasks on hand are varied and include erosion control, path maintenance, ditching, drystone dyking, tree planting, bracken control, collection of acorns and pine cones, beach clearance and surveying. These are important activities for the JMT, who, unlike many landowners in the Highlands, take their management responsibilities very seriously.

A few years after the purchase of Sandwood estate I was able to join a working party organised by the resident JMT conservation manager, Will Boyd-Wallis. About twenty of us met on the coast near Oldshoremore and erected our tents on the machair overlooking a sandy bay. It was an idyllic site with views south to the soaring cliffs on Handa Island, while behind us stretched familiar and much loved hills: Beinn Spionnaidh, Cranstackie, Foinaven, Arkle, Ben Stack, Ben More Assynt and Quinag. That first evening we walked across the seaweed-covered boulders to the tidal island of Eilean na h-Aiteig, which was bright with primroses, and later sat around a driftwood fire while the moon rose over the Minch.

The aim of this particular working party was to tackle the problem of sand blowing off the dunes and drifting over the roads, houses and grazing areas in the crofting townships of Blairmore and Balchrick. Although the growth of marram grass on many of the dunes has prevented serious erosion, there are several particularly vulnerable areas where the wind funnels through and has prevented marram grass establishing itself. 'Sometimes nature needs a little help and encouragement from mankind,' said Will. Our task was in two stages: firstly to stop the movement of sand, and secondly to plant marram grass on the stabilised area.

We carried in huge piles of brushwood (lopped branches of larch trees) to denuded areas of dunes, and then dug in the branches to make linear hedges rather like steeplechase jumps. The theory was that the sand would bank up against the brushwood rather than become widely dispersed by the wind. The technique works on exposed stretches of road that are vulnerable to wind-blown powder snow.

It was pleasant enough to work with convivial companions of all ages and from many walks of life, with plenty of tea breaks and in such a breathtaking environment. Sunday was a rest day in respect of the expectations of the Free Church of Scotland, and several mountains were climbed while others went rock climbing with Will at Sandwood Bay. As I dug with my spade in the shifting sands I did wonder whether the elements should be allowed to take their toll of JMT land. If the wind blows sand inland from the dunes, so be it. An equilibrium will eventually become established. A similar case has been made for stopping all artificial sea defences on Spurn Head, and allowing the sea to breach the headland. Do we put the preservation of wild land in its natural state, before the interests of those (crofters) who have reclaimed it in the past through life and death necessity? An interesting question.

In Praise of Whin Sill

A list of the most beautiful and spectacular natural features in northern England would include the low cliffs of the Farn Islands, the rock plinth supporting Bamburgh Castle, Crag Lough and the Roman Wall, the superb falls at High Force and Cauldron Snout, Cronkley Scar, Falcon Clints, and the broken south-facing escarpment of Cross Fell. For all these magnificent features we must thank a hard, grey, coarse-grained rock known as the Whin Sill.

About three hundred million years ago, an intrusion of volcanic rock forced its way between layers of limestone and spread south-west from the Northumberland coast. Since this molten igneous rock solidified underground it cooled slowly, producing quartz-dolerite with larger crystals than are found in basalt, which cooled more rapidly on the surface. This quartz-dolerite is the Whin Sill.

Not only does the Whin Sill provide us with wild and weathered outcrops, up to 200ft high in places, which are a joy to walk over and climb up, but in Upper Teesdale its effect on neighbouring beds of limestone has produced unusual conditions and a unique flora. Here the Whin Sill has metamorphosed the Melmerby Scar limestone, converting it into coarse crystalline marble. This 'sugar limestone' supports an arctic alpine flora which has survived the last ice age, and thus on Widebank Fell in May and June you can see mountain avens, spring gentians, the Teesdale sandwort, the hoary rock rose and the Teesdale violet.

Much of my early rock climbing was done in Northumberland. From my home in Corbridge we could reach the Wanneys and Crag Lough with ease, and my brothers and I polished off most of the climbs listed in the Northumbrian Mountaineering Club's old red guide, first published in 1950. Geoffrey Winthrop Young wrote the foreword to this guide, and his stirring message is still relevant today and well worth repeating:

> There is no nobler country than that of Northumberland, as it rolls processionally northwards to the Border in great waves of coloured and historic moorland, cresting upon the skyline into sudden and surprising crags, which crown for us the magnificent walking with admirable rock climbs. May the growing tide of northern climbers flow onward as great-heartedly.

The names of the climbs – Idiot's Delight, Sweethope Crack and Squeezy Bill – rekindle fond memories of the Wanneys, but the gritstone was often rather green and the holds rounded. The Whin Sill, however, is glorious rock to climb on, and Crag Lough on a warm summer's evening is unbeatable. Jointing of the Whin Sill has produced polygonal columns and towers 80ft high: Tarzan's Buttress, Raven's Tower, Centurion's Crack, Spuggies Gully, Grad's Groove, Battered Buttress and a host of other routes, full of character, give carefree climbing on sound rock, while swans glide on the lake below and reeds bend in the breeze. Above the crags, clouds move across a vast Northumbrian sky, and the ancient, hand-hewn blocks of stone, set firm in Hadrian's Wall, are there to greet you at the top of the climb.

Perhaps the very best stretch of our incomparable Pennine Way is that which follows the river Tees from Middleton-in-Teesdale to Cauldron Snout, and then heads west to High Cup Nick, Dufton and Cross Fell. Sadly the construction of the dam above Cauldron Snout and the reservoir of Cow Green has regulated the flow of the river Tees. No longer do spring floods thunder over High Force with a deafening roar, while rainbows arch over the brown peaty water. Nevertheless, the falls and cascades of the river Tees as it hurries over the beds of Whin Sill are always dramatic, and as Cauldron Snout is approached, the fells on either side close in, ending precipitously in the rough crags of Cronkley Scar and Falcon Clints.

Beyond Cauldron Snout the Pennine Way turns southwest and becomes even wilder, crossing bleak, peat-hagged fells until the Maize Beck is reached. This tributary of the Tees rises on Knock Fell and is a considerable river; some years ago a walker was drowned while attempting to cross it in spate. A footbridge has now been built to safeguard Pennine Way walkers, but on a recent visit in early February the Maize Beck had been stilled by the frost and was a mere ribbon of ice. We had walked up from Dufton, leaving the white-washed cottages of this charming village bathed in sunshine, and almost convincing ourselves that spring had arrived – only to be met by a piercing, arctic wind funnelling through the gorge of High Cup Nick. Here the Whin Sill has been scoured and eroded by glacial action producing a considerable escarpment with vertical cliffs, seamed buttresses and detached fingers of rock.

Leaving the unsightly radar station on Great Dun Fell with some relief, we took the broad switchback ridge which leads to Cross Fell, the highest of the Pennine Peaks at 2,930ft. In spite of the biting wind which penetrated all our clothing, we could appreciate the magnificence of our surroundings: to the north lay the vast bowl of Upper Teesdale, streaks of snow enhancing the bleakness of these desolate fells, while further down the dale Cow Green reservoir was covered with green ice. Beyond Teesdale the rarely visited Weardale fells of Burnhope Seat and Killhope Law carried a more or less complete snow covering. Thankfully the lenticular cloud which rarely leaves Cross Fell's summit had today lifted above the plateau, giving us distant views of Saddleback and High Street in Lakeland, while the Vale of Eden spread out to the south, bounded by Wild Boar Fell above Kirkby Stephen, with its characteristic cut-off summit, and the rounded Howgill Fells.

We sat cowering behind the windbreak on the summit of Cross Fell, blowing on our fingers and with our anorak hoods up; but the wind had deterred most other walkers, and from our solitary perch we could gaze happily over the finest walking country in England. Slow seepage of ground water above the impervious Whin Sill, and runnels from underground springs, had frozen to sheets of hard, translucent ice; to avoid these treacherous areas we chose to clamber down the boulder fields on the west side of Cross Fell and regain the path to Kirkland at a lower level. The Pennine Way walker proceeding north from Cross Fell must cover another 92 miles before he reaches his goal at Kirk Yetholm. The Whin Sill faces the elements with boldness and confidence, but our flesh is weak, and as the sun set and the frost intensified, we were happy to make for the warmth and friendliness of the Stag Inn at Dufton.

When the sun is shining and frost has iced the puddles and turned the path to iron, and the snow on the hills is firm to the tread, hill walkers rave about the conditions and chalk up days of high elation. But conditions following a really heavy snowfall can be a nightmare, when a thin crust covers a great depth of powder. Walking becomes exhausting with a heavy rucksack as one's boots break the crust and sink into the icing sugar below. Boulder fields become obstacle courses of leg-wrenching, ankle-twisting, hidden nooks and crannies.

Just such conditions existed a few years ago when I was due to be taking the school mountaineering club to the Lake District for the weekend. Would the venture be feasible, I wondered? Luckily the decision was made for me, because the A66 was blocked by drifting snow beyond Bowes, and there was no alternative route to the Lakes. I turned off at Barnard Castle and proceeded north for a weekend in Upper Teesdale, and since the road was blocked again well before Alston, we shouldered our packs and headed west across the fells towards Mickle Fell and High Cup Nick.

Two-and-a-half hours later we had only struggled as many miles through the deep snow, a hare lay frozen stiff beside the river, the party was tired and strung out and the light was beginning to fade. Visions of the 1951 Ben Alder tragedy when four men perished in a blizzard, and the 1971 Cairngorms tragedy, this time to a school party, flashed through my mind, but I hastily pushed them to one side. It was time to camp.

It is bad enough getting a camp organised when you have only yourself to worry about, but when you have inexperienced youngsters in your charge the whole business becomes phrenetic. With four adults and fourteen children we coped, just. Eighteen souls meant nine tents, and I swear that each was a different design. You try putting up a dome tent in 18in of snow, with a wicked wind blowing spindrift into your face and tangling the guy ropes, when the temperature is −10°C, when the 12ft poles become dissected inside their tight sleeves and, finally, when you have burrowed deep down through the snow to ground level and you find the turf is frozen rock hard and quite impenetrable to tent pegs – then the going is tough. Yes, I know this is routine stuff to Himalayan hardmen and the SAS, but it was adventure enough for the boys and, I have to admit, for me.

In the middle of our desperate antics a couple of seasoned skiers swished down the hillside on *langlauf* skis, located a deep bank of snow, produced a shovel from their mammoth packs and proceeded to dig a snow-hole for the night. Inspired by such professionalism the boys seized their ice-axes and dug and delved in like fashion, but with little real success. However, by scoring round a block of firm snow with an ice axe point it was possible to cut rectangular bricks of snow for wall building. Soon 3ft high protective walls surrounded each tent. Gino Watkins would have approved.

Hacking a hole in the ice of the river Tees, we collected water and retired into our tents to cook gargantuan meals. The stilled water froze into plates of ice, and fine powder snow blew through every crevice – but I don't think anyone would have exchanged their lot for the fireside. Sleeping bag, duvet jacket and a couple of jerseys fought off most of the cold, and any shivers were dispelled by thoughts of Hermann Buhl standing alone all night on his tiny ledge 26,000ft up on Nanga Parbat, or of Doug Scott and Dougal Haston in their snow cave at 28,000ft on Everest.

Another grey day and an icy wind blowing flurries of snow greeted us in the morning. A flaring primus had burnt a hole in one boy's nylon tent, and a few others had suffered ice-axe cuts whilst digging for the tent pegs, otherwise everyone was in good shape. There was no question of prolonging the exercise. In a virtual whiteout we plodded through a white world with waves of snowdrifts the only features. Ice gummed up our eyes and noses, and at one time we unwittingly strayed onto the frozen surface of Cow Green reservoir — but mindful of the chasm below the ice caused by drawdown, we strayed off again with alacrity. Finally, marker posts indicated the line of the road and we were able to regain the vehicles.

A fruitless exercise, many will say. It took a week to dry and repair the equipment and we missed a memorable Calcutta Cup match, but as Byron wrote:

> *Though sluggards deem it but a foolish chase,*
> *And marvel men should quit their easy chair,*
> *The toilsome way and long, long league to trace,*
> *Oh! there is sweetness in the mountain air,*
> *And life, that bloated ease can never hope to share.*

The Marsden-to-Edale
Classic

Of the many famous and historic long moorland walks over the Peak District, the Marsden-to-Edale is by far the most celebrated, twenty-five miles of rough peat, including the high tops of Black Hill, Bleaklow and Kinder Scout with gritstone outcrops, steep gullies and wooded valleys between. A traditional test piece for aspiring fellsmen and women, the route should be attempted in winter when the hours of daylight are strictly limited.

Some years ago, after a particularly gruelling outing on Bleaklow, my brother, Oliver, and I peeled off our soaking, stinking socks and trousers, threw them in the boot of the car and swore we would never return. But time is a great healer, and it was the smiling face of Ian MacAskill, the TV weather forecaster, predicting a frosty winter's day that turned our thoughts to the Marsden-to-Edale. After all, it was mid-January and the winter had not yet arrived; we were champing at the bit at the thought of black bogs frozen hard as iron, thin sunshine and an arctic blue sky.

Marsden at 7am was cold, grey and depressing. We laced up our boots by the car headlights and checked the Thermoses before setting off into the drizzly dawn up the dreary path beside the Wessenden reservoirs. How soft we had become. In the old days, at the beginning of the century, Cecil Dawson and his fellow bogtrotters would pad across the Pennines in gym shoes. Doubtless Dawson would have regarded us with as much contempt as Thesiger did Newby and Carless in the Hindu Kush. When he observed them blowing up their airbeds he announced, 'God, what a couple of pansies.'

There can be few Pennine fells that look less enticing than Black Hill when seen from the site of the old Isle of Skye Inn on Wessenden Head, particularly when it disappears into mist. An eroded ribbon runs south across saturated bog; this is in fact the Pennine Way and the National Park Authority has bridged some of the stream runnels with duckboards. In many places this seems to have made matters worse, for it has channelled boots into a line, thereby churning the peat into a knee-deep quagmire. To avoid these horrors the path has become wider by 150ft on each side.

Black Hill plateau is a wilderness of groughs, black mire and sizeable pools of standing water. With visibility down to fifteen yards progress slowed and we fell behind schedule. Yes, the forecast was wrong, there was no frost and no sunshine. Compass bearings are of minimal assistance on Black Hill because one's route is largely determined by a hunt for firm ground. Needless to say, from the summit trig point we strayed too far east and found ourselves off course in Crowden Little Brook. Nevertheless, an ascent of Wildboarclough onto Bleaklow is guaranteed to restore flagging spirits. The stream tumbles down its gritstone bed, which it has carved out of the moor, splashing over cascades and waterfalls which provide entertaining scrambles. The relief of clambering over firm, rough-textured rock after many miles of evil, energy-sapping, sucking bogs is quite overwhelming.

Naively optimistic, we dreamed of finding the perfect route across Bleaklow: a route that missed the groughs, and did not entail ignominiously scrabbling up huge banks of soft, black peat, but led you effortlessly to the Snake Pass. I doubt that such a route exists, and we blundered about frustratingly in thick, clinging mist, finally pinpointing our position as being in Doctor's Gate, off-route again and well on the way to Glossop. Wearily we plodded back over Coldharbour Moor and drained our flasks beside the A57.

Barely three hours of daylight left and Kinder still to cross. A difficult decision to make on a short winter's day. I had no appetite for heroics, and had Oliver suggested aborting the expedition and hitching round to Edale I would have agreed with alacrity. A wise and mature decision made in the light of years of experience, we could have argued – although in our gut we would have known that we had chickened out. However, the Pennine Way dog-legs across Kinder, rounding Ashop Head to Kinder Downfall, and a seductive length of 'improved' track was visible near the road. Could this be our salvation?

How magnificently firm and springy was the path, and what hypocrites we felt as we actually realised its artificiality. It is very easy to sit at home, pontificating as purists on the dreadful nature of 'improved' stretches of the Pennine Way. Reality is somewhat different. But after just 200 yards the path improvements ceased, and saturated bog continued onwards to the far horizon. With few regrets we left the Pennine Way path and headed due south over tussocky grass to Featherbed Top and the luxury of heather. Racing down to Ashop Clough we crossed the river and scrambled up to The Edge. Firm gritstone again – bliss.

In the fading light we forged on over the Kinder plateau on compass bearing, finding a deep runnel, with walls ten foot high, that ran in roughly the right direction. More gritstone outcrops, a deep valley falling away from the moor, inexorably steep grass, Grindsbrook, distant lights, a path, and we stumbled into Edale as night fell.

THE BOGTROTTERS

The Marsden-to-Edale was the first of the great marathon routes over the Pennines, and it wasn't long before Cecil Dawson and his colleagues, many from the Manchester Rucksack Club, sought stiffer challenges. Cecil Dawson was known as 'the Colonel', and he had legendary staying powers on marathon moorland crossings. With the severe access restrictions of the time, Dawson had to outwit and outpace the grouse moor keepers as well as contend with the natural difficulties of the terrain. Nevertheless he extended the Marsden-Edale to Colne-Edale and then Colne-Buxton, which was a full fifty miles.

In 1922 Fred Heardman pioneered the Three Inns Walk from Whalley Bridge to Marsden via the Cat and Fiddle, Snake Inn and Isle of Skye Inn; he later achieved the first double Marsden-Edale wearing gym shoes. Phil Altman tried to better Heardman's time, but died in the attempt on Bleaklow.

In 1968 Harry Gilliat, Don Morrison and Bill Woodward achieved a triple Marsden-Edale inside twenty-four hours, and in 1980 Rob Pearson of Dark Peak Harriers won a Marsden-Edale race in two hours and thirty-nine minutes. The longest and most demanding of all the pre-war bogtrotters' routes was the Tan Hill Inn to Cat and Fiddle, a distance of 120 miles and involving 20,000ft of ascent. In 1979 the champion ultra-long-distance fell runner, Mike Cudahy, ran this route in thirty-two hours.

Mike Cudahy's greatest feat was in 1984 when he ran the

full 270-mile Pennine Way in two days, twenty-two hours. This was Mike's eighth attempt at the record, and his account of the last stretch over the Cheviots – on a dark night with freezing wind, lashing rain, deep black bogs and protesting body, when his companions allowed him just seven minutes sleep in a wooden hut on the border – is already legendary.

As is so often the case when one record is established and announced by the media to be unassailable, it falls quite quickly. Thus it was that in 1989 another formidable ultra-long-distance fell runner, Michael Hartley, ran non-stop up the Pennine Way from Edale to Kirk Yetholm, clipping four-and-a-half hours off Mike Cudahy's record. Michael Hartley was a thirty-seven-year-old meter reader who did his rounds on foot. This exercise, combined with regular training sessions in the evenings and at weekends, enabled him to average twenty-four miles a day spread over the whole year.

Nowadays the ultra-long-distance fell-running calendar is full, with events taking place regularly. There is no lack of challenges for those inclined to take them up, from the Welsh 3,000s, the Bob Graham Round, the Long Distance Walkers Association's 100-mile circuits, the Skye Ridge, the Pennine Way or even the Munros.

An Teallach for the Connoisseur

Our boots crunched through the snow and splintered the ice on the puddles that had formed on the rutted track leading from Corrie Hallie to Achneigie. At the watershed adjacent to Loch Coire Chaorachain, whose surface of bottle-green ice sparkled in the sunshine, we turned right along the Shenavall path to be confronted by the east face of Sail Liath. The usual grey quartzite screes, so conspicuous in summer, had now been transformed into a white wall of snow curving upwards into a fringe of cornices cresting the ridge. Sail Liath is the bulky south-east outlier of the great Wester Ross peak of An Teallach (The Forge) and it takes a first sight of this huge giant to bring home the enormity of the challenge it offers.

An Teallach dominates the Great Wilderness area between Loch Maree and Little Loch Broom, and its characteristic serrated summit ridge makes it an unmistakable landmark, even from far distant hills such as Ben Hope, Ben Wyvis, the Affric peaks and the Cuillin of Skye. When you descend the zigzag A832 from Braemore Junction, recent clear-felling of forestry provides a sudden and almost overwhelming view of An Teallach's towers and buttresses which will quicken your pulse as you park in the Corrie Hallie layby.

In winter conditions An Teallach is a formidable proposition for the hill walker — indeed, in any season it requires care and commitment. While the so-called 'tourist route' from

Dundonnell presents no technical difficulties to a determined and fit party, the full traverse of the rocky crest should be left strictly to the mountaineer with a head for heights and considerable scrambling or basic rock-climbing experience. Along with the Aonach Eagach in Glen Coe, Liathach's Am Fasarinen Pinnacles and Sgurr nan Fhir Dhuibhe on Beinn Eighe, An Teallach ranks as the most serious ridge traverse on the mainland of Britain. The mountain has a bad accident record, and escape from its jagged pinnacles in severe weather is not easy.

Full winter conditions can occur on An Teallach in any month between November and April, but early spring is the best time for a traverse because the snow tends to be well consolidated and the days are longer. A minimum of nine hours should be allowed for a winter traverse from Corrie Hallie to Dundonnell, with the expectation of even more time if the conditions are not ideal. Thus it is essential to carry full climbing equipment, headtorch, emergency rations and a bivvy bag.

The narrow, cairned path which branches off from the Land Rover track to Achneigie crosses the shoulder of Sail Liath at 1,400ft and then gradually descends to Shenavall bothy in Strath na Sealga. This path should be left at its highest point and the broad ridge of Sail Liath climbed to the summit cairn at 3,100ft. A magnificent view now unfolds: the Coigach and Assynt peaks, the distant outlines of Quinag and Foinaven, Beinn Dearg, Ben Wyvis, the Fannichs and, nearby, across Strath na Sealga, Beinn a' Chlaidheimh and the exquisite horseshoe of Beinn Dearg Mhor.

After a night of hard frost the snow on Sail Liath was perfect, firm kicks of the boot provided small but secure steps, while ice-axes could be thrust in to a satisfying depth.

We made good progress over the switchback section immediately to the west of Sail Liath to the sharp little summit above Cadha Gobhlach (the Forked Pass) and down to the bealach overlooking Coire Toll an Lochain, where a tiny blue tent was pitched. Several steep and loose gullies run up to the main ridge from the corrie and they provide popular winter climbs. The snow squeaked underfoot and the sun shone from a blue sky: this was Scottish hill-walking at its exhilarating best.

The crux of the An Teallach traverse now loomed ahead: the negotiation of the Corrag Bhuidhe pinnacles, reached by a stiff climb. In summer a timid party can avoid the pinnacles by taking a sandy traverse path that contours under the rocks on the south side, returning to the ridge at the pointed summit of Sgurr Fiona. In winter, however, I cannot recommend this alternative because the path is usually covered by a sweep of snow set at a high angle and secure belays are more difficult to find than on the rock pinnacles themselves; besides which there is the threat of avalanches.

The sandstone pinnacles of Corrag Bhuidhe are fissured and split and ledges abound. If sufficient time and care are taken to clear the holds, a perfectly safe route can be found. Approaching the first pinnacle, a 40ft nose of slightly overhanging rock blocks your way, but a traverse left and a steep little wall provide the key to the problem and enable you to reach the crest; from here there is a dizzy view straight down into the corrie. Some of the pinnacles stand 10 or 15ft high, either directly on the ridge or slightly detached from it. We found a greater sense of security by weaving in and out of the chimneys and cracks, but almost any route would have been possible; the pinnacles provide an infinite number of bouldering problems of all grades. One final massive block overhanging the abyss and known as Lord Berkeley's Seat, is passed before the short ascent to Sgurr Fiona. Protected by the rope we faced into the slope and carefully kicked deep steps in the now rather sugary snow on the steep descent from the Seat.

Sgurr Fiona is An Teallach's finest top, and once gained, the more technical difficulties of the traverse are over. The very rarely climbed, but hugely rewarding, north-west ridge of An Teallach joins the main ridge at Sgurr Fiona, which was raised to Munro status by the Brown/Donaldson revisions of 1980. With icy slopes plunging down in all directions we squeezed onto a ledge beside the tiny cairn, and belayed ourselves and our rucksacks to ice-axes thrust into the snow to enjoy a late lunch: this amazing perch can have few rivals outside the Cuillin.

An Teallach's principal summit, Bidein a' Ghlas Thuill, at 3,484ft, rises half a mile to the north across a low bealach. Great care should be taken on the descent from Sgurr Fiona to this curved bealach because the wind whips through it, glazing the snow to a hard sheen, and huge cliffs overhung with cornices fall away to the north, while on the south side, unrelentingly steep slopes descend 2,000ft to Loch na Sealga.

We plodded wearily up the broad and bouldery ridge to Bidein a' Ghlas Thuill, another fine, sharp summit with a narrow and gendarmed subsidiary ridge running east to Glas Mheall Liath. But it was a clear afternoon, and we were rewarded by an enchanting and unrivalled view of the indented coastline of Wester Ross, the waves racing over the sands of Gruinard Bay, Gruinard Island, the Summer Isles beyond Beinn Ghobhlach, the islands and skerries of Enard and Edrachillis Bay ringed by breakers, and Stoer Point lighthouse catching the sun. Looking back south we could appreciate fully the vast scale of the Corrag Bhuidhe buttresses as they plunged down towards the lochan.

It is best to keep to the ridge as it drops gradually down northwards from Bidein a' Ghlas Thuill. A line of low cairns leads on from the bealach under Glas Mheall Mor, traversing the main bulk of the mountain to reach the unnamed glen which runs down towards Dundonnell. This path follows the burn until it passes under fearsome-looking boiler-plate slabs on the north side of Glas Mheall Mor. At this point it crosses the burn and becomes rather boggy and tiresome on the final descent to Dundonnell Hotel: a warm and welcoming hostelry at all times of the year.

BROCKEN SPECTRE

If winter provides the sternest challenge on An Teallach, other times of the year can produce exceptional and unexpected conditions. Our ever-changing climate is so often the bugbear of British mountaineers: whole weeks washed out in the Cuillin, the Llanberis Pass wet and greasy for that long-planned summer weekend, a sudden thaw on Ben Nevis in March. It is little wonder that, given the chance, we head south to the blue skies and sun-warmed rocks. But very occasionally the quirks of our weather system can throw up a truly brilliant day, one that provides new levels of exhilaration.

A year or two ago in October, the West of Scotland suffered one of its worst autumn gales in memory. Walls of white water crashed over the low cliffs at Reiff; at Sandwood Bay giant waves swept through the dunes carrying boulders and tree trunks into the loch beyond; Foinaven, plastered white, rose majestically into a blue sky and we waded through knee deep snow to gain the summits of Cul Mor and Ben More Assynt. But then a thick and freezing blanket of cloud rolled in from the Atlantic, filling the glens and obscuring all the views. Swarthy East Europeans from the factory ships in Loch Broom thronged the streets of Ullapool, standing smoking in doorways with their collars turned up against the persistent drizzle.

Bored by inaction we donned our wet-weather gear and set off up the Achneigie track from Corrie Hallie bound for An Teallach. Half-way up Sail Liath, slipping on the greasy quartzite boulders while the mist swirled around, we contemplated cutting our losses and descending to Shenavall bothy to eat our sandwiches and watch the deer. Yet five minutes later a watery disc appeared in the sky together with a hint of blue haze, and almost immediately we broke out above the clouds into warm autumn sunshine.

It was shirt-sleeve order on the 3,100ft summit of Sail Liath, and we sat blinking beside the cairn while we opened the Thermos and took in the scene with incredulity. A layer of thick white mist lay over the Highlands to a height of about 2,500ft; only Munros and a few Corbetts emerged above the cotton wool, but every wrinkle and fissure of these was highlighted by the intense rays of the sun. As we gazed in wonderment round every point of the compass, all the favourites could be seen: Foinaven, Ben More Assynt, the Beinn Dearg hills, the flat table-top of Wyvis, the Fannichs, Cairngorms, Mullach Coire Mhic Fhearchair, the Affric peaks, Beinn a' Chlaidheimh, Torridon, the Cuillin and Flowerdale hills – all hove into view. Our pleasure in greeting them was like the joy of meeting long-lost friends.

Nearby, across Strath na Sealga, towered one of Scotland's classic Corbetts, Beinn Dearg Mhor, with layers of fleecy clouds drifting past its buttresses of black rock. Immediately to the west beckoned the pinnacles of Corrag

Bhuidhe, the spire of Sgurr Fiona and An Teallach's main summit, Bidein a' Ghlas Thuill, still streaked with snow. As we descended to Cadha Gobhlach we could see that the vast amphitheatre containing Loch Toll an Lochain was filled with white mist, and the sun projected our shadows in a giant and perfect 'brocken spectre'. Haloes of rainbow colours surrounded our heads, and when we waved, the spectre waved back in unison.

As the day progressed the mist gradually evaporated, leaving warm rock, and traversing the pinnacles on coarse-grained sandstone was sheer delight. We lingered long on Bidein a' Ghlas Thuill, reluctant to leave our perch with its taste of heaven. Most of the principal glens of the Western Highlands run east–west between high ridges, thus we could look over line upon line of hills until they merged into distant horizons. By four o'clock the cloud cover had completely cleared, revealing the sands of Gruinard Bay and Mellon Udrigle, and the Summer Islands floating on the bluest of seas.

Apart from Trisha, Cathy and myself, only three other people traversed An Teallach on that day of days. We greeted each other emotionally, with full hearts and lumps in our throats, not quite believing we were in the real world. Yet within 500ft of the top, on the Dundonnell path, the curtain came down abruptly as we re-entered the zone of freezing mist, hoar-covered moor grass and sheets of ice.

Dinner at the Dundonnell Hotel, where the staff sympathised with us over the assumed claggy weather, rounded off one of the most perfect mountain days that one can hope to enjoy in this life. Once again our beloved Highlands had rewarded us richly, and this roller-coaster of a day above the clouds will command for ever a special place in our memories.

THE NORTH-WEST RIDGE OF AN TEALLACH

Over the years I have enjoyed the classic traverse of An Teallach many times, and from the sharp summit cone of Sgurr Fiona I have often appraised, with increasing fascination, the long north-west ridge which runs away over Sgurr Creag an Eich and Sgurr Ruadh towards Gruinard Bay. When finally I came to climb An Teallach by this ridge I was overjoyed by the experience. It is a magnificent route: demanding, interesting, diverse, exposed, and as a viewpoint, it surpasses the classic traverse. Although it has no rock architecture to rival the Corrag Bhuidhe buttresses or Lord Berkeley's Seat, it can provide scrambling of peerless quality in an airy situation on the rocky nose of Sgurr Ruadh.

The north-west ridge meets the main backbone of An Teallach at the summit of Sgurr Fiona, whence alternative finishes are possible: thus you can either proceed south-east over the Corrag Bhuidhe buttresses to Sail Liath and descend to meet the Shenavall to Corrie Hallie path; or you can descend steeply northwards to the bealach under Bidein a' Ghlas Thuill, climb easily to the summit of this peak, and return via the shoulder of Glas Mheall Mor to Dundonnell. Nowadays the north-west ridge is my preferred route up An Teallach. The classic traverse syphons off the Munro baggers and the rock scramblers, and you are unlikely to see another bootprint, let alone another party on the ridge. It is truly a connoisseur's route.

Park at the layby just beyond Ardessie on the shore of Little Loch Broom. A sign on the roadside announces Ardessie Falls, and certainly an attractive little cascade foams over a step of black rock by the bridge: but what few people realise is that the Ardessie Falls proper lie a few hundred feet up the rough hillside. A twisting, boggy path leads to a number of deep gorges overhung with rowan, down which the burn thunders; in places, more open amphitheatres of rock display some impressive waterfalls and deep, mysterious pools where we have swum on hot summer afternoons.

After the top waterfall the path becomes indistinct, but the banks of the burn should be followed over the lip of moorland into a long, shallow glen under the steep and scree-covered east face of that huge plum pudding of a mountain, Sail Mhor. Straight ahead looms the rocky nose of Sgurr Ruadh, which looks black and forbidding. Cross the easternmost tributary of the Allt Airdessaidh and make straight for a conspicuous grassy gully running up to the summit of Sgurr Ruadh; there is much dead ground to cover, but the going gets easier as boulder-strewn sandstone slabs replace tussocks and hags.

The grassy gully is desperately steep, but could be ascended to gain Sgurr Ruadh; however, a far more enjoyable route is to walk round to the north side and scramble up the rock nose. There are plenty of good holds, terraces, gullies and ledges, and the situation is reminiscent of the direct ascent of Ben Mor Coigach from Culnacraig. As you climb higher, so an entrancing view unfolds. Lochans fill every hollow in the moorland, the light reflects on the broad expanse of sand in Gruinard Bay, while to the north behind the shoulder of Beinn Ghobhlach, the peaks of Coigach and Assynt roll away to the horizon: Ben Mor, Cul Mor, Suilven, Canisp, Quinag, Conival and Ben More Assynt.

Sgurr Ruadh has two summits, and on a recent occasion we sat on the southernmost top and ate our sandwiches in warm sunshine while banks of cloud drifted slowly down Loch na Sealga. A herd of wild goats emerged from behind some rocks and gazed at us inquisitively. Their coats were long and shaggy, the nannies' mottled grey and the young billies' black. This was one of several herds which roam throughout the Great Wilderness.

The ridge is quite narrow at first, then rises gradually to Pt 792m which looks across wild Coire Mor an Teallaich to Bidein a' Ghlas Thuill. In October this remote corrie echoes to the roaring of stags. Throughout this first section of ridge broken cliffs fall away steeply to Loch na Sealga while tors, slabs, boulders and other sandstone debris abound. It is exhilarating to follow the edge of the cliffs with uplifting views of everyone's favourite miniatures, Beinn Dearg Mhor and Bheag, seen to their best advantage across the Strath.

At Sgurr Creag an Eich the ridge narrows dramatically and swings north-east, giving unusual and impressive views of the south side of An Teallach's main ridge as it sawtooths over Corrag Bhuidhe. It gives good representation of the exposure on Corrag Bhuidhe, for here, on the south side, we see impossibly steep slopes plunging down 2,500ft to Strath na Sealga, which rival the vertical northern cliffs above Loch Toll an Lochain.

After a section of ridge which is razor-sharp, the rocks fan out and descend quite steeply to a lonely, windswept bealach under Sgurr Fiona. It is important to scramble up the rather ill-defined ridge ahead which leads straight to the sharp little summit of Sgurr Fiona; straying too far on either side will land you on horrid, steep, loose rocks. There is barely room to swing a cat on Sgurr Fiona's summit, let alone lie down for a nap. This is just as well because, however tempting a long rest in the sun might be, you are a long, long way from home, and cannot relax. The descent from Sgurr Fiona in any direction is tricky, and I have had to cut steps in sheets of ice as late as mid-May.

The north-west ridge is not necessarily an easy option, and you should allow the same amount of time as for the main traverse — that is, eight to ten hours. Likewise, take ice-axe and crampons if there is any chance of meeting snow or ice. Whichever route of descent you choose to take from Sgurr Fiona, you will probably end up at the Dundonnell Hotel. Who knows, you might even get a lift for the three miles back along the road to Ardessie to collect your car. That would be the icing on the cake to complete this truly splendid mountain day.

Winter Snow in Swaledale

After a week of gales and torrential rain the River Ouse in York had risen to ten feet above normal. Brown water was swirling under Lendal Bridge, the Clifton meadows were flooded, and waves were lapping the bar of the King's Arms. Then miraculously the wind dropped, the clouds rolled away and the temperature plummeted. From the top of Crayke Hill we could see the characteristic nose of Pen Hill above Leyburn and the massive whaleback of Great Whernside gleaming white in the sharp air. Some real winter conditions at last, after months of clag and depressing talk of global warming.

The decision was easy: with the AA reporting Hartside blocked and the A66 passable only with care, the deepest snow was in the north-west and that meant Swaledale. Swaledale: the name alone sends the pulse racing for it is the grandest, wildest and loneliest of the great Yorkshire dales. Its gateway is Richmond, an historic town with tiers of ancient houses rising above the river, dominated by the castle with its magnificent Norman keep. The railway never penetrated Swaledale, and the bustle of the lead-mining era has passed on, leaving relics and derelict workings in some of the gills. Sheep farming, holiday cottages and retirement homes now characterise the dale, and the stone-built villages of Reeth, Low Row, Gunnerside, Muker, Thwaite and Keld are as tranquil and beautiful as any in England.

A small group of walkers were zipping up their snow

gaiters at Thwaite, before taking the broad Pennine Way track up Great Shunner Fell. A few farmers were taking bales of hay to huddled groups of sheep on the snowy wastes; and plumes of wood smoke rose from cottage chimneys straight up into the clear blue sky, spreading a delicious aroma through the still air; otherwise the dale was deserted. Trisha and I crunched through frozen snow under a stand of beech trees overlooking Wain Wath Force, whose peaty waters were partly frozen. The tributary streams were a mass of tinkling icicles, while smooth bulges of green ice had spread over the banks.

Raven Seat farm in Whitsun Dale stands at the focal point of the upper Swaledale horseshoe and is one of the most isolated farms in Yorkshire. The brilliant morning sun reflected from the deep mantle of snow on the semi-circle of high fells, the intensity of the light dazzling our eyes: Lovely Seat, Great Shunner Fell, High Seat, Robert's Seat and Rogan's Seat, names derived from the Norse *saetr*, meaning 'summer pasture farm'. The complete horseshoe walk extending as far west as Mallerstang Edge and Nine Standards Rigg is just as varied and wild, and almost as challenging, as the notorious Derwent Watershed Walk.

We stopped to check the map, and were nuzzled by a small flock of gentle Swaledale sheep. In summer there is a path of sorts leading north-east from Raven Seat over the rough fells to Tan Hill, but today we were in a white world, save for the gritstone outcrops of Low Whitsundale Edge, a stand of skeleton trees and the sprinkling of solid stone barns which so typify the lower Swaledale fells. Walking was exhausting work. The surface crust broke at almost every step, plunging our boots into deep powder snow and raising a mist of microscopic crystals which changed the sunbeams to rainbows. Hollows and gills had drifted over, and at times we fell headlong into the icing sugar from which recovery was difficult. However, the gaunt building on the skyline beckoned: the Tan Hill Inn, at 1,732ft the highest pub in England.

With two fires burning, the inn was a haven of warmth and hospitality. Although this legendary inn is solid and unpretentious, with stone walls a yard thick, it has been spoilt by the fitting of ugly UPVC windows and doors which were featured in a TV advertising campaign. The inn was built for drovers, packmen and miners who worked shallow seams of coal on the surrounding moors for hundreds of years. The miners lived in primitive buildings called shops, bringing a week's food and returning to their families down the dale on Sundays. The mines have long since been abandoned, but the area is still pitted with shafts.

Tan Hill Inn boasts a stirring history, and it oozes character from every seam. The modest snows of our sparkling day were put into perspective by vivid photographs of winter blizzards piling drifts half-way to the eaves. The inn is an important staging post on the Pennine Way (120 miles from Edale, 130 miles from Kirk Yetholm), and it is the starting point for one of Britain's greatest challenge walks, the Tan–Cat, which links Tan Hill with the Cat and Fiddle, the two highest inns in the land.

It is not hard to imagine the scene in 1953 when a small party from the Rucksack Club left Tan Hill for the 120-mile, 20,000ft of ascent, marathon walk. It was completed by three of the party: Ted Courtenay, Vin Desmond and Frank Williamson. Twenty-six years later the record for the Tan–Cat was held by John Richardson at thirty-seven hours, but this was soon broken by an astonishing margin of five hours, by Mike Cudahy. Six years later Mike reduced the record still further to twenty-nine hours and eleven minutes.

When we emerged from the bar, the slanting rays of the afternoon sun were lighting up Mickle Fell, rising hugely beyond Stainmore. This superb hill, which is on Ministry of Defence controlled land, was the highest in Yorkshire before the Maude Commission boundary changes placed it firmly in County Durham. Deep snow completely covered the Pennine Way track running east of West Stone Dale to Keld, and after floundering for half an hour, we swallowed our pride and sought the road. The sun set quickly, and in the shadows, the frost nipped our faces. An energetic young farmer was out on his tractor, spreading muck on the pure white snow of the meadows, but most dale dwellers had pulled up their chairs and were stoking their fires with logs. Reluctantly we left this unique corner of upland Britain and headed home, the mournful eyes of the sheep reflecting in the car's headlights.

STORIES AND LEGENDS

*'His record of plunging into 729 icy tarns will probably
never be equalled.'*

Munro and the Baggers

The rain sweeps in curtains across the bleak expanse of Rannoch Moor, the largest and most inhospitable tract of saturated peat in Britain. The grey day dawns to show ragged clouds clinging to the black cliffs of Glencoe, and the burns are ribbons of white foam. Climbers, thankful perhaps that the weather has blotted out all hopes of another epic on the greasy slabs of Glen Etive, lazily stretch a hand out of their down sleeping bags to light the stove. Motorists swishing by on the A82 turn up the heater another notch and switch the wipers to double speed. Snug with their creature comforts they can afford to spare a thought for the poor beggar plodding, head down, through the heather on his way towards the hills of the Black Mount.

But our lonely soul needs no sympathy: he is bound for a new Munro, and a bright fire burns within him, sustaining him over the miles of peat hag and boulder slopes. This fire was first kindled by Sir Hugh Munro in 1891. The *Scottish Mountaineering Club Journal* of that year carried a list of the 3,000ft mountains in Scotland, a list prepared by Munro after years of poring over maps and careful research in the field with an expensive aneroid. It contained 538 tops and 283 separate mountains, but this was later revised by Sir Hugh to 543 tops and 276 separate mountains. At once the Munros provided a framework for hill walkers in Scotland, and the highly addictive pursuit of 'Munro-bagging' began.

Contrary to popular belief Munro himself never completed

the ascent of all the mountains on his list. He failed by just three: the Inaccessible Pinnacle of Sgurr Dearg (Munro was no rock climber), and Carn Ealar and Carn Cloich-mhuillin in the Cairngorms, which he was saving for his final peak to be followed by a party at his home at Lindertis in Fife. Sadly he died of pneumonia in 1918 while operating a canteen for French troops at Tarascon in France.

The first Munroist was the Reverend A.E. Robertson who made history in September 1901 when he climbed Meall Dearg on the Aonach Eagach ridge. Meall Dearg was Robertson's final Munro, and he kissed the cairn first and then his wife. Since 1901 the number of Munroists has increased rapidly, and the rise is now exponential. For example I was the 101st Munroist in 1972, and the thousandth completed in 1991; the latest figure that I have – at the end of 1998 – is 2000. In my active Munro-climbing years it was unusual to meet a fellow walker on a remote hill outside the summer season, and if you did, he or she was sure to be on the same pilgrimage. I still remember with satisfaction the raw Easter day when I reached the summit cairn of Spidean Mialach, having traversed the ridge from Gleouraich, at the very same moment as another walker who had approached from Quoich dam to the south. We nodded to each other: 'One ninety-eight,' he said. 'Two thirty-five,' I replied, and we turned away and continued our respective journeys, me with a slight spring in my step and he with stooped shoulders.

Who was this man Munro, in whose footsteps we tread? Does he deserve the devotion and respect of his followers? Would he approve of our obsessional strivings to reach mere topographical points in the Scottish Highlands? Sir Hugh was a major contributor to the early editions of the *Scottish Mountaineering Club Journal*, and from his writings and from the many appreciations of him following his death, I can state categorically that the answer to these questions is 'Yes'.

Sir Hugh was associated with the SMC from its foundation, and he almost never failed to attend a club meet or the annual dinner. He said on his election to President in 1894 that he held the honour in higher esteem than if he had been made Prime Minister of Great Britain. It is worth taking a few examples from his writings to illustrate his single-minded devotion to the remote hills – though before doing so we should appreciate the very different character of the Highlands in Munro's time.

The big estates and deer forests were thriving, and Sir Hugh knew many of the lairds personally; thus it was always possible for him to obtain accommodation in the shooting lodges and bothies that abounded. Larachantivore in Strath na Sealga was inhabited, as was the old lodge of Benula at Luib-na-damph west of Loch Mullardoch; the latter was a two-storey house served by a carriageway from Invercannich. Now, however, both road and lodge are under the raised water of the loch, and the area is remote indeed. In Munro's time the head keeper would send a man as a guide for parties traversing Mam Soul and Carn Eige, and he would supply ponies. Walkers could stay with Mrs Scott at Alltbeath cottage in Glen Affric, and then cross the hills to Mrs Finlayson's at Benula Lodge.

Sir Hugh was often transported by his man in a 'dogcart' to the base of the mountains. Later he bought one of the first motor cars, and the roads were sufficiently good for him to drive around, even to places as remote as Kinlochhourn.

Hotels were comparatively cheap. In 1904 complete board, including packed lunch, afternoon tea and bath was 5s 6d at Kingshouse Hotel, and 8s at the Sligachan Hotel on Skye. But, as we shall see, Munro was not often pampered.

January 1890. Munro was alone on the Carn Liath range in deep powder snow which was raised in columns 100ft high by the wind. The snow penetrated everything, filling his pockets and drifting between his shirt and waistcoat where it melted and froze into a solid wedge of ice. Back home they had to scrape him down with a knife to get the frozen snow off.

March 1890. A solo walk by Munro from Dalwhinnie. Crossing the burns on the ice he traversed the Aonach Beag, Beinn Eibhinn ridge and was back in Dalwhinnie after a four-teen-hour day in deep snow all the time. The following day he climbed Beinn Bheoil and Ben Alder in a blizzard, descending via Benalder cottage to Loch Rannochside where he obtained lodgings.

February 1892. Munro left Lynwilg Inn at 8.45am, much regretting the late start. He ascended Cairn Gorm and Ben Macdui in dense freezing mist. A navigational error led him to descend towards Loch Avon instead of Loch Etchachan. It was now after sunset, but he retraced his steps and made another attempt to find the correct route – this ended above cliffs. Finally, in darkness, he reached Derry Lodge where he was entertained by the head stalker and his wife. Munro blamed the late start for his trouble, but his fitness and reserves gave him a good margin of safety.

May 1898. Munro wrote. 'Who has not regretted the hour lost in the morning?' Accordingly he set out in the after-noon and cycled to Spital of Glenshee from Lindertis. He started walking at 11pm, and in poor weather knocked off six big mountains, returning home at 8pm the following evening.

March 1990. While staying at the Aultguish Inn, Ross-shire, Munro had two disastrous days which tarnished his reputation. On the first day he left the inn after lunch for Am Faochagach, but the snow needed a lot of step-cutting, and coming down Strath Vaich he was unable to cross a stream and had to detour to a keeper's house. He then mounted a horse, but still arrived back at the inn after midnight.

A day later, in the company of H.G. Lawson, he climbed Liath Mhor Fannaich, Sgurr Mor, Sgurr nan Clach Geala and Sgurr nan Each. While they were descending northwards towards Loch a' Bhraoin they had difficulty fording a stream and became benighted. For light they had precisely three matches: the first showed the map to be folded upside-down, the second blew out, and the third gave them insufficient information. Freezing cold, they blundered about all night, finally reaching the road at 7am to find Munro's driver still waiting with a fire alight and hot cocoa ready.

March 1904. Munro liked to arrive at SMC meets a day early to have a solitary day getting the feel of the hills and assessing the conditions. Before the 1904 Easter meet he cycled from Aviemore to Loch Einich and climbed Sron na Lairig in a ferocious blizzard, exceeding anything he had ever experienced. Watchers on the shore of Loch an Eilein timed the spray being blown from one end of the loch to the other at 100mph.

July 1908. Munro and W. Garden made a night ascent of An Sgarsoch. They walked up Glen Tilt to the Memorial Bridge in heavy rain, finding the rivers Tilt and Tarf in high flood. They reached An Sgarsoch's cairn at 1.05am in thick mist, but their matches were wet and they could read neither map nor compass. Much to Munro's distress, for he had not climbed it, they abandoned Carn Ealar, and knowing that the wind was from the north, were able to descend to the Geldie. The bridge at Geldie Lodge had been swept away and they had to make a long detour to cross the bridge at the junction of the Tarf and Bynack. They reached Linn of Dee at 8.10am.

We can see from Munro's writings that his days were always long, and that he hated to waste a minute of them. He would rather set out for the hills late at night after dinner, than risk missing an hour of daylight because of a late start in the morning.

The Reverend A.E. Robertson, the first Munroist, had a very different, more relaxed approach to the hills than Sir Hugh. Robertson was a gentleman climber who enjoyed his position in society, and he demanded the best in everything. He bought his ice-axe from Simond, his aneroid from Lord Kelvin, his compass from White's and his boots from James Wright of Edinburgh. Apart from these essential items of equipment he travelled light, knowing that emergency accommodation was never very far away. For bad weather he used a heavy German Wettermantel cape which went everywhere with him. He was a talented craftsman, and made the table for the Charles Inglis-Clarke Memorial Hut under Ben Nevis.

At the turn of the century, the leisured life and social status of gentlemen of the cloth gave them opportunities to take long holidays in the hills. Robertson's motivation seems to have come more from the physical satisfaction gained from the ascents than from any feeling of 'nearer my God to thee', because he frequently climbed on Sundays, defying local opinion against exertions of any kind on the Sabbath. His logbooks never mentioned wildlife or natural history, but had much to say about the contents of his lunchbox – and he was never averse to enjoying the good things of life. He writes, 'We found Ben Doran an awful grind, but we lay on the snow for an hour on the summit, basking and smoking our pipes and revelling in the view. The descent provided us with a 2,000ft glissade.'

Robertson managed to arrange three-month holidays in both 1898 and 1899, during which time he polished off nearly 150 Munros, using a bicycle to reach inaccessible places such as the west end of Loch Mullardoch, Monar Lodge in Glen Strathfarrar and Kinlochquoich. He was an enthusiastic member of the Cyclists Touring Club: he and his second wife, Winifred, used a tandem to travel around the Highlands. Winifred was also a keen hill walker who climbed over 200 Munros.

Like Munro, he used the shelter provided by the keepers' and stalkers' cottages, although he was more discerning. After Ladhar Bheinn he intended spending the night at Skiary, but was so put off by the dirty room and the lack of beer or whisky that he went on to Kinlochhourn. However, he records pleasant hospitality with keepers at Steall, Glen Dessarry, Carnoch and Kinlochquoich. He writes, 'Make me of the shepherd's houses for the people in the glen are not spoilt by the vulgar products of modern civilisation and are kind, courteous and hospitable. In all my wanderings I have never been refused a night's shelter in a keeper's house or shepherd's shieling.'

Robertson had a wry sense of humour; for instance, on one expedition he hired a trap to Loch Ericht Lodge. Beside the Culra burn he met a party of men supposed to be mending the path, but all fast asleep. 'I gave a shout, and how they jumped – they thought I was Sir John Ramsden the laird who was half expected up that day.'

Since their publication in 1891 Munro's Tables have been chopped and changed and debated with considerable heat. It is a topic on which everyone has strong feelings, and it is worth taking a brief look at their history. Sir Hugh's first list consisted of 283 separate mountains, but a few years later the Ordnance Survey produced revised 6in maps for Scotland, and these threw up certain discrepancies. Sir Hugh started a revision of his lists, but died before he could complete the task. What constituted a distinct and separate mountain was arrived at after careful consideration by Munro, but he never published his criteria.

In 1921 a new list of 276 mountains was published by the SMC, based on research carried out by J.R. Young, A.W. Peacock and others on Sir Hugh's notes and card index. Still not satisfied, the SMC set up a committee in 1933 to advise on Munro's Tables and they reported that The Tables was too much of an historical document to alter, and the only changes that should be made to the 1921 list should be corrections of proved errors. Thus more accurate surveying elevated four more mountains and demoted one, making 279 in all. But in 1981 the SMC blessed further revisions suggested by Brown and Donaldson, which promoted four more mountains and demoted seven, leaving a total of 276. Since 1981, one further peak has been shown to exceed 3,000ft, making 277.

The most recent revision was carried out in 1997. This was based not on resurveys, but on what Sir Hugh might have adopted. Ironically Sgor an Iubhair, which was promoted in 1981, has now been demoted. When I broke the news of Sgor an Iubhair to a couple of friends they gnashed their teeth in rage because they could still remember their night-mare foray from Kinlochleven just to bag the peak on a week-end of gales and torrential rain. Now they are told that all that effort was wasted.

The problem of having a subjective list has been realised for a long time, and many other categories of mountain have been proposed. Lists based on definitive measurements should do away with any arguments, but since mountain heights can be defined in feet or metres and the necessary drop on all sides to give separate mountain status is debatable, we still have a plethora of different classifications. Hill baggers can choose from the following:

Munros 284 mountains in Scotland over 3,000ft. Chosen at the whim of the SMC.
Corbetts 221 mountains in Scotland between 2,500 and 3,000ft with a drop of 500ft on all sides.
Murdos 444 mountains in Scotland over 3,000ft with a 100ft drop on all sides.
Donalds This classification is now split in two.
Old Donalds 87 mountains in the Scottish Lowlands that exceed 2,000ft with a 100ft drop on all sides. An historic but unfashionable list.
New Donalds 118 mountains in Scotland south of the Highland boundary fault that exceed 2,000ft with a drop of 100ft all round.
Grahams 224 mountains in Scotland between the heights of 2,000 and 2,499ft with a drop of at least 500ft all round.
Hewitts 525 mountains in England, Wales and Ireland over 2,000ft with a 100ft drop on all sides.
Nuttalls 433 mountains in England and Wales over 2,000ft with a 50ft drop on all sides. John and Anne Nuttall

personally surveyed each hill on the list using equipment approved by the OS.

Marilyns Named after Marilyn Munro. The 1,551 hills of Britain that, irrespective of height, have a 500ft fall on all sides.

What should the aspiring hill-bagger go for? The Munros still command easily the highest status, followed by the Corbetts, but the Marilyns are catching up fast. However, before you grab your boots and a copy of Marilyn's Tables you should appreciate that to complete them all you will have to climb Stac Lee and several other ferocious rock pinnacles in the St Kilda group. Apart from the difficulty of obtaining permission, the resulting disturbance of several thousand breeding gannets should not take precedence over inflating your ego. Yet aspiring Marilyn-baggers can start off easily enough: how about a round of golf on the Cliffe Hill course outside Lewes in Sussex, followed by an opera at neighbouring Glyndebourne? Such a day will give you your first Marilyn – just 1,550 to go!

If you are really bitten by the Munro/Marilyn/Nuttall bug there can be no peace; you could never climb everything in a single lifetime. The task reminds me of Sisyphus of Corinth who was condemned by the Gods to roll a stone up a hill, but every time he got near the summit the stone rolled back down again. To return to the Munros: these are achievable by anyone with enough determination. To the uninitiated, Munro-bagging must seem a very unrewarding pastime. Do those rare days of crisp snow and panoramic views, or those brief moments of satisfaction when another tick is placed in Munro's Tables, make up for the cold, the wet and the clinging mists? Of course they do, many times over.

Every Munroist develops a deep love of the Highlands.

He or she has explored their remotest glens, has crossed their highest plateaus, has scrambled along their rockiest crests. From Ben Hope to Ben Lomond and from Mount Keen to Mull, he has toiled up slopes of heather and scree and has stridden across broad ridges with a glint in his eye and a delight that ever increases with experience. The Munroist soon discovers the Highlands to be a fascinating environment. I get a kick whenever I see eagles, ptarmigan, snow bunting, foxes, mountain hares and deer. The smell of bog myrtle and heather, and the startling colours of orchids, saxifrages, snow gentians and lichens make me realise how lucky I am to be a Munroist. Where the Highlands are concerned I am an unashamed romantic.

Martin Moran, who completed a non-stop traverse of all the Munros over the winter of 1984–85, is a shining example of non-whingeing in adversity – though even he complains occasionally. After an appalling day on Ben Lui he wrote, 'Your nylon leggings sag to the knees, sloshing audibly at every pace. Numb, white knuckles are clenched and curled into the shelter of cagoule sleeves. A warm puddle slops about in your boots, and icy raindrops somehow penetrate your Goretex armoury to trickle down the neck and back. Then you stop and the wet chill attacks, reducing you to a shivering wreck in half an hour.'

We have all stood by the car after such a day, hands too cold to unlock the door, fumbling with zips and buttons, exposed skin white and wrinkled, the growing pile of sodden clothing resembling washing removed from a machine with the spin-dry function out of operation.

Sir Hugh Munro has a lot to answer for; yet the trials and tribulations of such a day are all forgotten when the magic tick is placed against another hill.

Running the Munros

In 1990 Hugh Symonds, the English fell-running champion, completed the Munros without using mechanical transport in just sixty-seven days, on a sponsored run for Intermediate Technology.

Hugh is a mathematics teacher at Sedbergh School which sits beside the river Rawthey in the shadow of the Howgill Hills in Cumbria. Winder, the southernmost Howgill, rises straight up behind the town and its name appears in the Sedbergh School song. No wonder the Howgills have inspired generations of schoolboys and their teachers to enjoy exploration and endeavour throughout the world: Freddie Spencer-Chapman, war hero and conqueror of Chomolhari; Robert Swan, the intrepid adventurer to the Arctic and Antarctic; and recently, Hugh Symonds, fell runner extraordinary, who makes a habit of running up Winder before breakfast every day for sheer exuberance.

In 1990 Sedbergh School granted Hugh a sabbatical term, and as a complete change from teaching, he decided to learn more about the hills of Scotland by attempting to run round all the Munros. When Hugh left for Ben Hope in April, he had set himself a target of one hundred days to climb the 277 Scottish Munros, the four Lakeland 3,000s and the fifteen Welsh 3,000s. In early September, on a golden late summer's day, I drove through Wensleydale and Garsdale to Sedbergh to talk to Hugh and to hear how the mountain run had gone. Hugh, his wife Pauline and their three children were still brimming over with excitement at their amazing achievement. Hugh took sixty-seven days to complete the Munros, running all the way between the mountains, rowing across to Skye for the Cuillin, and sailing to Mull for Ben

More. He finished the 296 3,000ft mountains on the mainland of Britain in eighty-three days, and still feeling strong, ran straight down from Snowdon to Holyhead, caught the night ferry and then ran round the Irish 3,000s, finishing on Brandon Mountain just ninety-seven days after leaving for Ben Hope.

Pauline was the sheet anchor of the entire run. Driving a motor caravan, she never once failed to arrive at the rendezvous on time with dry clothes and a substantial meal ready. She dealt with the liaison with the support runners and the media, besides shopping and the regular classes which had to be given to their children, a condition stipulated by the local authority for allowing them to miss a term's formal education.

April had left the north-west Highlands with a covering of fresh snow which necessitated the use of an ice-axe together with studded running shoes, particularly on An Teallach, a mountain which impressed Hugh more than any other outside the Cuillin. On the Fannichs, the day's programme had to be cut short when a blizzard blasted a contact lens out of his eyes. Further south, on that superb mountain Sgurr nan Ceathreamhnan, Hugh experienced the terrifying phenomenon of St Elmo's Fire during a sudden storm which deposited 6in of snow on the ridges. St Elmo's is the glow produced by the discharge of atmospheric electricity on rocks, accompanied by crackling and fizzing. That day he traversed the entire Affric Ridge from Mullardoch dam to Dorusduain, including the outlier A' Ghlas-bheinn, which defeated his pacemakers.

Two days later, having climbed the seven Munros of the South Cluanie ridge, followed by Sgurr na Sgine and the Saddle, he was looking forward to a decent night's sleep when a message came through that slack tide, necessary for the rowing boat crossing to Skye, was at 6.45am the next day, rather than 1pm as planned. Hugh had to continue running late into the night in order to reach the slipway at Glenelg in time.

But Skye was a revelation to Hugh, and the weather was kind. He left the road near Elgol, and in one fifteen-hour day, ran through Camasunary, across the 'bad step' to Coruisk and Gars Bheinn, and then traversed the main ridge to Sgurr nan Gillean before descending to Sligachan for the night. Because he was climbing only the Munros he was able to by-pass the tricky Thearlaich-Dubh Gap, Bidein Druim nan Ramh and the Bhasteir Tooth. The following day he described as one of his happiest as he unwound from the Cuillin traverse, gently jogging over Blaven to Kylerhea, thence a smooth crossing of the narrows in his rowing boat to reach Glenelg.

One of the reasons why Hugh's enthusiasm for the Highlands remained undiluted, even after sixty-seven arduous days, was because he strove to minimise his use of roads, although this was not always pragmatic. Thus he would strike straight for the objective, even if it meant crossing trackless wastes of rugged terrain, and the descent and reascent of sub-sidiary glens. For example, Hugh approached Ben More Assynt from the north, traversing some of the wildest country in Britain, rather than taking the trade route from Inchnadamph. These pure routes introduced him to the loneliest and loveliest nooks and crannies in the Highlands, and he was rarely too exhausted to appreciate them.

Throughout the summer Hugh was free from injury and his speed exceeded expectations. Gradually he was getting ahead of schedule, particularly when he moved east to the Grampians. This meant, however, that every night maps had to be spread out and new plans made for the next day. Hugh kept up his energy with large meals. In addition to piled-up platefuls of potatoes, pasta and rice, he demolished twenty-four Christmas puddings in ninety-seven days.

Late July saw Hugh and his family enjoying the Irish hills, particularly those in Co Kerry; like Hamish Brown, they were captivated by Brandon Mountain, the final peak of all. Appropriately they will call the Dales barn they are converting into a home, 'Brandon Cottage'.

He Who Hesitates is Lost

It was late November in 1990 and we were in Lakeland enjoying the sharp ridge over Rough Crag and Long Stile, which rises from the head of Haweswater to the summit of High Street. Above Caspel Gate the grass was thickly covered with hoar frost, and we startled a flock of snow bunting which skittered away like fallen leaves in the wind, disappearing into the depths of Riggindale. Caspel Gate tarn was fringed with ice, and in the combes below, the keen wind was ruffling the surface of Blea Water and Small Water. Well muffled against the cold, Trisha and I mused in wonderment on the two legendary characters who had swum in every tarn in Lakeland – and thus it was that a month later I spent an enthralling morning talking to Colin Dodgson in his beautiful house above Grasmere. He built the house himself, stone by stone; through its large picture window we enjoyed fleeting glimpses of the huge bulk of Sargeant Man as storm clouds raced down the dale.

Colin was then eighty years old, having spent his working life running a shop and café in Grasmere. His great friend was Tim Tyson, the local shoemaker, and together they would walk in the hills on Sundays, their only day off work. Tarns became suitable objectives for these Sunday outings, but soon what started as a mere diversion, became an obsession. Their explorations of every nook and cranny in Lakeland were thorough, in addition they scrutinised large-scale maps, and they sought advice from all quarters – and so the list of tarns grew longer and longer. Regularly every Sunday, in all seasons, they plunged into the icy, lonely tarns. Finally, when they could find no more, Colin's logbook recorded a total of 463 tarns, though a year or two later this was raised to 534 tarns and 195 pools. The distinction between 'tarn' and 'pool' should be regarded in the same light as that between Munro 'separate mountain' and 'top', and is best left ill-defined.

'But didn't you perish with cold?' I stuttered in amazement, 'particularly when you had to break the ice?' 'Oh no,' replied Colin with a smile; 'The secret was not to hesitate but to strip quickly, dive in, jump out, dry off and get dressed immediately. It did no harm to Tim, either. He lived to eighty-three, and swam in hundreds of icy tarns when he was over seventy.' But if you think swimming in 729 different tarns, and building your own house, is enough for one lifetime, you will gasp at Colin's other achievements. In 1951 he became the ninth person to climb all the Munros and tops. The majority of his ascents were between October and March when he could more easily leave his business interests; many ascents were with Tim Tyson.

Colin started his love affair with Scotland (he is a proud member of the SMC) in 1931. That year he cycled to Carlisle and put his bike on the train for Glasgow: from there he cycled to Fort William and on to Aviemore, climbing the Scottish 4,000ers on the way. Not being able to afford the fare home, he cycled back to Grasmere. A year later he visited the far north-west with his girl friend, on a tandem.

In 1933 Colin bought an Austin Seven which was extremely useful in getting up the remote glens. For example, in 1933 Loch Mullardoch had not been dammed and the water level raised and he could drive along the excellent track on the north shore to obtain accommodation at Ben Ula

Lodge under Beinn Fhionnaidh. Colin would obtain prior permission from landowners and this enabled him to drive into the heart of the hills to such places as Bruar Lodge, Derry Lodge and Forest Lodge. An Austin Ten followed; in those days he was able to enjoy traffic-free roads. One day he left Grasmere at 5am, and was still able to climb Ben Stack (near Laxford Bridge, Sutherland) in the last rays of the evening sun.

Colin and Tim shunned backpacking, preferring to travel light and return to base by evening. This meant long days in the hills, and indeed, there was one notable holiday in Kintail when they never saw their tent in daylight, because they always left before dawn and returned after nightfall. In general they disregarded the weather, and Colin ruefully conceded that their ex-army gas capes were hopelessly inadequate; overtrousers were unknown, and when it rained they just accepted that they would get wet. They never wore crampons, although Colin admitted they would often have been useful in saving hours of step cutting. At the height of his Munro-climbing activities, Colin took a weekend off to complete the classic Lakeland marathon circuit established by Dr Wakefield and extended by Eustace Thomas. This was well before the foundation of the forty-two-peak Bob Graham Club in 1971.

Colin was a close friend of the exceptional Scottish walker and climber, Willie Docharty, who presented him with copies of his privately published books listing all the 2,500–3,000ft mountains and (later) the 2,000–2,500ft mountains. Having completed the Munros, Colin set to work on Docharty's daunting lists: 590 mountains on the first list, and 683 on the second. It goes without saying that the English and Welsh 2,000ft peaks followed. Sadly, Tim Tyson died in 1967, but Colin pressed on alone; even when he was over seventy years old he could manage fifteen-hour days in the hills. He never had an accident.

Colin's last 2,000ft peak was Beinn a' Chearcaill above Loch Maree, which he remembered gave outstanding views into Coire Mhic Fhearchair on Beinn Eighe. He rated the 2,000–2,500 footers just as enjoyable as the Munros, although his three favourite peaks are An Teallach, Liathach and Suilven. He recalled with joy, a family of foxes playing on the summit of Foinaven.

Never expert rock climbers, Colin and Tim approached the Inaccessible Pinnacle of Sgurr Dearg with some trepidation. Colin led up the long east ridge, but somehow Tim lost the end of the rope and Colin arrived at the summit with 100ft of loose rope trailing behind. He was forced to descend solo, too. When I visited him he was still active in the hills, and included in his plans for his eighty-first year were ascents of Ben Nevis, Scafell Pike and Snowdon for the umpteenth time. His legs were as sound as ever, which tends to undermine the theory that constant physical activity in the cold and wet leads to arthritis in later life. He has never used walking poles.

Surrounded by friends, a member of four different Lake District choirs, and kept busy by a large garden, Colin still leads a full and active life. He derives much satisfaction from the knowledge that his record of plunging into 729 icy tarns will probably never be equalled!

Tapping George

In the 1870s the Midland Railway Company, anxious to have their own link to Scotland, staked all on the construction of the Settle-to-Carlisle line. It was a mammoth task, for the high Pennines were unforgiving: thousands of tons of gravel would sink without trace into the black peat bogs, embankments would be swept away by floods, and construction sites would be devastated by storms.

The most difficult section of all was at Ribblehead where the line had to cross an exposed plateau at a height of over 1,000ft before reaching the formidable obstacle of Blea Moor. The notoriously steep incline from Horton-in-Ribblesdale to Blea Moor is known to this day as the Long Drag because double-headed steam locomotives had to be used to pull the heavy freight trains. The engineers decided to build a viaduct across Ribblehead and to tunnel through Blea Moor. The viaduct was to have twenty-four arches, while the tunnel would be 2,600 yards long.

A huge shanty town grew up at Batty Moss, Ribblehead, to accommodate thousands of navvies from all over the British Isles. Life was tough and brutal, with fights, hard drinking and womanising, while outbreaks of smallpox ravaged the workforce. A forest of gravestones in the tiny churchyard at Chapel-le-Dale bears witness to the mortality rate. George was one of many skilled stone masons working on the massive tiers, up to 165ft in height, which support the arches of the viaduct. By January 1874 the seventh tier from the north end was nearing completion, and was ready to have its hollow inside filled with rubble, when a sudden gust of wind caused George to lose his footing and plunge into the abyss.

Night was falling and the shrieking of the gale drowned George's cries. Life was cheap on construction sites in Victorian England, and his fellow workers, assuming him to be dead, mumbled a prayer and returned to their shacks. George, injured and helpless, tapped all night with his hammer in a desperate attempt to alert a rescue team, but to no avail. Rubble was tipped into the tier the next morning, entombing George for ever.

Many Three Peaks walkers, returning at dusk to Ribblehead, listen with horror to Tapping George as they pass under the seventh arch of the viaduct. Tap, tap, tap goes the hammer. The walkers shudder with fear, quicken their step, and hasten to the cheerful bar at the Station Inn for a pint. As mists roll down to Ribblehead from Whernside, or when darkness descends and the wind howls through the arches at one of the loneliest places in England, George still taps away inside his tomb. He has waited over one hundred years for release, but his pleas have gone unanswered.

Under
the Coroner's Shadow

Ireturned home from the Harrogate Trade Fair, mind reeling from the impact of acres of superb outdoor clothing and climbing equipment. That night, however, perhaps as a result of over-stimulation, I lay tossing and turning, plagued by a nightmare. Its scene is a hut somewhere in the Lake District, where a dozen school children are spending an adventure weekend supervised by three adults: Bob, Mike and Liz. It is late March, and there is still some winter snow on the tops.

At eight o'clock Mike struggles out of his sleeping bag and, holding his head, staggers to the front door. He has drunk far too much beer the previous night and is bursting for a pee. Blinking in the bright sunlight, he shakes his head in disbelief that it is not raining and bellows, 'Wakey, wakey, rise and shine!' An hour later breakfast is well under way. Burnt porridge is being slopped into bowls laid out on the trestle table, while sausages are rapidly charring in the oven which has inadvertently been turned to maximum.

Bob is the proud possessor of a Mountain Walking Leaders Certificate, and has recently attended a training week for the winter certificate at Glenmore Lodge; he is overall leader of the party and is laying down the law: 'Today we shall attempt to climb Helvellyn. This will be a tough proposition and we must be prepared for every eventuality. I want all of you to pack ice-axe, crampons, sleeping bag, exposure bag, spare jersey, spare socks, spare laces, two pairs of gloves, balaclava helmet, snow goggles, climbing harness with kara-biner, safety helmet, anorak, over-trousers, lunch pack, water bottle, emergency rations, first-aid kit, torch, whistle, compass, map and route card. One rope, one deadman and one shovel for digging snow holes will be carried between four. You can't be too careful in the unpredictable and often vicious British climate.'

One of the boys, Peter, is sent a mile down the road to the nearest telephone box with 10p and instructions to phone Windermere 5151 for the latest Lakeland weather forecast. Four girls are instructed to make the sandwiches for lunch, and the remainder of the party is occupied in menial tasks such as scraping the porridge pan, sweeping the dormitory and scrubbing the washroom. Bob and two of the brighter children sit down at the table to start writing out the route cards. A route card for each child is mandatory practice, laid down by the Local Education Authority, but their prepara-tion is time-consuming and tedious. Compass bearings, changes of direction, height gained and lost and estimated times are computed feverishly. Mike and Bob argue over the exact details of Naismith's Rule.

Time passes. It is now 10.30am. A few clouds drift over the sun and preparations for departure are not going too well. Peter returns having raised only an irate farmer on 1515; he is bollocked and despatched again to ring 5151 this time. Liz is trying to stem the flow of blood from the finger of one of the girls, cut while attempting to open a tin of corned beef for the sandwiches.

Mike's aspirins are beginning to take effect and he is showing off his climbing prowess to the children by travers-ing a few feet along the outside of the wall of the hut. Mike climbed Middlefell Buttress in Langdale (excluding pitch one) the previous weekend and is feeling tigerish, but he soon has the wind taken out of his sails by fifteen-year-old Simon, who solos the wall, the overhanging eaves and the roof, wearing only trainers.

At 11.30am Steve is sent to the village to find a responsible person (policeman, vicar, doctor, lawyer or teacher) to receive the route card and the list of the entire party, their names and addresses, schools, ages, next of kin and estimated time of return. Meanwhile the dormitory is a shambles of clothing, magazines, sweet papers and crisp packets; but by 12.30am all the rucksacks have been packed and checked and the party herded into the mini-bus ready for departure.

The route is to be Grisedale Tarn, Dollywagon Pike and thence to Helvellyn. Bob takes the lead wearing a woolly hat, snow gaiters and a Whillans harness festooned with chocks and pegs. His 85-litre pack towers over his head and shoulders. Liz is appointed 'tail-end Charlie'. After five minutes Wendy is sent back to the bus to deposit her Sony Walkman; she returns sullen and resentful. 'Dammit, there's music enough in the hills,' grunts Bob.

The party, sweating and weary under their huge loads, gets strung out. Dave stops to plaster his heels for he has borrowed his brother's boots which are two sizes too small. Finally, everyone collapses by the tarn and delves for their sandwiches. Bill throws a stone into the tarn and is reprimanded by Bob: 'Never throw stones in the mountains, you never know who might be there.' Bill turns away in disgust mumbling, 'No bloody frogmen in Grisedale Tarn.'

A horribly eroded path winds up Dollywagon Pike and morale falls further. The pace of the slowest is very slow indeed, and the line of figures moves erratically, like the

Klondikers climbing the Chilkoot Pass, and heels are getting kicked. Mike, realising that opening time at the Pheasant is rapidly approaching, suggests to Bob that he take the stragglers back down, while Bob and the others continue to Helvellyn. 'Can't be done,' says Bob; 'Regulations permit only those leaders with MWLCs to be in charge of parties above 2,000ft. Dollywaggon Pike is 2,810ft so you must stay with me. Just think what the coroner would say if an accident happened.'

On the summit of Dollywagon Pike a few patches of wet snow are found, and there is feverish activity with ice-axes, crampons and shovels. More time is lost. Many of the children are hungry and are nibbling at their emergency ration Mars Bars. A thin mist begins to envelope the party. Bob busies himself with compass and notebook, taking bearings in case resection becomes necessary. In spite of the 'I want to go on, Sir'; 'This isn't the top, Sir'; and 'I want to do a Munro, Sir', and other protestations, he makes the courageous decision to retreat.

'It is no disgrace to fail on a mountain. Discretion is the better part of valour,' he informs the company. 'Now get into line and keep your distance.' He swallows hard, tightens his woggle, turns about, and digs the heels of his massive boots into the eroded shale as he begins the descent.

At this point I awoke shivering with horror, but thankful that I was safely in my bed and that this ghastly outing was all a dream. I turned over, cranked the electric blanket control knob up another notch, and slept until morning.

Ice Warrior

It was close on four o'clock when three men crunched through the snow to the half-buried concrete trig point, sat down with a grunt, pulled up their hoods against the bitter wind and began fumbling in their rucksacks for food. Each was cocooned alone with his thoughts, and for five minutes no one said anything. The weak January sun had already dipped towards the horizon producing a diffuse, livid green light, against which was silhouetted the cruel spire of Sgurr na Ciche, while in the far distance the Cuillin of Skye rose in a jagged line like Baba Yaga's iron teeth. Dave, who had been studiously examining the map, suddenly rose to his feet. 'There's a Munro top just two miles away along the north-east ridge; if we get a move on we could bag it before nightfall.'

'Get lost,' replied Mark, tilting back his head and opening his mouth to receive the last drops of oil from a tin of sardines. 'We'll be pushed to make the glen as it is. I'm knackered, and Pete's knee is playing up again.'

'Well, I'm going on alone,' retorted Dave; 'Goodness knows when I'll be up here again. See you back at camp for a late supper and a pint at the Invergarry. Here, take this will you mate, I don't want to be lumbered unnecessarily.' He chucked a polythene bag of spare clothes in the direction of Mark, and set off with a loping stride along the the ridge. He did not spare himself, and an hour later was scrabbling up verglassed rocks on the. final slopes of his objective. Adrenalin was flowing fast, his chest was heaving and his breath came in gasps, but he managed a wolfish grin as he scribbled an entry in his notebook and muttered, '431 done, 137 to go.'

Dave was certainly obsessional, and indeed, if it hadn't been for Hilary and the twins he'd have chucked in his job and done the Munro round, tops and all, non-stop in winter and completely unsupported. That would have shown the likes of Hamish Brown, Martin Moran and the other pundits, he mused with relish.

It was some time before he realised that the light had faded seriously. The surrounding mountains were mere black shapes, and the glow from the western sky barely illuminated the rocks. 'Christ, I must hurry,' he hissed. 'How the hell do I get down this sodding mountain?'

The correct bearing was roughly due north; he'd had the good sense to memorise that fact earlier in the day. But the snow was glazed with ice, and he suffered some bruising falls before he met a long ribbon of firm névé which appeared to descend a narrow corrie towards the glen. Great! The snow was runnable, too, and he raced down in giant steps, revelling in the free expression of his exuberance. Although his legs were plunging knee deep into the snow his momentum carried him on effortlessly.

But suddenly, a foot did not emerge from the snow. With the faintest 'crump', an entire section of thin crust broke away and disappeared into the stream bed underneath the snow ribbon. Dave shot down ten feet into the hole and came to rest on the boulders. Embedded in snow, in pitch darkness and totally disorientated, he screamed. But his muffled cries barely reached the surface — and anyway, there wasn't another soul within miles.

A wave of icy water washed over his back and head and brought him to his senses. His body, together with the snow crust, had effectively plugged the narrow passage through which the burn flowed tempestuously, swollen with meltwater. The water rose swiftly, gurgling and foaming round his body in its helter-skelter dash down to the glen. In seconds he would be drowned. Fighting like a madman Dave somehow clawed his way back up the crumbling walls of his tomb and lay gasping and exhausted on the snow.

It was the shudders racking his body, and the agonising aches in his limbs, that brought him back to his senses and the reality of his position. His rucksack and ice-axe were gone, but he dragged his dripping body off the snow and stumbled down the rough hillside towards the glen. Boulder fields and deep heather were meat and drink to Dave for he had, over the years, negotiated hundreds of thousands of feet of such ground. Tonight, however, as the sky cleared and the moon rose, a vice-like frost gripped the Highlands, striking fear into Dave's heart.

His mind was racing, but it was crystal clear. He knew the score, knew the odds were stacked against him – but by Christ, he wasn't done yet, not by a long chalk. 'Keep moving, damn you, keep moving.' He drove himself down towards the glen, with no feeling for the knocks and scrapes.

But by seven o'clock his arms were numb and useless, with less co-ordinated movement than a rag doll's. Soon afterwards he was unable to stand, his legs buckled, and he crawled to a hollow beside a large boulder to seek shelter. Sheep had used this refuge before him and the ground was littered with dried pellets of dung. But almost as soon as he stopped moving his clothes froze stiff as cardboard, and to his horror he noticed a thin, glistening film of ice had formed over his entire body. He was rapidly turning into a knight in armour.

Using his teeth he pulled back his sleeve to read his watch.

7.30pm. Oh God! Hilary would be settling Ben and Jane to sleep before going downstairs to watch EastEnders. 'When's Daddy coming home?' Ben would be asking. When indeed. Tears rolled down his cheeks and he moaned softly.

Later he fell into a fitful sleep. In his dreams he was back in Cornwall, climbing on the sun-drenched cliff of Chair Ladder with Hilary, and moving effortlessly up the rough granite. But something was dreadfully wrong, he was unable to make the final mantleshelf, his arms turned to jelly and he fell backwards, turning over and over and over. The sensation was ecstatic and he pushed his face into the heather to prolong the dream. When he opened his eyes the moon had risen further, and light clouds were scudding across the sky. However, it was really too much effort to keep his eyes open. His lids dropped again and his breathing slowed and became shallower as his chest tightened...

The sharp smell of peat and dung, the staccato barking of a fox and the distant roar of a stag echoing around his beloved hills, were his last sensations before consciousness ebbed away for ever.